Praise for *Hollywood Virgin*

"I've always believed in the power of storytelling, with honesty and authenticity. *Hollywood Virgin*, along with its unique soundtrack, provides an inspiring and uplifting experience. I can't wait for y'all to meet the Jason I know and love."

—Jessica Simpson
singer, fashion designer

"*Hollywood Virgin* is a masterclass in resilience, offering an unfiltered look at an industry that many aspire to. A must-read Hollywood love/hate letter for anyone desiring a little peek behind the curtain."

—Christopher Gialanella
publisher of *LOS ANGELES MAGAZINE*

"*Hollywood Virgin* is the unlikely success story of Jason Felts, who made all of his dreams come true and learned a lot of lessons in the process. I'm so proud of everything Jason has accomplished. But most of all, I'm proud to call him my friend."

—Sir Richard Branson
from the Foreword

"Felts captivates, detailing a (not always first-class) journey filled with aspiration, struggle, self-awareness, and super success. A masterclass in perseverance and authenticity in an industry that often lacks both. A must-read for anyone looking to blaze their own trail and keep it real."

—Lance Bass
singer of N'SYNC

"A look back at the surreal life of one of my closest friends. His memoir made me laugh and cry. Hollywood chewed him up, but didn't spit him out."

—Ashlee Simpson-Ross
singer, songwriter, and actress

"*Hollywood Virgin* is filled with laughs and a behind-the scenes account of life working for one of the most iconic brands of our time."

—Brian Kelly
The Points Guy

"An executive's well-written account of his journey through filmland, of which I had a small window into; never losing sight of the wonder and optimism that makes moviemaking exciting."

—Oliver Stone
director, screenwriter, producer, and author

"If you want to learn how to build, and how to lead, Jason Felts knows. *Hollywood Virgin* shows how dreams happen. FYI, this book will help you to 'Focus Your Ideas.'"

—will.i.am, singer
songwriter, producer, and entrepreneur

HOLLYWOOD VIRGIN

HOLLYWOOD VIRGIN

BREAKiNG iNTO AND OUT OF SHOW BUSiNESS

JASON FELTS

FOREWORD BY SIR RICHARD BRANSON

WILEY

Published by John Wiley & Sons, Inc., Hoboken, New Jersey.
Published simultaneously in Canada.

For general information on our other products and services or for technical support, please contact our Customer Care Department within the United States at (800) 762-2974, outside the United States at (317) 572-3993 or fax (317) 572-4002.

Wiley also publishes its books in a variety of electronic formats. Some content that appears in print may not be available in electronic formats. For more information about Wiley products, visit our web site at www.wiley.com.

Library of Congress Cataloging-in-Publication Data is Available:

ISBN 9781394323838 (Cloth)
ISBN 9781394323845 (ePub)
ISBN 9781394323852 (ePDF)

Cover Design: Paul McCarthy
Back Cover Photograph: Michelle Brody

SKY10093708_121824

You hold in your hands one of the last books to not be written by AI. Hopefully, that's not true. But know that, despite some name changes, everything in here is true and was written by a real person with a real sense of humor, in a real bathrobe. So, in that spirit, this book is dedicated to you, dear reader, and artificial bots everywhere, who only wish they could be like us.

Contents

Prologue

MY ENTIRE LIFE has been shaped by music. When I was little, the sounds of classic rock and Motown hits filled every room of our house. Road trips with my family included not just the radio but the entire evolution of music technology from 8-tracks to cassette tapes, compact discs, and MP3. Despite where the music was coming from, it would always include quizzing by my dad—*Quick . . . name this artist!* After school, I was glued to MTV, and in high school I went through the requisite era of loving pop songs and most singles on Casey Kasem's *Top 40*. Every significant moment in my life is marked by a particular song or band I was into or heard at that time. Eventually, I ended up developing my own tastes and favorite genres, which are wide-ranging. There isn't much music I *don't* like.

So it's no wonder I ended up working for one of the most iconic music brands in the world and then running music festivals. But more on that later. For now, all you need to know is that at the end of each chapter is a music cue to a song that correlates, to me, with that precise time in my life. I listened to these exact songs, in this order, as I wrote the book. From start to finish, they are a musical accompaniment to this book, and my entire life. I challenge you to figure out exactly who each song is dedicated to from my story. Regardless, I hope you'll use them to enhance your reading experience and take a journey with me that I never in a million years imagined I'd go on. I'm so grateful for every minute and wouldn't change a thing. So, as I sit here in this bathrobe, typing these last words, I invite you to hear the story of how I lost my virginity, in every way, in Hollywood.

The following QR codes will take you to the music cue listed at the end of each chapter. Each song either conveys how I was feeling at that point in my life OR is dedicated to someone from that chapter. I will leave it to you, and with any luck you will know.

Apple Music

Spotify

Foreword

by Sir Richard Branson

ALMOST 20 YEARS AGO, I was at my home on Necker Island for what was going to be a wonderful celebration week. I've always made it a habit to invite old and new friends alike to come spend time on Necker and discuss the next big ideas, innovations, and movements. That particular week included a few accomplished entrepreneurs and a few kids (20- and 30-something-year-olds) who were making moves in the entertainment industry. One of them was a tall, scrawny, blonde-haired bloke named Jason Felts. I've always said that one of the most underrated keys to success is keeping it fun. One of the first things I noticed and immediately liked about Jason was that this kid sure knew how to have fun.

As my friendship with him grew in the coming months and years, I've learned that he really epitomizes the adage, "Work hard, play hard." While we had a ton of fun, it also was clear to me that Jason had ambition and big dreams. So, of course, he would be invited back. One evening, on another trip to Necker, I put him on the spot in the middle of a dinner with more than 20 other guests. Around the huge, alligator-shaped table sat some prominent founders in technology and other industries. Jason was substantially younger and earlier in their career than most of the other dinner guests. As all the other accomplished guests spent the majority of dinner sharing their recent achievements, awards, and pitched various ideas, I turned to the attentive (but quiet) young man adjacent to me and proclaimed, "Jason, why don't you get up" (motioning him with my hand to hop from his chair) "Go on . . . introduce yourself . . . tell us what you're up to." He looked a little taken aback but stood up with a smile and began talking. But the table was just too big and not everyone could hear him.

Again, with the motion of my hand, now as I shoved the glassware to the sides, "Go on, get up on the table. A little louder so everyone can hear," I suggested, springing attention onto him, as I am known to do. If he was nervous, he didn't show it. Without flinching he jumped up and began walking the table like a runway. What intrigued me was that he didn't just talk about what he'd accomplished in his career so far, but the future he envisioned within entertainment and how he dared to be different in such an ego-driven industry. Later when I apologized for casting the spotlight onto him, he told me that he didn't think anyone around that table would be very impressed by his career, considering who the other guests were and what they had accomplished. He was much more interested in talking about what was possible in the future than what had happened in the past. We had that in common.

It was on that trip to Necker that I shared my story of Virgin Records, and we floated the idea of building out a Virgin production company. That was when I learned a second value Jason and I share: if you aren't sure how to accomplish something, just say yes and figure out how later. When I asked Jason to email me and Gordon McCallum a business plan to see if this could work, I later learned that he immediately went home and Googled "how to write a business plan." I maybe knew he wasn't totally sure what he was doing. But I felt sure I'd found a partner who could figure out the "how." And have fun along the way. You really can't ask for more in a friend and business partner.

You'll have to read on to learn about all the ups and downs of Jason's life thus far and his Hollywood career. Together we've sat in the Lincoln bedroom of the White House, sipped fireside martinis with President Obama, had our fair share of Hobie cat races, walked movie premiere red carpets, fundraised with purpose for Virgin Unite, and laughed our asses off along the way. I'm so proud of everything Jason has accomplished. But most of all, I'm proud to call him my friend.

Hollywood Virgin is the unlikely success story of a small-town, Southern boy who made all of his dreams come true and learned a lot of lessons in the process. I happen to believe that his success is not mostly due to his talent or work ethic, though he has those in spades. No, I believe the biggest driver of Jason's success is his instinct to always do what is right. He's a person of integrity. That's the kind of person one should most want to be around. I'm honored to be a part of his story, be called his mentor, and excited for you to dive into these entertaining and enlightening pages. Like me, Jason certainly didn't learn by following the rules. He learned by doing, failing, getting up, and trying again. He trusted his gut and put other people first. If a secret to life exists, I'd say it's that.

PART

I

Ready, Set, Action

1

Peaches

"PEACHES!" DOC BAKER barked. "Get in here!"

By Peaches, he meant me. Doc Baker started calling me that during the first week of my tenure as the high school football team's trainer, when I was just a freshman. I didn't like the nickname, honestly. And I didn't quite understand it. Later in life I realized there was something obvious about me that I didn't see yet. I suppose, looking back, I was a "light in the loafers" teenage boy in the heart of rural Texas in the 1990s, working in the most macho setting imaginable. It was everything you're probably thinking – muscular boys who look more like men throwing each other around every day and being led by actual men who cursed and talked about women with a strong Southern drawl. I was different, a fish out of water. I guess . . . I was Peaches.

I didn't even care that much about sports; I preferred music. This was due in large part to my father's constant practice of educating me on not only who performed a certain Motown song but also the story behind the song. It was a trivia game we often played, and still do even to this day. But when we had moved from Memphis, Tennessee, to Rowlett, Texas, the year before, the band teacher wouldn't let me play alto saxophone anymore. I loved it, but apparently Lakeview Centennial High School had enough alto sax players. They wanted me to play tenor sax, which is a long, gigantic instrument, much bigger than the alto I loved. I was about 115 pounds (soaking wet) and wasn't strong enough to manhandle it, so I passed.

I was devastated and looking for something else to do in my new town at my new school when Doc Baker mentioned that they needed football trainers. He was my health teacher, and not even a doctor, but that's what we all called him anyway. I had no idea what being a trainer entailed, I just knew enough to know that high school football in Texas is A THING. It truly was the TV show *Friday Night Lights* come to life. I was intrigued. Brokenhearted by my saxophone rejection, and following a short, boring stint in FFA (Future Farmers of America), I figured maybe becoming a part of the cool thing would help.

During my first tour of the facilities, I realized that being a trainer, in a lot of ways, meant being in charge. I was responsible for making sure the players got what they needed to play their best. They were led by Coach Watkins, who at the time was the winningest high school football coach in Texas history, which meant the place was a well-oiled machine with a lot of high expectations. Trainers were organized and attentive. They were responsible for ensuring the players operated at the highest level because they had the support behind them, whatever that meant. I remember thinking on that first day, *these are the people who really make it happen on Friday night.* They were leaders, not followers. And that was a feeling I aspired to.

I was psyched about the opportunity to become a trainer, until Doc broke the news that all the positions had been quickly filled, but I could work for the hardware room, reporting directly to Coach Watkins. That's where all the players go to get their chin straps adjusted, helmets fitted, jerseys tailored, and so on. I wasn't exactly thrilled by this – it didn't seem nearly as exciting as being a trainer, who ensured players were mentally and physically prepared to win. Teammates, parents, and spectators alike all expected a strong team, and trainers were vital to that.

So was the hardware guy, but I didn't see it that way yet. It was lower down the food chain and much less glamorous than the role of a trainer. But I came to enjoy it. I ran that hardware room. And the players loved me. They felt like I was the one truly taking care of them because I had to care about the seemingly smaller things – if their mouthguard fit right or their shoes were too tight. I did my job well and gained respect. The hardware room was where I was that day when Doc Baker yelled my name. Well, the name he and the entire team called me, anyway.

"Peaches! Get in here!" he hollered as I walked to his office. "You're up."

"What?" I replied.

"There's an open trainer position and you're taking it. You're going to learn how to wrap ankles and do electrotherapy. We practice every day, and two-a-days in summer. Games on Fridays, during season. You need to be at all of it," he replied. "Tell your parents you won't make any family vacation this year."

I was ready, and nervous, but also a little relieved. The training room was farther from the showers than the hardware room. I was already having a hard enough time not walking by more than I needed to. My confused 14-year-old brain had no idea what was even happening. As far as I knew, I had no interest in anyone. I didn't know the term for it at the time, but I considered myself to be asexual. I wasn't interested in girls, but being interested in boys was something I couldn't conceptualize. In my conservative, smaller town, Southern Baptist world, men married women. End of story. I didn't want to marry a woman, so I must want to be married to no one. That's all I could understand at the time. My curiosity to compare my skinny, hairless body to naked, hairier, muscular boys would be easier kept at bay if I were farther from the showers. Plus, now I had some real responsibility, and I've always liked that.

At school, that was my identity: football trainer. But at home, I was doing one of two things – either researching anything related to entertainment or watching recorded copies of *Entertainment Tonight*. With the invention of the DVD on the horizon, videocassette recorders were lower in price, and I managed to buy one with my babysitting money. For $109, at Circuit City, it was my first purchase with my own money. I also had signed up for something called Columbia House, which was a music and video subscription program. For 1¢ and then the low, low price of $19/month they'd send you six videos a month. I built up my own little movie collection by also buying blank tapes to record and watch *Entertainment Tonight*, *Star Search*, and other shows that gave me a peek into Hollywood, a world very far from my own existence. To me, Hollywood had everything. Movie stars! Money! Culture! Beautiful people!

Don't get me wrong, I had a fantastic childhood. My parents deeply care for me and my three younger brothers, and our house was full to the brim with love. This love came in many forms: listening, encouraging, teaching, reprimanding. As an adult I see now that it also came judgement-free and with unwavering understanding that although we were all dealt the same deck of cards, we were different, and they loved that about us. They supported us, and still do, in anything we've ever wanted to do. At the risk of sounding cliché, I truly owe them everything. Still, it was becoming clear that I wanted something more than what small-town Texas could offer.

I enjoyed watching celebrities and entertainers on these shows, but soon I was curious about more than what I could see on TV. I was interested in the behind-the-scenes stuff, the gigantic complex engine that is the entertainment industry. I dreamed of Hollywood, but not to be a celebrity. There's a famous scene from the movie *Pretty Woman*, where a man walks down Hollywood Boulevard screaming, "What's your dream? Everybody's got a dream. What's your dream?" The first time I saw that film it was on one of those video home system tapes Columbia House sent me. I heard that line and rewound it to watch again. I knew my dream was to move to Hollywood and do something. I just didn't know exactly what.

Many days after school, my best friend Melissa and I would rush home and begin filming our own homemade videos. We'd been best friends ever since we met at the bus stop on our first day in high school. Confidently swinging her red purse, she had offered me a Tic Tac and told me I had Oreos in my teeth. Turns out I didn't, it was 8:00 a.m. But what I did have was old school metal braces and the week before had made the unfortunate decision to go with black rubber bands. I thought black was cool, and as the new kid, was trying to make a big impression on the first day. The only impression it seemed to leave on people was that I likely snacked on Oreos all day. But Melissa is kind and one of my best friends still to this day. She and I recorded many "music videos" together, as well as the "Melissa Winfrey Show," in which we mimicked the interviewees and celebrities we'd seen on *The Oprah Winfrey Show*, then at the height of its popularity. Occasionally, because of our casting needs, I'd be on camera, but I never enjoyed it. One need only briefly watch those old episodes we made (and we recently have!) to strongly affirm that I was, without a doubt, an innocent, naive, closeted gay kid. I liked the planning and execution of the videos, not the acting. I liked *producing* them. I was far more interested in the people behind the scenes. I wanted to be one of the people who actually *made things happen.*

Back then, directors, producers, and celebrities were easier to reach. I literally bought a book at a bookfair that listed the celebrity fan club addresses and phone numbers. *Fan clubs, that's not too impressive,* you might be thinking. But in the 1990s, many celebrities ran their own fan clubs. I swear to God, one time I called up Jason Bateman's fan club and he actually answered. Worst-case scenario, or perhaps best case for me, you could reach their manager or assistant. Because I could often get these assistants and managers on the phone via fan clubs and publicly listed phone numbers – and I was more interested in them than the actors anyway – I'd ask them millions of questions in my squeaky drawl. *How did you get that job? What's it like working with Wesley Snipes? What should I be doing now? What job should I look for? What skills are important? Should I go to college?* It was a gold mine! Somehow I even convinced my parents to let me have a phone in my room with my own phone line. I even still remember the number: 412-3530. I was, after all, a football trainer for the Lakeview Centennial Patriots and had a booming babysitting empire in Lake Bend Estates. I needed to be reachable. I used it to make these long-distance calls to actors' fan clubs and their management, and when that first month's bill came due my parents were up in arms. I didn't know long-distance calls cost money; I was just a kid. It was hundreds of dollars. From then on out, I was only allowed 10 calls per month, so I used them wisely. *I'm at my limit, so the Tim Allen (aka Tim the Tool Man Taylor) fan club will just have to wait until next month.*

No matter, though, because I could write as many letters as my heart desired. Stamps were cheap, and my determination was strong. I wrote to entertainers, executives, and even iconic cultural figures. I told them how much I admired them and, of course, asked for advice. Frequently in return, I received handwritten letters and signed headshots. I still have them all, somewhere deep in storage, including a handwritten letter from former First Lady Jackie Kennedy Onassis. At the time, for reasons I could not explain then, the entertainer I was most fixated on was John Ritter from *Three's Company.* In that beloved 1970s and 1980s sitcom, John portrayed the struggling culinary student

Jack Tripper, who spent most of the time pretending to be gay so he could live with his two female roommates and keep the old-fashioned landlords appeased. I'd record the reruns most days after school, and it was on that show that I heard the word *gay* for the first time. Hell, it was the first time I was introduced to the concept of homosexuality. Jack had a switch he would flip. With his female roommates, he was traditionally masculine and spoke with a deeper voice. He stepped heavy and drank beer. But when the older landlords were around, he had to act *gay*. This meant talking with a higher voice, a lighter step, and being a bit flamboyant. When Doc Baker called me Peaches, I worried that he saw a little Jack in me. Gay Jack seemed like someone they'd call Peaches. *Do I act like that?* But I related to him. His character was also just fun, happy, and the life of the party.

Because John Ritter was my breakout favorite entertainer at the time, I wanted to get in touch and was extra dogged in my efforts. When my family happened to be taking a cross-country vacation (not during football season, of course), we found ourselves in Los Angeles for a few nights. I took the opportunity to call and leave a message for John's assistant, Susan Wilcox, and let her know I'd be in the area and would love to meet her and John. I was too naive to even know how crazy this was at the time. All I knew was, in a previous call, she had offered me sound advice, and it was a shot. I told her what motel we were staying at in nearby Marina Del Rey, hung up the phone, and went about my way. On our last afternoon in LA, as our family returned from Venice Beach, the front desk attendant told me I had a message waiting. My mom, surprised, asked the attendant, "You have a message for Jason Felts?" *Oh my god*, I thought. I knew exactly who it was. It had to be! The attendant handed me the message she had transcribed on my behalf: "Call Susan from John Ritter's office ... invite you and your family out to come visit the set tomorrow." Tomorrow?! We were leaving tomorrow! We were on a tightly packed schedule, a cross-country vacation with our closest family friends. There were two dozen of us, and I knew my schedule wasn't going to be a priority. I was devastated. Although hopeful because Susan had returned my call, my dreams of meeting John Ritter soon were slipping through my fingers. Why did I have to go back to Texas? It just felt so right in Los Angeles.

I called Susan back and told her as much. As a credit to how wonderful she is, she invited my mom and me to come back in a few months and ensured us spots at a taping of *Hearts Afire*, John's then-current show. My hopes of meeting John were still alive, but getting out to LA again was no easy feat. I didn't have a lot of wants as a kid, and we certainly weren't rich. I would define my upbringing as economy class financially and upper class emotionally, with plenty of coupons and SkyMiles as my parents' ancillary currency. My mom used a coupon to get a discount on my new pair of pants, and my dad used all of his frequent flier miles from traveling for work as a beverage salesman to get us back out to Los Angeles for the taping. Several months later, my mom and I attended and sat right next to Bill Clinton's brother, Roger, and his family. (Apparently he was an actor and musician. Who knew?) Though I idolized John Ritter, and seeing him in person was amazing, he wasn't the main object of my focus during the taping. My eyes were on the producers, the suited-up executives, the director in the chair yelling "Cut!" and plenty of other people whose job titles I certainly didn't know. They were important in my young mind because they were busy pointing and instructing and concerned with the bigger picture of it all. I wanted to know how the production crew made it all come together. How did they actually make it happen?

On my first LA trip earlier that year, I had insisted on going on one of those double decker bus tours around the city. I wanted to see all the gorgeous Hollywood houses and people from atop the famous giant bus! I thought it would be like all of those pictures in my tiny Texas bedroom coming to life. And it really was. We drove down Rodeo Drive in Beverly Hills, and my family likes to remind me that I actually spoke out loud, "God, they all look so rich and tan!" A little gauche, I know. But hey, I was a teenage boy from the South. I had strong values and a moral compass, but I wouldn't have minded being rich and tan. Over the course of my career, a lot about Hollywood ended up not being how I thought it would be. But the abundance of tan and rich people has never disappointed.

As we drove through Hollywood, the guy on the mic pointed out all of the celebrity homes. Lucille Ball, Michael Jackson, Al Pacino. Of course, I recognized all of these names. Until we got to the biggest house on the tour. It belonged to someone named Aaron Spelling, a name I'd never heard before. And believe me, there weren't too many celebrity names I hadn't heard before. The tour guide informed us eager passengers that Spelling was a producer, famous for so many of the big TV hits around that time: *Charlie's Angels*, *The Love Boat*, *Dynasty*, *Beverly Hills 90210*, and *Melrose Place* to name a few. *A producer*, I thought. *A producer has the biggest house on the block!* I had assumed the most successful people were actors because they were the famous ones. Working behind the scenes in movies had appealed to me for a long time, and now this trip solidified my calling further. In a lot of ways, I felt my experience as the high school football trainer was grooming me for it.

I also learned that producers had a much longer project list than actors. Actors are time-limited in the projects they choose. They have to be there, all day, almost always because their job is to be on screen. But producers can do a lot more. They can have their hands in many different creative projects. That "jack-of-many-trades" aspect of the job interested me. I knew early in life that I didn't want to be a one-trick pony. I loved movies, many genres of shows, and all types of entertainment. I didn't want to be put in a box. My interests varied; I wanted my life to as well.

With my illusions of grandeur firmly cemented and my mind made up after my short flirtations with LA, I was more determined than ever to get to Hollywood. Though I knew I had to finish high school first, I still felt I needed to make connections and perhaps even find a job that put me in the company of "entertainment people." Meet the right people and learn more. That was my main aim. I was going to convert those calls I'd been making into knowledge and relationships. I knew if I kept doing that, I was moving in the right direction and would eventually get somewhere. In fact, I had a poster hanging on my closet door at home that illustrated a perfect California setting: a big mansion, a few cars, and an ocean view. It read JUSTIFICATION FOR HIGHER EDUCATION. *But I don't want to go to school*, I often thought. *I want to be creative.*

Living in Texas, though, those right people and right rooms were pretty damn hard to come by. There aren't any gateway jobs to Hollywood in Rowlett, Texas. I regularly scoured the newspaper and the community board at my school for any kind of job even remotely connected to entertainment. Any flavor of low-level interning or assisting I'd take it. But alas, there was nothing. That is, until one day I was doing my normal exploration, and saw that the television show *Walker, Texas Ranger* was going into production for another season. It would be returning to a neighboring suburb, Las Colinas. Perfect! Chuck Norris wasn't my favorite actor and *Walker, Texas Ranger* wasn't my type of show, but beggars can't be choosers. This, and the children's show *Barney*, were the only two things shooting in my area. And *Barney* was one of the only shows I was less interested in than *Walker, Texas Ranger*. If this was my only way in, I'd do it. I really, really wanted to work in casting or production, so I relentlessly called the casting director, Barbara Brinkley. Have you ever heard a more Hollywood name than Barbara Brinkley? She seemed straight out of central casting herself and was very tough to get a hold of. But I was resolute. Eventually, I managed to actually get her on the phone.

"I want to learn," I said. "Put me anywhere behind the scenes and I swear I'll be a help."

"No," she said briskly. "All we need are extras at this time. If you want to be in the show, send me your headshot." And she abruptly hung up.

I didn't want to be on screen, but now I desperately wanted to meet Barbara Brinkley. So, if this was the only way to do it, then so be it. At the time, I didn't even know what a headshot was. Without explaining why, I had Melissa take a few pictures of me leaning against a tree in my front yard. I got to one-hour photo quickly to develop the roll and mailed the picture off to Barbara Brinkley. I just love saying her first and last name together each time. Of course, my "headshot" was accompanied by what I felt was the most inspired letter about why I should be picked for the show. It was absolutely cringeworthy, but the naive intent was genuine. Within a few months, I got word that I would be a single-scene extra cast member in one episode of *Walker, Texas Ranger*. The rest of the details would be revealed when I got there.

When I showed up on set that day, it turned out that my role was to be Prisoner 3, one of a few prisoners sitting behind bars in a juvenile detention center. This was as Texas as Ranger Walker got. They had me dress in baggy jeans and a T-shirt. I greeted the fellow extras and got into position. "Action!" they yelled, and the producers and the actors with lines did their thing outside the jail cell, while I sat there silently in the background. *I want to get to Hollywood*, I thought, *what am I doing here?* It didn't feel right, and I hated it. But I still had hopes of meeting Barbara Brinkley. This could still be worth it.

After my short scene was over, I ran up to the casting assistant whom I had checked in with earlier that morning. "Hi, I'm Jason Felts," I said with confidence, as if they would remember. "I wrote Mrs. Brinkley a letter, and I'd like to meet her. We even spoke on the phone," I proclaimed, as if that carried weight.

"Oh, Brinkley? She's in LA. She works in LA," the assistant replied. She'd been there the whole time. Barbara Brinkley wasn't even on that set. She was the boss, and she was in LA. I felt just as far from my dreams as I'd ever been. I had to get to a babysitting job, so I hopped in the car, and slammed the door. As my mom drove away from the studio, I vividly remember the LeAnn Rhimes song, "One Way Ticket" playing on the radio.

It was at that moment that I thought, *I gotta get the heck* outta here.

> *And buy a one-way ticket on a westbound*
>   *train. . .*
> *See how far I can go. . .*

CUE: "One Way Ticket" by LeAnn Rhimes

2

California, Here I Come

NEEDLESS TO SAY, *Walker, Texas Ranger* was the end of my acting career, but it certainly wasn't the end of my pursuit of Hollywood. Right before the final semester of my senior year of high school, my father unexpectedly and devastatingly lost his job – the very corporate job that had moved us to Texas many years prior. It felt like we were going to lose everything: our home, our cars, our family livelihood. And we basically did. My father is quite literally my hero and the most honest and hardest worker I know. Well, tied with my mom. She worked tirelessly raising us and taking care of just about every detail in our lives. I inherited my work ethic from them both equally.

It felt so unfair that dad had lost his job, and I remember wondering, *How could it even be possible that a company just fires someone after so many years and so much dedication?* I didn't understand corporate politics at the time, or how leadership changes often have a domino effect creating full regime shifts, and with it, merciless job cuts. All I knew was, my father was a dedicated company man, and worked tirelessly zigzagging across the country for that company. And just like that, he was written off.

Although my mother also worked tirelessly at home raising us, my dad was the primary income earner. I lay awake wondering how our family would survive with no substantial income. *Should I get my GED and go to work to help my family?* The thought crossed my mind. It felt

13

like an option, though my parents would never allow it. They made the tough decision to let our home go back to the bank, sell our prized family van, and move back to Virginia where my father could more easily get a new job and start over. Yet I was happy and thriving at my high school and had everything going for me. Starting over at a new school when I was so deeply enmeshed in my final year and with so much opportunity ahead would certainly stifle my spirit and dreams. Fortunately, our family friends, the Blairs, offered to host me for my last semester of high school and get me set up with a job. My parents were supportive, and so it was decided. I was to stay behind in Texas while my family moved back across the country. It was bittersweet. I missed my parents and little brothers terribly but was so grateful for my time with the Blairs.

It was my senior year of high school, and I was now a head student trainer of the football team. By then, Doc Baker had taken a liking to me and said I should go to Southern Methodist University (SMU) to study sports medicine. This did have some appeal; I knew SMU as the place where many successful people I knew in Texas went to school, and although I didn't have the grades or money to get in on my own, it wouldn't matter. This is when I first learned that "it's who you know, not what you know." SMU is in the heart of Dallas and had a strong local alumni network, which presented plenty of opportunity for me. In fact, Doc knew the head trainer, Cash Birdwell (you can't make these names up), for the football team and said he could get me in to work under him. No problem. I mean, we were in Texas and the good ole boys' network does govern most decisions. Occasionally I mentioned to Doc that actually, I was considering moving out to Hollywood instead. "Peaches goes to Hollywood," he said in his Southern drawl, as I confessed my dream. He thought that was just crazy. So I was seriously considering his offer. I still had no idea how I was going to get to Hollywood, and SMU was a sure thing. The easy path. Plus, I liked being a trainer well enough. *Do I make a career out of it?* I often wondered.

I was almost at graduation, and money wasn't growing on trees. Times were tight, and I needed to figure out what path to take: SMU to be a trainer, or something else? Hollywood after graduation just wasn't in the cards . . . yet. That year, I had a few different jobs. I had worked at a one-hour photo lab, which my curious self enjoyed as it gave me a glimpse into what was going on with everybody's lives. Call me nosy, but this was fun and sometimes gave me juicy food for thought. I would make up captions and stories in my head, almost as if I was writing a script from someone's pack of developed photos. I also worked at a telemarketing firm where I basically called people up all evening, reading a transcript soliciting them to refinance their mortgages. I was almost 18 and barely even knew what a mortgage was! It was miserable, but I was saving for my future. Whatever that might be.

My last semester of high school, after a brief stint working in the file room at Yellow Rose landscape company, Mrs. Blair got me hired by her real estate broker. The office happened to be right down the street from SMU. Often, I'd sit at my workstation looking toward the campus and daydream about what it'd be like to go to college there, study sports medicine, and stay with Henry S. Miller Real Estate. I mean, I was getting pretty good at it. That is, being the young buck who was installing and training middle-aged agents how to work computer programs. Those big-haired Southern ladies loved me, and I loved them. Mrs. Blair also regularly tried to talk me into staying rather than entertaining my Hollywood ambitions. It seemed like everyone was invested in keeping me in Texas.

Occasionally, I was still babysitting on nights and weekends. One of my regular clients had turned into more of a nannying gig. The mother's name was Mary. Mary was unlike anyone I'd met before. Originally from Boston, she was refined, well mannered, and had exquisite taste. She liked the finer things in life including unique foods, the theater, and fashion brands I'd never even heard of. She was different and interesting, and I liked her instantly. My Gran (my mom's mother) had once given me a copy of the book *Miss Manners' Guide to Excruciatingly Correct Behavior*, and Mary was someone who actually appreciated my intimate knowledge of where salad forks should go and how to properly leave a table. But more than anything else, Mary took my dreams of Hollywood seriously. She asked lots of questions, and she never encouraged me to stay in Texas like everyone else.

So there I was working the real estate job whenever I could, going to school during the day, and nannying Mary's kids many nights and weekends. One afternoon, I arrived at Mary's house, and the kids were back in their rooms watching television and doing homework. Mary's husband said "Hi" quickly as he shot out the door to catch a flight, something they were both often doing as I arrived. As I put my jacket on a hook and walked toward the refrigerator, a note caught my eye. Mary's family fridge, otherwise pristine, had a Post-it note stuck squarely at eye level. As I approached I saw that it read, "Jason—We're moving to Cali. You're coming with us. Pick a school."

That was it. No further information. Instantly my mind was racing. I went about my normal duties and took care of the kids. *What did this mean? They're moving to California? And I'm coming? But why? Is this for real? Couldn't they have possibly left me some more information?!*

When Mary came home later that night she said, "The kids are going to their friend's house; do you want to go grab some dinner?" We went to a local Italian place and when we arrived she said, "I'm not very hungry, do you want to split a pizza?" I'd never split a meal with an adult before. I felt cool and like an equal. I left it to Mary to choose, and I recall being a little troubled because it had leaves (basil) all over it. She explained that it was "gourmet." Then we launched into a conversation about our collective futures, and we were splitting food. This was the start of our friendship. I could already tell that she was going to be more important to me than just an employer.

"Are you guys really moving to California?" I asked.

"Yes. I've wanted to move for a while, and I've always wanted to live in San Diego. I've been there a few times and loved it."

"Where is San Diego?" I asked immediately.

"It's about an hour and a half south of Los Angeles," she replied.

Oh my God, I thought, *that's so close to LA! Presently I'm 24 whole hours away, but I could be only one and a half! But where would I go to school? Would I like San Diego? What would I tell my parents?*

"But you are so great with the kids, and we'd love for you to come. What do you think?" she asked.

"I don't know," I answered honestly. The offer sounded great and something inside me leaped at the thought of moving to California, of course. But I could hear Doc Baker and Mrs. Blair in my head, telling me to stay put. I told Mary I'd think about it.

The next week, Mary started defining what the California nanny job would entail. I'd live in their home, and ensure they all had dinner and got to their various obligations. I could go to college during the day once the kids were off to school, and they would pay me a small fee. Outside of that, my time was my own with no restrictions. They would even provide a Mercedes for me to use. I had a great offer on the table to do something I knew I could do, and most important, I could be in California. It felt irresponsible and even ungrateful to walk away from it. But Texas was what I knew. It had stability. It's where my friends were. It was my comfort zone. I was on a fence and did not know on which side to jump.

The following day, I was back babysitting and took Trevor, their youngest son, through a drive-thru to get some food. We were sitting in the line staring straight ahead, when out of the corner of my eye I saw Trevor turn toward me and say, "J?"

I turned to look down at his little cheeky face and said, "Yeah?"

"You're coming to California with us, right?" he asked.

"Yup. I'm coming to California with you," I said quickly before my mind even made a conscious choice. It just came out. I half-blamed it on Trevor's approach; his sweet, little kid eyes were begging me to go with him. Though, honestly, I knew deep down I'd decided the minute I read the Post-it. This was the chance I'd been looking for my entire short life and there was no way I was passing it up now.

Within a week I had told everyone the plan. Though plenty of people in my life didn't understand, and even thought I was making a huge mistake, my parents always supported my decision and asked all the right questions to ensure I had considered the pros and cons of the direction fully. I think it was easy for my parents to not be upset about my moving to California because we had already been separated since they moved to Virginia. Being apart from them was already difficult, and occasionally I wonder if leaving for California was that much easier because in many ways I had been on my own for a while. Another person who supported the decision immediately was my childhood best friend, Melissa. She knew about my years of letter writing and cold-calls to Hollywood in my bedroom adorned with signed pictures of entertainers. Having gotten married and pregnant at 18, she shared with me that I simply had nothing to lose and that I must go – for both of us.

But the person I was always most concerned with impressing was my Gran. I never stressed much what my parents thought; as long as I didn't do anything too stupid, I had their approval.

But Gran was different. She was more judgmental and held a high bar. My Gramps, Gran's husband, was a Baptist preacher. This came with some strict rules for living (especially for my mom and her siblings), which included using your manners, attending church, not touching alcohol, and of course marrying "traditionally," while ruling with an iron fist. Her approval meant the world to me because she was tougher to impress. I worked hard for her approval, and I almost always got it. I am convinced that she and I connected on a deeper level than she did with other family members. We had an understanding that I can't fully explain. Most of my relatives had a difficult relationship with her, which looked like frustration or rolling their eyes at her behaviors. But not me. For better or worse, I studied her and worked for her affection. And she thought I hung the moon. I felt an underlying expectation to keep holding it up.

Once when I was about eight years old, my brothers and I were in one of those kitschy museum gift shops with Gran. I was pursuing the name keychains that are staples at places like this. As I excitedly found "JASON," Gran came up behind me and looked at it and flipped it over. "Jason means healer in Hebrew," she read. "You are going to be a healer." It was one of those off-handed comments that she likely wouldn't even have remembered, but it meant everything to me. *I'm going to be a healer*, I thought. Still to this day, I think about that all the time. It left an indelible mark on me, and I've always wanted to live up to the title. Gran bought the cheap piece of plastic for me, a constant reminder of who I was meant to be.

That keychain was one of three things that I'll always remember Gran gave me. The Miss Manners book was another, and the third was what she called a *worry stone*. It was a slick little stone that she gifted me one day and told me to rub it any time I had a worry. She gave it to me apropos of nothing except that I'm sure she could tell that at a young age I already struggled with anxiety. I retain those three physical reminders of her with me today. They were visible expressions of who she was, and who she wanted me to be. Fortunately, it turned out that Gran also supported my decision to move to California. Though it was unconventional, she told me she was proud of me for going after my dreams, as long as I attended college. Even though, of course, it meant I wouldn't get to see her nearly as much – hardly ever. It meant I'd see all of my family much less, even less than when they moved to Virginia. But I knew that we'd still keep in touch constantly. We've always been the kind of family who were up in each other's business in the best possible way.

Mrs. Blair, several friends, and some of the realtors from the office hit me with all of the hard questions and objections that I knew were coming. "Where are you going to go to college?" "You hardly know Mary." "You won't be able to afford it." Etcetera, etcetera.

"I'll go to community college for a while and I know them well enough," I said, though I realized they were raising some good points. An awkward laugh and "I'll figure it out" was my answer for everything. I admit the questioning gave me some pause, but I was moving to California, and that felt like enough for now.

Eventually, the naysayers in my life stopped trying to talk me out of moving. They had witnessed my drive – er, obsession – since I was in middle school, and when I said, "I'll figure it out," I think they believed that. I was so excited about the upcoming big move to San Diego that one day I randomly went to one of those rent-to-own places that sells whole room packages worth of furniture. Mary had made it clear that I would be living with them rent-free. But hell, I wanted to contribute *something* and wasn't going to presume they'd buy me a bunch of furniture, too. I was trying to decide how much to get when I called up Mary and asked, "Do you know how big is my bedroom? I'm buying a bedroom suite. I've picked out a bed, dresser, and nightstands so far."

"Jason," she replied with her signature cackle, "don't buy all that. Your room is a good size, but I can put together your bedroom. And it's pronounced *sweet* by the way, not *suit*. If you're dead set on buying something, just get a bed, and we'll have the movers put it on the truck."

As moving day got nearer and nearer I graduated high school, given up ever going to SMU, quit my real estate job, and sold my car. I let go of the *Friday Night Lights* lifestyle and everything I'd ever known. All I packed was my clothes and the bed I'd financed in 18 equal payments of $38.99 from the rent-to-own company. The house Mary and her husband, Vinny, had built in Del Mar wasn't quite done yet when we moved, so for the first week in San Diego we lived in the famed Hotel Del Coronado. Actually, when Mary first told me the house wasn't finished yet, I feared the migration west might be in jeopardy. *This was all just too good to be true and is falling through at the last minute!* But that worry was for naught, as everything went off without a hitch.

I arrived on a different flight and met Vinny in baggage claim at the airport. We drove out to the hotel together. It was hard to believe just months prior, he had placed that Post-it note on the refrigerator, and now here we were, cruising down the California freeway. "This was Mary's dream, and I understand yours also, yeah?" As I nodded, I vividly remember his next words: "Open the sunroof, pal. Let's do this."

And with that, we rode down the highway, wind in our faces. All of it was gorgeous to me. Palm trees were everywhere, and I was fixated on all the California license plates. Something about them made it all seem so real. I was in California, these cars were in California, these people lived in California, *I* lived in California! Later at the hotel, Mary had pulled out her credit card and driver's license to check in. The lady at the desk took it and looked from the card to Mary, "Oh, you're from Texas?" she asked. Mary looked over at me with a wry smile and said, "Not anymore." She let out her signature cackle, which became a secret language between us that signaled mischief from that day forward. The very next week, Mary and I went down to the DMV and got our own California driver's licenses and plates for my Mercedes. I put the plate on that sporty red beauty and finally let it sink in – I had made it. I was officially a Californian.

***

Life working for and living with Mary and family was good. I'd enrolled in community college, so I attended classes while the kids were in school and took care of them in the afternoons, evenings, and on some weekends. Any chance I got, when I didn't have classes or the kids were busy with their friends, I'd drive the hour and a half up to Los Angeles and literally just drive around. I didn't have the money to stay in a hotel or eat anywhere fancy, but I didn't care. All I wanted to do was be there. I'd wind through the streets of Hollywood, or drive down Rodeo Drive (which, of course, I pronounced like the Texas kind of rodeo for way longer than I'd like to admit) and take it all in. I was a living, walking, human dream sponge. After cruising or walking around for a while, I'd drive the hour and a half back to San Diego. I did that more times than I can count, hoping and praying I would never get in trouble for racking the miles up on that Mercedes. I wanted to understand the roads and how to get to, from, and around LA. I wasn't living there, but knowing how to get around the large city made me feel like I belonged, like I wasn't just visiting.

In one of my college classes, a man named David Mirisch was set to be a guest speaker. I'll go ahead and briefly explain who this is, but do yourself a favor and Google him. The man is a legend. If you have any interest at all in the entertainment industry, the Mirisch name is one you should know. I had been looking forward to his visit to our class for a long time. David lived in San Diego, but he was as Hollywood as they came. Dubbed "The Man Behind the Golden Stars," his famous family produced over 72 movies, including *West Side Story* and *Some Like It Hot*, and won 28 Academy Awards. David did everything from discover Farrah Fawcett to create the Los Angeles Rams Cheerleaders. He handled the public relations careers of stars like Raquel Welch, Pat Boone, Perry Como, and nearly 500 others.

I was too green to pay much attention to this at the time, but one of the most incredible things about David was and is his focus on philanthropy. All told, he's raised millions and millions of dollars using his relationships with entertainers to host celebrity events for causes he cared about that supported so many. He was the epitome of using his influence for good and was an early influence on me that one must give back to be fulfilled. (This will go on to play a big part in my life to come, but I'll save that for a later chapter.) David was exactly the kind of Hollywood person I found most interesting, influential, successful, and powerful. Outside of his circles, he wasn't particularly famous. I was intrigued at how someone could have so much success, financial freedom, and do so much good without compromising their personal life or giving up their anonymity for fame. That felt like success.

I was excited to hear David Mirisch guest speak in my class. So I was absolutely devastated when Mary told me I had to be at the house to meet a painter the day he was scheduled to speak. *A painter,* I thought. *Seriously!?* I missed the class, but afterward I decided I would try to reach out to David personally to meet him, using my absence from class as a way in. I begged my professor to give me David's phone number so I could call him, but he wouldn't do it. In hindsight, I don't blame him for not wanting to potentially subject David to the whims of his teenage students whenever they felt like reaching out. But he didn't know who he was dealing with.

By now, I was an expert in finding phone numbers of the hardest-to-reach and had mastered the art of the "I'm a bit of a nobody, but can I ask you a favor?" cold-call. I called 411 and there was no David Mirisch listed, but there was a David Mirisch Enterprises. (Okay, so maybe not too much sleuthing required this time, but it definitely took a little guts, especially because my professor made it clear I was "not to contact Mr. Mirisch.") The automated robot voice on the line asked if I wanted to be connected automatically, and I pressed one for "yes." David's assistant picked up immediately. "Good afternoon, David Mirisch Enterprises," she said with grace. With all the confidence I could muster, I simply asked "May I speak with Mr. Mirisch?" Shockingly, she said, "Sure," and put me right through.

"Hello?" said a raspy low voice on the other end of the line.

"Uh, hi, uh, Mr. Mirisch, my name is Jason Felts, and I'm in the class you spoke to the other day at Mira Costa and uh . . ." I fumbled for a minute. It was intimidating being connected to him so quickly, and I wasn't prepared. I thought I would be leaving a message. My mind was racing and then, suddenly, something clicked, and I had a moment of clarity. Maybe it was all of the practice I'd had before, maybe my determination took over and I knew this was a huge shot that I couldn't afford to blow, but my voice steadied and I said, "I had to work the other day, and I was unable to be there. I was very disappointed and was so looking forward to it. My teacher would not give me your number. But I found it. Could I please come by your office to meet you sometime soon?"

"Sure" he replied. "I live on La Costa golf course. Here's my address. I'll see you Thursday at noon."

"Well, actually, I can't on Thursday," I said, "but I could possibly come on Friday. . ."

"I'll see you Thursday at noon," he said again. *Message received.* Looked like I'd be missing another class because there was no way I was skipping this meeting. I couldn't believe what had just happened. I had a meeting with Mr. Mirisch! At his house! I had learned this lesson a few times already in my stint as a small-town Hollywood cold-caller, but once again I was reminded that it never, ever, ever hurts to call and ask. In fact, I'd go as far to say that it's almost always to your benefit to ask. The worst thing that can happen is that someone says no, and the best is that it might just change your life.

Soon, I was driving up La Costa, passing mansion after mansion until I arrived at one of the most beautiful Spanish houses I had ever seen, right on the golf course. An elegant blonde woman whisked past me as I was let in. Later I learned this was David's wife, Sandy. The entrance of this home just oozed California. An assistant of some kind met me at the door and showed me out to the bungalow where David worked. He greeted me kindly with a firm handshake, and we exchanged pleasantries as I found a seat on a chair and tried not to sweat through my new $18 dress shirt. Almost immediately he looked at me and kindly asked, "What can I help you with?"

I followed the same pattern as before, at first fumbling along and telling him how I'd like to learn everything I can about Hollywood and it's my dream to live and work there, and so on. But soon I could tell I was losing him a little. Inspired by his directness, I cut to the chase and found the same steadiness and bluntness as I had before. "Sir, I'm living and going to school here in San Diego but I'm trying to make my way up to Los Angeles. You're the closest to Hollywood that I can find right now, and I'd like to work for you."

He clocked me for a second and replied simply, "Well, I don't hire guys."

Confused, my reply was short. "Why?" I asked.

"My experience with assistants is that women have a stronger work ethic." I knew that this was just patently untrue. There are plenty of lazy guys out there, but I've always had a very strong work ethic. My dad worked hard. Vinny worked hard. What a bizarre rule to have. "Well, I work hard," I said.

"But do you work smart?" he responded. (A clarification I now remind others is much different than working hard.) He continued, "Also, I have an assistant, Lisa, and don't really need any more help right now." I was still trying to decide whether to get up and go or try and talk him into it when he said, "But if you want to glue some pictures onto this poster board for an event we're having this weekend, you can hang out for a while and do that."

"You mean, right now?" I asked.

"Yes, right now. Inside with my assistant. Go introduce yourself." And so I did. I got down on the floor with his assistant and literally started gluing pictures to a poster board. I was still disappointed that he'd so quickly said he wouldn't hire me, but I was willing to play this out. As his assistant and I glued and made signage for the event, I got to know her much better. She was grateful for my (free) help and asked if I'd be willing to come back the next day. Of course I was, and David didn't seem to care one way or the other. So I went back the next day – and the next day and the next.

I kept getting invited back (by her) and within a few weeks I was on the payroll working very part-time doing random, absolute grunt work. I embraced the grind and did anything and everything required. I gave up my weekends of driving aimlessly to Los Angeles and any type of social life. I worked long hours for minimal pay because I wanted to be there. As simple as the job was, and although it was on the fringes of Hollywood, I felt I was on a path toward my dreams. I was getting closer, anyway. Eventually David took notice, and after seven months when Lisa left for a new job in Hollywood, I become his assistant. I found out later that he'd had one male assistant earlier in his career who was lazy, and it soured him for a long time.

What I did in that first year for David is called "paying your dues." I fetched coffee, filed papers, typed memos, picked up packages, took out the trash, ran errands, and did all the things that nobody else wanted to do but absolutely had to be done. Bottom of the food chain stuff. But in entertainment, and in a lot of other industries I imagine, it's how you start. I carried a lot of water, literally and figuratively. At the celebrity golf tournaments, I often did have to carry huge jugs of water to fill up dispensers. Then I'd run to the men's locker room if I was lucky, or a closet at the country club if I wasn't, change into my presentable clothes and out of my soaking wet ones, strap on my name tag and walkie talkie, and get back out onto the red carpet to greet sponsors and celebrity players. It wasn't glamorous. But it taught me a lot.

One of the more interesting, grunt-like, dues-paying things I was tasked with was typing up David's letters. This was just before email, so everything went through the regular mail system. He'd write them out on a legal pad, and I'd type them up on a computer. He proofed them and signed them, and I stamped them and mailed them. It was a whole four-part system. He proofed those letters with a red pen, and I'd have to go back and retype them up with the corrections made. It was like I was back in grade school again, except I applied myself harder than I ever had before.

At this point, Mary's kids had established a lot of friends in San Diego, so my nanny duties weren't needed every single day. I am not proud of it, but I started to skip my college classes more frequently to put in the hours at work. Something Gran could never know about. My career was more important to me than school had ever been. I desperately wanted to avoid having that red pen mark up the letters. I know this kind of exact correspondence process sounds primitive today, but I still believe this kind of intimate working relationship with a mentor is one of the most valuable things anyone can do for their career. Getting a look at what David said and to whom and learning why he made the decisions he did, it was like learning from the grand master. Yes, I was fetching his lunch and painstakingly typing up letters, but who cares? I was observing and absorbing how things worked, and that was invaluable.

Similarly, I got to do the common Hollywood assisting task of "rolling calls." This meant I'd listen in when David took calls, usually twice a day, once in the morning and once in the afternoon, and take notes. Often we'd make or take up to 20 calls in just a few hours, and it went something like this. I'd get someone on the line, "Hi, John, I have David Mirisch holding for you." David and John got on the line and I listened intently. Before the call ended David might say something like, "Alright, well let me talk to Jane about that first, and I'll get back to you tomorrow morning." Now this was something I definitely needed to keep track of and make sure that whatever was supposed to get run by Jane did, and then relay that back to John when David said he would. It also often sounded like reminding David, "Before you rolled the next person you mentioned you wanted to talk to Jane first; do you want me to get her on the line?" You had to listen, take notes, anticipate David's needs, and react. Each conversation dictated the next and created a task list for the rest of the day. And David wasn't directly instructing any of it; I was just hearing what needed to be done and taking initiative. That's what good assistants do. That *is* working smart.

Information is power, and as an assistant, you gain a lot of information. Watching David roll calls was like gaining my bachelor's degree in entertainment. Which was the only degree I ever really wanted, anyway. Rolling calls enables you to learn who is who, who has influence and power and who doesn't, who has leverage and connections, who could and couldn't negotiate, and sometimes who was in really deep trouble (and maybe even how to get them out of it). This kind of info did come in handy occasionally when I made business decisions later down the road. I got an early education in navigating the industry, including the hierarchy among the talent's assistant, manager, agent, attorney, business manager, and publicist.

Back in Texas, Doc Baker had told me as I departed west that there is no better experience than physical experience – actually doing it and getting your hands dirty, so to speak. You're only going to learn so much from a book, or even from school. How much can you learn from a map of Istanbul without actually visiting? You have to get on the ground and go walk around Turkey. You know what I mean? You have to get in the rooms where decisions are made, relationships are formed, and the foundation of everything you eventually see on the big screen is laid. I wasn't making any decisions yet, and most of the time I was still rolling calls or gluing pictures onto poster board, but I was in close proximity to some real Hollywood power and the people who were everything I believed I wanted to be.

Careers in entertainment have no set, direct path. People end up there from all different walks of life and by all different means. Unlike becoming a doctor or a lawyer, there's no certification you can get that ensures you a job or qualifies you for the next step. The one thing you can do that works every time is put yourself in those rooms to meet the people who are making things happen. I had a long way to go, but I had made it into a room with one important decision-maker, so I was going to learn everything I possibly could from that opportunity.

CUE: "Big Time" by Peter Gabriel

3

Do Better

David was a great teacher – a formidable teacher. He had a keen ability to teach you things right in the moment, in the middle of the action. He didn't wait until some employee review, or even the end of the day. He always took the opportunity to teach and correct immediately and calmly, often in front of others. Not on purpose or in an attempt to embarrass you (although it often *was* embarrassing), but because the moment was happening among others and the efficient thing to do for everyone was make it a point then, and move on. He never intentionally shamed anyone. I wanted nothing more than to please and impress him, so I lived my entire work life trying to soak up everything he knew and garner his attention without doing anything that required the kind of corrective teaching that stopped me dead.

One particular instance when I garnered this wrong kind of attention was the first time I attended the Victor Awards in 1997. This was an awards show in which the National Academy of Sports Editors honored the country's most accomplished athletes. It was basically the West Coast version of the ESPY Awards. I didn't know a lot about sports, and I honestly didn't care much about them, either. I'd played a little baseball and soccer as a kid but it didn't take me long to realize that I didn't like sports at all. Although I had been a football trainer, that was less about sports and more about the production of a Texas high school football game experience. The lights, the fans, and the talent – I mean players. I knew the fact that I got to attend the Victor Awards three years in a row impressed my dad and brothers, who love sports. Over the years I got to meet some of the greats like Shaquille O'Neal, Michael Jordan, Wayne Gretzky, James Worthy, Oscar De La Hoya, Florence Joyner, and Caitlyn Jenner (pre-transition).

At the first Victor Awards that I attended, I was tasked with picking up the legendary baseball player and manager Yogi Berra from the airport and driving him back to the famous Las Vegas Hilton where the event was being held. The venue also happened to house the very stage where Elvis Presley performed his residency 20 years prior, mind you. Although established way before my time, it was a distinguished theater, and I felt honored to wear my first backstage pass and ride the very elevator Elvis rode night after night. The massive stage was historic, and just being in its presence was exhilarating. Despite not knowing much about sports and probably only learning who Yogi Berra was earlier that week, I was wide-eyed and excited. This was a big job and I was eager to nail it. One of the things that David made very certain to do anytime there was a major VIP airport pickup was print out specific directions that the driver was supposed to take. Las Vegas is a vast city with tons of routes and traffic. When the timing window of delivering a VIP somewhere for an event is small, these kinds of things matter a lot. And remember, there was no GPS or even MapQuest at that time. Just written directions and a folded paper map.

I had my directions in hand, understood my task, and headed off to the airport. When the man landed, I walked right up and said with authority, "Mr. Berra, I'm Jason. I'll be your driver." He was short in stature but big in aura and replied back warmly, "My friends call me Yogi." His wife was with him, so the three of us headed out to the van.

As we drove down the highway, I started to notice that traffic was bad. I began to worry that the directions I'd received might not get us there in time and took it on myself to find another route. I didn't know Vegas well, but I'd done this airport drive a few times now. Admittedly, I was pretty unfamiliar with the town. I turned down one street thinking it would get us there faster, but we hit more traffic. I turned down another street hoping it was a short cut and again hit even more traffic. I made turn after turn until I was pretty lost. I tried to maintain a sense of calm and confidence for my VIP passengers, but at that point, Yogi was supposed to have been at the hotel a while ago. He was receiving an award that night, and we were cutting it super close. To make matters worse, while I was battling traffic, Yogi and his wife were discussing their need to shower and change before the show. Time and traffic were not on my side.

I'd also brought along a baseball I intended to ask him to sign. Not for me, of course. All due respect to Mr. Berra, but I didn't revere athletes like that. I wanted him to sign it for my dad because I knew he'd love it. Because we were just sitting in traffic with nothing but time to kill, I figured I'd ask him then. During one particularly long stretch of sitting bumper to bumper, I grabbed the baseball, turned around and said, "Mr. Berra, while we wait, would you mind signing this baseball for my dad?"

"Of course," he replied. He was nothing but kind and gracious during the whole ordeal.

Finally, after much circling and wrong turns, we did make it back to the theater. As we pulled up, I spotted David standing there, clipboard in hand, looking unusually anxious. I got out of the van, nervous but chipper as always, trying to act like everything was fine. "Aw, man, traffic was so bad. Good thing we made it!" I proclaimed.

David stared at me and asked, "Did you take the route I gave you?"

Yogi chimed in and said something like, "Well we sure did make a lot of turns!" "Yeh, like a bunch of curveballs," I added with an awkward half-laugh.

Now David was glaring at me, talking through his smile. "You weren't supposed to take a lot of turns. You were supposed to stay on the route. Always stay on the route."

As he was talking, I saw his eyes glance down and notice the baseball I was holding with Yogi's signature on it. Then he gave me one of those famous, helpful but humiliating lessons in the moment that stuck with me forever. He turned and looked at Yogi and said, "I'm so sorry, Yogi. I sent one of my young drivers to pick you up, and he had very specific instructions to stay on the route we mapped out to get here. Unfortunately, that didn't happen in this instance and I apologize. I also notice that he has a baseball in his hand with your signature on it and that's just not appropriate. He knows better, and I'm very sorry about that as well."

I was mortified. Did I know better? Was the signature a rule that I didn't remember? I had only been trying to help and do the right thing. And wanted to do something nice for my dad. Yogi and his wife walked inside the backstage of the theater. No shower, no change of clothes. Then David turned back to me, and softly and politely only said two words: "Do better." *Okay yes, I gotta do better,* I thought. But I admit to feeling a little defensive. I was just trying to help by taking a shortcut from the freeway traffic and doing something nice for my dad. I thought I'd made the right judgment call in the moment.

But as I reflected, I realized that I hadn't trusted David or represented him well. When someone gives me instructions, they're for a specific reason, and I should follow them. Asking for an autograph minutes after meeting him wasn't a classy thing to do, and I'd completely missed that social cue. Years later, when I was leading entertainment for Virgin, I'd go on to use these same words with my team occasionally. Sometimes specific feedback is helpful. But sometimes, instead of reprimanding, all you need to make a person self-reflect on where they went wrong is to simply tell them: *It's okay; do better.* And I did do better after that. David called me to a higher standard that day, and I worked even harder and smarter to meet it. It proved both a teaching and learning moment.

***

The Victor Awards turned out to be full of learning experiences . . . including walking in on an incredibly famous A-list NBA star having a drug and sex orgy while I was trying to drop off his jacket he'd left backstage. Lesson learned: even if you're given a room key for gift bag reasons, NEVER walk in announced. I also experienced my first nightclub during Victor Awards weekend. It was customary to hit the Vegas clubs after the show, and Vegas night clubs aren't like other clubs. They are like regular clubs but on steroids: massive in size and containing any vice you could possibly desire. A far cry from the small Texas dives I had once frequented. I handled and transported talent after the Yogi Berra incident without a flaw, and David recognized that. So on the night after the show, he took his son Michael and me aside and said, "The talent wants to go to a club, so you two are going to take them." Michael had been in the nightlife business in Hollywood and promoted some of the biggest clubs, including the famed Roxbury. I could tell he was excited because this was totally his arena. Like an understudy, I felt I was just along for the ride.

We hopped in two limos and got chauffeured with some of the celebrities around to various clubs who stayed out most of the night partying. For most of the night though, I was working, fetching drinks for the table around what I learned was called *bottle service*. I didn't actually drink much yet and was mostly playing waiter. But by early morning at the last club, I was persuaded by others to relax a little and have a shot and then a drink before Michael came over to me and shouted over the music, "Paris wants to go to her hotel, so you take her back."

"What?" I replied. I was so confused. We were in Las Vegas and he was saying something about Paris.

"Paris," he said again and pointed to a beautiful blonde girl sitting on the top of a booth. "Paris Hilton."

"What?" I asked again, unable to hear. "Take Paris to the Hilton?" I asked.

Michael was getting frustrated with me, I could tell. I looked between him and the girl he was pointing at a couple of times, waiting for the situation to compute. Was I supposed to know who this was? I still was unclear. Michael was acting like she was a celebrity but I'd never heard of her. Hell, she just looked like another pretty, blonde girl to me. There were plenty of those in the room. Paris wasn't famous yet, by the way. This was before *The Simple Life* shot her into public consciousness. "Just call the limo," Michael said, exasperated.

Within minutes, the limo arrived and Paris walked out of the club hand-in-hand with some actor from *Married with Children.* I acted as an escort and instructed the driver to take us back to the Hilton. We all got into the back of the limo and the two began immediately making out right in front of me. It was awkward to say the least. Also, I was later told that I was meant to ride in the front, which I really wished I had done. *Just mind your own business*, I thought as I sat staring out the window at the Las Vegas strip flying past. It was pretty hard to do that with their kissing reflections in the window, so I squirmed in my seat until I found an angle that didn't have them in it. I knew who the actor was from television, but I was still trying to figure out who this girl was. *I guess this is Paris*, I thought. *Or is she from Paris?* I wondered. Still unclear. *That must be a nickname. I mean, no one is actually named* Paris.

Fortunately, we quickly arrived at the hotel, and they stopped the lip lock. They got out of the car, and I followed them to ensure they got in okay. I guessed that was my job, but I'd never actually done this before. Sure enough, as soon as we walked in the door, Paris stopped and said, "Oh, wait, I don't have my key." I panicked and realized Michael might have sent me with them for this reason. It wasn't uncommon for us to "take care of the talent" by keeping track of their room keys, or carrying extras ourselves, to ensure they didn't have to worry about a thing. My walkie talkie was out of range to dispatch Michael, and I didn't have any numbers to call. Handling celebrity hotel room keys broke me out in a mild sweat after witnessing the orgy earlier that evening. I wasn't sure how I was going to help these people into their room. Possibly sensing my panic, Paris looked at me and said, "Don't worry," with some sweet sass. She flipped her hair as she turned and walked away. Strolling with confidence over to the front desk she said, "I need a key to the presidential suite, please."

"Sure thing, name?" the front desk lady asked.

"Paris Hilton."

Hilton. Paris Hilton. Take Paris to the Hilton. This was her hotel. I finally got it. And they didn't even ask for an ID. She smiled, snatched the key card, took her friend's hand, and turned back to me. "Thanks, sweetie," she said with genuine warmth. I was a good five years older than her, but she acted so much cooler and way more worldly than me. I watched them disappear into the elevator, relieved that I'd delivered them safely. I went back to pass out in my own hotel room before I had to get up a few hours later to wrap the event and head back home.

***

Within two years, I went from moonlighting as one of David's three free interns while working full-time for Mary, to being David's primary assistant and occasionally helping watch Mary's kids, who were teenagers now. They were in high school, much more self-sufficient, and I was ready to dedicate myself full-time to David Mirisch Enterprises. But I couldn't continue to live with Mary rent-free and drive her Mercedes if I wasn't actually working for her anymore. I had evolved, but still I was nervous to give up these comforts. I had a gorgeous red sports car and lived in a beautiful home in Del Mar; it was a big deal for me to give that up. But I knew I had to. It would be selfish, and Mary had already done so much for me. I was on a path headed somewhere else, and it was time.

I began hunting around for a cheap, used car, when word reached my Aunt Karen (thanks to my mom) in Cincinnati that I was in need. She called me up one day and said, "Jason, I'm proud of you and everything you've accomplished already. I'll loan you money for your new car and you can make monthly payments on it to me with some interest." Great! But first, I needed to learn what interest was. Seriously, I had no clue. Aunt Karen taught me what interest meant, and how to calculate it. She also told me exactly step-by-step how to research pre-owned cars, check the maintenance record, check the value, and so on. It was a lot of education in a few calls. Eventually I found a maroon Nissan 240SX, a little two-door. It rattled a lot, but it was mine. It had a unique scratch on the back and bumper, and it's that very scratch that I recognized many years later after I upgraded. A young, good-looking actress type hopped out of it in the grocery store parking lot. I imagined she was fresh to LA with big dreams, like I was back then. My old rattlebox of a car had served me well, and I hoped it would for her, too.

The guy I bought the car from was an architect named Ira. I showed up at his house in West Hollywood one morning to check it out. When I entered, he kindly introduced me to his domestic partner. I had never seen two men living together before – two men who weren't just roommates. There were pictures of them up everywhere, and judging by the large wedding picture on the wall, they loved each other. I noticed there was family in their wedding pictures, too. It seemed like everyone approved. Naively, I thought this was strange. *These guys can't be actually married; men can't marry each other*, I thought. Of course, legally, that was still true back then. But that's not what I meant. I was still resistant to the idea that two men could love each other, be married, and be happy. This was perplexing to me.

Ira took me for a test drive and on the way back he asked me what my plans were. "I'm hoping to move up here, to Hollywood," I replied.

He turned and looked at me and said, "just be careful what circle you surround yourself with up here. You seem like a nice kid." Aunt Karen transferred me the money, I picked up the cashier's check from the bank, and I transferred the title.

Meanwhile, back at Mirisch Enterprises, I started to get more vocal with David about my aspirations. Now I had my own car, and I was hoping to move to Los Angeles within the year, and I'd like to dedicate myself to him full-time in the meantime. I had basically stopped working for Mary, and I couldn't afford to pay her rent with my small salary from David, though I didn't admit this to anyone at the time. I just told her that I knew if I stayed, I'd get sucked back into doing nanny tasks, and it was too hard to live where you used to work, which was also the truth. She completely understood. I'd always been clear about my ambitions, and she'd been supportive from day one.

When I mentioned to David and his wife, Sandy, that I intended to move out of Mary's and focus on building my career, they quickly offered up Sandy's office as a temporary guest room to me. It was so gracious and unexpected, and I will forever be grateful for the thoughtful transition that they made possible. I lived there for about four months and worked constantly with and for David until I could get something set up in LA. I knew I couldn't work for him full-time anymore when I moved, but I also knew that was the direction I needed to go. Soon enough, Sandy connected me with a transitional job at a friend's real estate office in LA, and I loosely had a lead on an affordable apartment in Burbank. Just as I'd set out to do, within six months of quitting my nannying job, I found myself driving my little Nissan right out of San Diego and up the coast to LA. This time, for good.

CUE: "Unwritten" by Natasha Bedingfield

4

Eight's Company

AT AN EVENT in San Diego with David a few months prior, I'd met an actor from the TV show *Freaks and Geeks*, which was very popular at the time. We got to talking, and I mentioned I was trying to make my way up to LA. "Well, I've got a spot in my apartment opening up in a few weeks," he said. "It's yours if you want it." That was all it took. I didn't ask a single question or do any research on this guy – or the place – whatsoever. I was in. I gave my notice to David, packed up my belongings, and headed up the coast, beyond excited. With a tiny bit of income lined up, an apartment I knew nothing about, and my new (old) Nissan, I felt like I was finally living my dream. I was going to Hollywood, baby!

My new home was located deep in the valley. Burbank is near many of the studio lots, where shows and movies are filmed, and is also known for its cheap and high-density housing. It's an early stop for wannabe actors, writers, and producers, hoping to make it big and someday own a mansion in Beverly Hills or a beach house in Malibu. Anybody who lands in Hollywood in search of their dreams, ends up in the valley first. I, too, was fresh off the proverbial plane (from bougie Del Mar), headed to my obligatory first home to pay my dues in Burbank.

In a small moving truck, with a trailer attached hauling my Nissan, I drove past apartment complex after apartment complex before finally arriving at the address my barely an acquaintance actor friend named

Riley had given me over the phone. I walked up and knocked on the door and a very model-like, half-asleep guy about my age opened the door. It was about 11 in the morning. "Uh, hi," I said. "I'm supposed to move in here today."

It took a minute for this to register, but he finally replied, "Oh, yeah, you're taking my spot. I'm Ben; come on in."

"Actually," I said, "Could you help me move in a few pieces of furniture really quickly? I'm double-parked out front."

Ben looked really annoyed, but he agreed and stepped out to the curb. The moving truck contained some boxes, bags full of clothes, and the furniture from my bedroom suite setup from Mary's. It was heavy, real wood furniture that matched the rest of my previous, gorgeous bedroom in Del Mar. The bed was finally all paid off, and I was proud of my possessions. Ben took one look in the back of that truck and said, "Dude, I don't know where you're going to put all of this, that's a lot of stuff." *Interesting*, I thought. It was just one bedroom's worth of furniture. I figured I better go in and have a look around before we dragged this stuff inside to see what Ben meant. He must be exaggerating or making an excuse not to help unload.

It was then that I learned I had agreed to move into a two-bedroom, one-and-a-half-bath apartment that housed seven other guys, eight including me. Ben was right, my furniture was barely going to fit inside this place. I barely fit inside this place! None of the other guys were there at the time, they were all out on auditions or shooting something or working their in-between gigs. It turned out, like Riley, they were all various forms of actors trying to make it big. Anyway, I couldn't just leave my furniture in the moving truck. It had to come in. And I had to return the truck. After Ben and I squeezed my stuff into the apartment, within an hour he had finished loading his few belongings into his car and moved out, handing me his key.

Alone in the apartment, I surveyed my new living situation. I took in the interesting décor and smells. This was new terrain. As I peeked inside the one full bathroom containing the one shower, it looked like a Sephora had erupted up all over the counter. Every manner of creams, serums, cleansers, body sprays, and colognes were scattered about. Anything that was invented to keep you hot and young, or mask a smell, these guys had it. As I examined it all, I had no idea what any of that stuff was for, and I had never consumed or encountered guys who used anything like them. My bathroom regime included Crest toothpaste, Old Spice deodorant, and Jergens lotion that I used wherever dry, feet and face alike. At first, I actually thought there must be girls living there because of the makeup. This was well before I learned that it was pretty customary for men to dab on a little powder or concealer to blot the shine before heading to an audition where they'd be on camera. (Or that some men do wear makeup and they don't need a reason beyond that they want to, for that matter.)

I sat down in the quiet living room alone, still excited about finally residing in LA, but a little more apprehensive about what this would be like. I spent the next few hours there alone, wondering what to do with myself. Soon, I heard a loud bang on the door and walked over to open it. A big, sweaty man stood in the doorway, and his uniform read that he was with a furniture rental company. "I'm here for your refrigerator," he said, as if I was supposed to know what he meant.

Confused, all I could think to say was, "What?"

"I'm here to get your refrigerator," he repeated. "You guys are behind on your bill, and this is a rented refrigerator so no pay, no stay." I can still hear that line in my head.

He shoved past me, unplugged the refrigerator, and began strapping it to the dolly. I was new to having roommates, but I knew this was a huge problem. I mean, I didn't have super high standards, but I wanted to live in a place with a refrigerator. That didn't feel like too much to ask. As he strapped it to the dolly, I inquired a little to gain more insight into this strange situation I now found myself in. The sweat-dripping furniture man shared with me that the name on the bill was "Lane" and he apparently lived here, too. So now I'm aware of two of my roommates, Riley and Lane, and one former roommate, Ben. *Five more to go,* I thought.

The man wheeled out the refrigerator with everything in it, food, beer, and all. For the first time, I began to worry a bit. I was now living in an apartment with too many roommates and no refrigerator. How was this going to work? This had all happened while none of them were home and during my first few hours here. What if they came home and were angry that I squeezed all of my furniture in this already overstuffed apartment? What if I was blamed for letting the man take the fridge? I'm not sure what I could have done differently, but I certainly didn't try to stop him. I really was just hoping Riley would arrive home first because he was the only person I halfway knew.

He didn't. As evening came around, one by one they started rolling in. I had situated myself upstairs now, trying to distance myself from whatever instant reaction would occur when they realized they had no more refrigerator. I could hear them downstairs, rowdy and high-fiving as they each walked in, asking how auditions went, and so on. Finally, I sheepishly and nervously walked downstairs to the group.

"I'm Jason," I said with a half-wave.

"Oh, yeah," one of them replied. "Riley said you'd be moving in. What's up, man?"

As I was about to reply and start bonding, someone noticed and belted out, "Hey, where's the fridge?!"

"A guy came and got it earlier," I quickly replied. "He said someone named Lane hadn't paid the bill or something."

This response triggered a chain reaction from everyone cursing Lane and trying to get him on the phone. *Shit*, I thought. *I probably just got Lane in trouble*. This wasn't going well at all. What if Lane was some huge seven-foot guy who's about to come home and kick my ass? While they scrambled, I looked around at my new roommates. None of them had an ounce of fat or ugly on them anywhere to be found. Something stirred in me. I was still completely out of touch with my sexuality, but I did somehow understand that living in such close quarters with seven hot model-level guys might be tricky for me. And at that point, I wasn't exactly sure why, but I was beginning to feel slightly uncomfortable. Like maybe, I wouldn't fit in here.

Finally, Riley got home, and I was relieved to learn that I would be sharing one of the two rooms upstairs with just him. The other bedroom was shared by three people, the living room housed two more, and the remaining poor soul slept in the downstairs bathtub. I'd soon come to learn that eight was the very least amount of people that ever slept in this apartment, as these guys had many girls and buddies crash regularly. It was a far cry from having my own bedroom in Del Mar.

Eventually every one of my seven roommates came home and said hi or did some version of nod and walk past me, with a few making comments about how much of my stuff was now shoved into whatever corner it would fit in. Conversation turned to pregaming and going out that night. The LA lifestyle of a struggling actor, or anyone new to the industry, is to go out clubbing until two in the morning, maybe hit a house party, and then come home in the wee hours of the morning, wake up about 10 o'clock to hustle all day, and start the whole thing all over again.

This night though, the problem was we no longer had a refrigerator full of beer. They had decided the destination of choice was a place called Miyagi's, but pregaming was a huge part of the drill. With no beer, it wasn't possible. Eager to make a good impression and feeling guilty about throwing Lane under the bus, I offered to buy the beer. I remember specifically only having $333 in my bank account, but still, getting the beer seemed like a good first move. This unfortunately set the precedent that "Jason will buy the beer" from then on out. Not a great rule for someone who was barely employed. But as Dale Carnegie would say, I won friends and influenced people quickly. And that seemed a necessity in this new town.

After I picked up the beer and before kicking off the night, I sat on the edge of a planter at my new building to ring my parents and let them know I had made it to LA. I rambled and rambled about how great it was, and of course they were happy for me. It's how they always reacted to my dream chasing. Never discouraging, and always reminding me to be safe. I returned with the beer and everyone seemed a little more content. We engaged in a round of "three showers in an hour." The water heater only produced enough hot water to get through about three showers an hour, so some got a hot shower and the rest of the guys got a cold one. Apparently, this was a nightly game. There was always a competition for almost everything around there. Who got to use the shower, get ready in front of the mirror, use the toilet, control the TV. Every morning when we got up and night before we went out there were doors banging all over the place and eight men clamoring for one bathroom. The guy who slept in the downstairs bathroom got that one all to himself as a small consolation prize – I suppose for, you know, having to sleep in it.

After everyone got ready in the one (very disgusting, might I add) bathroom, we all piled into three cars and headed to Miyagi's. This was my first time officially going "out" in Hollywood. I had barely been in LA for 12 hours. As we pulled up to the place, it was packed. We parked and walked toward the side entrance when Riley pulled me aside and said, "Hey, run up and tell the doorman that you've got the guy from *Freaks and Geeks* here with his crew."

"Like I'm your manager or something?" I asked confused.

"Yeah, exactly," he said. "Like you're handling it." I wasn't sure what "handling it" meant, but took from context clues that I was supposed to act like I was in charge and my companions were people this club wanted to have inside.

Though not a complete novice, given my days with Mirisch, this one was a first for me. But I was prepared to be a team player and did it just like Riley said. I wasn't feeling super confident and was surprised when the bouncer lifted the rope and ushered us in. *Wow, that easy*, I thought. I felt powerful and confident, and I enjoyed watching each of my new roommates walk past me with varying nods of appreciation. There was a huge line waiting to get in, and we skipped right to the front. As soon as we were in, I forgot about the furniture, our tiny apartment, the missing fridge, and everything else that had worried me that afternoon. The guys accepted me now. I'd been honest about the fridge! I moved in my oversized furniture! I took the cold shower! I'd bought the beer! And I'd gotten us in! It was official, I was in Hollywood, and I had a crew.

It was an amazing night. It felt like a movie. Pamela Anderson was even there with her entourage, and we spent the night in their shadow. Thanks to the encouragement of my roommates, I drank more than I ever had in my life. For the past few years I'd either been living with Mary as her kids' nanny, or for a brief stint with my 70-year-old boss. Drinking was not yet a real part of my life. We partied all night and got home about three o'clock. I vomited in the very planter I'd been sitting on nine hours earlier when I called my mom and dad to tell them I'd made it safely to LA. I was still safe in LA, just now extremely intoxicated.

The very next day I had to get up for my first day of my new job. My boss, Ms. Josephs, ran her real estate business out of small office in Beverly Hills. Though the admin gig was temporary and part-time, I was appreciative. It was only my first day, and I was completely hungover and miserable, but I powered through. This became my routine. Like I said, it was the routine of everyone, really. It just seemed to be what they all did; it was the lifestyle. Out every night drinking, connecting with peers, and then rallying the next morning hungover for work. I was the only nonactor of the group, which meant I became the designated person to always act as the "manager," because I was told that "talent never approach the club first or calls to get on the list." Not that these guys were huge stars at all; they were working actors/waiters living a threadbare existence with seven other dudes. But no one else needed to know that. Fake it till you make it, believe it till you become it, and all that crap.

I even set up an email address, HollywoodMGR@aol.com, on an AOL account I still shared with my Gran. With this email address, I'd message clubs and hot spot bars to gain us entry and some special treatment. The guys insisted I was a "great talker," which fueled me, and only encouraged me to further outdo myself. Occasionally my Gran would joke that she couldn't sign into her account because "the manager must be doing deals in Hollywood."

I constantly emailed back-and-forth with these hot spots, and pretty soon we were showing up at clubs and bars and I was asking for the promoters by name. "Eric told me to ask for him," "I'm Jason; let Tommy know we are here," that kind of thing. The rope would lift and the door would swing open. I even started doing research on the latest spots and essentially became the de facto nightlife planner of the group. I still had my connection with Michael, David Mirisch's club promoter son, to help get us access to some of the hard ones, which only won me more points with my newfound crew. I felt that was how I could contribute. Riley once said I should start a service called "do LA," because we knew how to *do LA*. I thought about it, but my liver begged me not to. Although it would never be a profession for me, I could get us into the hottest spots and that counted as me pulling my weight. Meanwhile, the guys were busy hustling, appearing in the occasional TV series or film, living paycheck to paycheck, and managing a revolving door of beautiful girls along the way.

This was when I first started questioning why I didn't have any sexual feelings or real attraction to anyone. I was either extremely intimidated by the semi-famous quality of the girls in our orbit and often shoved into the "friend zone," or was managing my periodic temptation to look a tad too long when one of my male roommates had his shirt off. Which, by the way, was all the time. In an apartment overflowing with testosterone, I fought that hard, and some seemed to notice. It didn't take long for all of them to start convincing me that

I needed to get laid. One time they called me, all huddled around the phone, playing that line from *Happy Gilmore* that goes, "I just like to putt from the rough." They laughed with hysterics and hung up.

Confused at first, I eventually realized what they were insinuating. Also, once they cut all of my boxer brief into thong underwear. I opened up my drawer one evening and there they were. Crudely cut like women's panties. It was a crude and misogynistic joke, and I knew what it meant. To them, I was Peaches. They didn't call me that, of course. Mercifully that nickname stayed in Texas. But that's how they saw me: different, not hyper masculine, soft, possibly gay. It was these experiences and how they made me feel that caused me concern that I could lose my new crew if I glanced in the wrong direction again. It was clear that I should bury any remote curiosity that I had about possibly being attracted to men immediately. If I couldn't, the consequences were simple: this could all go away. I thought Hollywood could reject me, just as fast as it had accepted me. From that moment forward, I focused on work and decided I'd curb all curiosity with the same sex. My focus was my job, my new life in Los Angeles, being a friend and contributing roommate, and trying to build a life that my parents would be proud of.

But my roommates were still determined to "get me laid." This all came to a head one night when several of the roommates egged on one of the beautiful girls to go into my bedroom. I had chatted with her briefly that night and, unbeknownst to me, the roommates were sure this one would not put me in the "friend zone." She caved to the peer pressure and entered, finding me changing clothes. There I was, naked – a literal virgin – and apparently about to learn how to have intercourse with a girl. She started the process for us and my heart beat through my chest. I was shaking. Sensing my awkwardness and nervousness, she suddenly stopped. As we sat on the edge of the bed, I started to cry. I felt so inadequate. *What a complete loser. What the hell is wrong with me?* I kept repeating in my head. *She's gorgeous and she's really nice. Isn't this what I was supposed to be doing in my 20s?* But I didn't say anything. I just cried, silently.

She obviously felt sorry for me, and then I noticed she started to tear up as well. Almost as if she understood my pain and confusion, and my fear that something was broken inside me. She hugged me tightly, and we fell asleep, her hand clinging to arm. The next morning, as I exited the room, I was cheered on by a few of my (immature) roommates. She followed close behind me as I turned back, dreading her expression might give me away as a failure. Instead, she smiled sweetly at me, a subtle sign that she would keep our secret. She gave me a hug and left, letting the guys assume whatever they wanted. We still run into each other periodically. She has since become successful and famous, and is dating a wonderful woman. That evening created a unique bond, and a shared secret. The experience that night only further solidified that I was still as confused as they come, so instead of dealing with that, I would focus on building my career. Whatever else was happening in my head, my sexuality was on the backburner.

***

After about six months, I couldn't take living in that apartment anymore. We were grown men. We had jobs. They might not all have been respectable jobs yet, but they were jobs nonetheless. There was income, enough to party every night. We deserved a better living situation. Riley still might have been the leader of the pack and spiritual center of the group, but I had carved out a spot of my own as a designated manager type – seemingly taking care of everyone, providing advice when solicited, and suggesting somewhat reasonable life decisions. With Riley enlisted to help, I began to make my case that we should move. This was the first big change I was able to implement. We needed to get a bigger place, we needed to grow the fuck up. We also needed to get out of the newcomer haven of Burbank. Everyone agreed.

We found a house in an area called Sherman Oaks, Colbath Avenue to be exact, and decided to all move together. It was more expensive, of course, but everyone had their own bedroom, and we had a few extra bathrooms to share. I also had enough sway now that I laid down some ground rules and made it clear that everyone had to start minimally cleaning up. You could keep your bedroom however you wanted, but the chores for the communal areas were divided and everyone had to contribute, which was a real teeth pull at times. The house was amazing. There was even room enough to put all my stuff in appropriate places, instead of stacked in corners as it had been in the apartment.

The house even felt like Los Angeles, with a main house and a bungalow guest house. And the best part about it was that in the center of the property was a huge outdoor area and jacuzzi that became the center of our social lives. I couldn't help but associate it with the pool that sat between the apartments in the show *Melrose Place*. We had huge backyard parties where we crammed too many people in the already large hot tub. For the unprepared ladies who were invited back after a night at the club, the roommates kept many different sizes of bikinis on hand in the laundry room to accommodate. How gentlemanly of them. Soon enough it became known as the house with all the hot, C-list actors. Some were even inching their way up to the B-list. For a few years, most of young Hollywood passed through a party or two of ours at one time or another. The first regular at the house to break it big was Anna Faris. She landed her starring role in the Scary Movie franchise and never looked back. I remember thinking, *It can happen that quick.* There were plenty of times where I played manager/parent, waking up in the middle of the night to check on a roommate or two who'd done a little too much ecstasy, because I was afraid they'd stop breathing. We had fun, but they scared me sometimes.

I continued to channel all of my energy and focus into building my career. I appreciated the spirit of my roommates, but I didn't want to be like them. I didn't want to live a hand-to-mouth existence and continue to be the butt of many jokes. I wanted to be successful, and although I didn't have a road map to get there, I definitely knew what I *didn't* want.

Riley actually called me up a few months ago, now a successful, constantly working actor, and happily married with a cute kid. I had not talked to him in over a decade. Unsolicited, he apologized for the way he and the roommates had treated me back in those days. It meant a lot and proved what I had always intuited: we were all just dumb, ignorant, guys making mistakes and trying our best to find ourselves. But I hadn't lost sight of what I came out to Hollywood for in the first place, even if I temporarily got distracted by one thing or another. I spent my days balancing that temporary admin job, college classes (to make Gran happy), and partying. But I wanted more for my life and I missed learning from David. It was time for a real job. It was time to curb the partying and get serious.

CUE: "Time of Our Lives" by Pitbull featuring NeYo

5

Ovitz and Favors

WHILE I WAS working part-time at the real estate office, I was aggressively trying to get a full-time job at a place called Artist Management Group (AMG), run by infamous Hollywood mogul Michael Ovitz. The AMG office was, in my opinion, the nicest in Beverly Hills with its fair share of marble. It had its own beautiful, valet-focused parking garage, a sign of success in that town. No other parking garage was lit like a museum, with priceless Lichtenstein and others art adorning the walls and rows on rows of exotic cars backed into their spots. It was north of Wilshire Boulevard, where I wanted to be. I was learning quickly that, unlike North Dallas where people evaluate you based on the answers to "What's your name, and what's your daddy do?" Hollywood is all about your physical address and the image you project. To the naive, perception is reality. The office where I worked was in Beverly Hills, but south of Wilshire. Although, it was nice, it was still just a few blocks too far south. This meant it was close to the action, but not quite where all the power players were located. Power agents, managers, and producers who were running shit – they did everything that I wanted to do in addition to being where I wanted to be.

Ovitz had previously founded and run a company for a long time called Creative Artists Agency, or CAA for short, arguably one of the most powerful talent agencies in the world. For a short period of time,

Michael Eisner, the former chairman of Disney, hired him to run the studio. After an embarrassing and public falling out with Disney and Eisner, Ovitz abruptly left. He blamed his fall at Disney on a clash with Eisner and on the "Gay Mafia" (his exact words). For his next act, he had formed AMG, a full-service management company. There were a handful of prestigious management companies in Hollywood at the time, but AMG was new, redefining, and revered.

Between the AMG building and my part-time job was a tiny place called Mulberry Pizza. It was the cheapest, quickest spot on the block, and you could buy it by the slice. I ate there almost every day for lunch. One of the other regulars whom I had seen multiple times before was a woman named Kara. We always seemed to sit across from each other, her head always buried in a script. After making eye contact a few times, it felt necessary to one day finally say hi to her.

She was friendly and took interest, "You from around here?"

"No, ma'am," I replied.

"Ma'am!" she said, taken aback with a pause. "Cute, I like that."

She looked to be in her late 30s, was an agent's assistant, and was really impressed by my manners. I was still in my early 20s. I told her where I was from and what I did for work. "You don't sound too inspired," she said about my job. That was an understatement.

"Gotta pay my dues," I said.

"I guess so," she said. "There are a lot of places to pay them around here. Which one are you eyeing?" she asked.

The answer came easy and fast, "AMG."

Her face revealed that she knew it well. "Oh, I have some close friends over there; I could introduce you," she said casually, as if she hadn't just made my entire week. "There's a cocktails thing at Caffe Luna on Thursday. It's kind of an agent trainee–assistant mixer thing. You should come."

I tried to play it cool as we exchanged numbers. "If you call me and I don't answer, just leave a message," I said.

"Ooh, busy guy," she teased.

I wasn't, really, I was just overly conscious of my cellphone minutes. I paid for less than 100 a month and voicemails were free. If someone left a voicemail, I could call them back from another phone, like the office, and didn't have to spend minutes. A genius workaround, I thought.

We set it up, and I did attend the mixer. Kara introduced me to a few people, and a cocktail or two in she proclaimed, "Jason's cool; get him an interview or something." With Kara's endorsement, some of my new AMG "friends" agreed to set up an interview for a bit of a flunky, bottom-of-the-barrel job I assumed. I was willing to do a mailroom/ messenger/coffee run/whatever sort of job. I didn't mind too much. If it was at AMG, I wanted in. At that time, film scripts were still being mostly printed out, hole-punched, stuck together with metal brads, and packed into envelopes. They needed to be delivered around the office and elsewhere. This was a role that constantly needed filling at a bustling firm. I felt my experience with David could help get me in the door I desperately wanted to go into. I always knew I'd have to start from the bottom and could turn that into a stepping stone to something bigger. I knew people desperately wanted a job at a place like AMG or CAA. I learned that there were Harvard and Stanford grads working in the mail room for $5 or so an hour just to get a shot at working their way up to manager someday. I mean, I only had a couple years of community college under my belt, so I figured I was doing pretty well.

I knew I had to dress nice for the interview, and that ties were mandatory at AMG, so I wore the only suit I had and my brown lace-up Dockers boat shoes, the nicest shoes I owned. It wasn't a good look, but I didn't know any different at the time. As soon as I walked through the gorgeous double glass doors, and took in the sterile reception, I felt as if I'd done something wrong. People glanced me up and down as they walked past, but I had no idea why. There was elaborate, expensive art on all the walls and marble so shiny I could see my reflection in it. The office was majestic in my eyes, and oozed class, just as I had imagined. I did well enough in the interview that I got the flunky entry-level job. I had to find replacement batteries for Blackberry phones from the first day, while fetching endless ice blended coffee constantly. Most relevant to the actual business, my first mornings were spent scanning all of the daily trade publications, like the *Hollywood Reporter* and *Variety*, to highlight all the mentions of AMG clients and deliver these to certain managers – or their assistants. I suppose this was to make them aware of what had been written about their client in the last 24 hours, positive or negative. It sounds archaic, but it was what I was asked to do. And you do what you are told to do.

With the advent of the internet and today's social media, this practice is nonexistent now.

I also helped out delivering the mail, packages, buckslip memos, and those scripts all around the office. Apparently, there was a higher position to the one I filled, where a select few could actually deliver packages to a client's house on behalf of the firm when a more personal touch was required. That would be exciting – one day you could find yourself at Ben Stiller or Will Ferrell's house, delivering them a package. Those select jobs were rumored to be offered only to people with nicer cars and they must be black or silver, I was informed. I didn't stay long enough to get promoted, and I'm not sure my Nissan and I would have been qualified. Toward the end of my very short tenure there I did get to semi-temp on a desk (which is basically filling in for the second assistant – the assistant's assistant) if you call it that, rolling a few calls like I did with Mirisch. I enjoyed the few times I got to do that, because it really gave me quick study into who was who within a subset of the industry.

I only had two real interactions with the infamous Michael Ovitz. The first, I was walking down one of the corridors in the office that seemed to all tilt toward his own office. My hands were full of scripts. This is when I took the leap and said, "Good morning," and he nodded his head, sort of, at me without replying. Though he was a small-statured guy, he was feared, and it was understood that you don't talk to him unless you're pretty high up the food chain. He had a reputation. But I didn't care. You say good morning to someone when you pass them that early. That's how I was raised. He was notorious at CAA for having employees read *The Art of War*, the military strategy book by Sun Tzu. Apparently, he thought there was something to be learned about agenting, management, or life in the book. Maybe there is . . . for a certain personality.

My second interaction with Ovitz was on another morning when I was dropping stuff off at various offices or desks, like I did as instructed or needed. On this particular morning, his assistant wasn't stationed outside Ovitz's office yet. He'd never paid me much attention before, so I proceeded to drop the package off on his actual desk, in front of him, with a chipper, "Gooood morning, sir!" As I turned to walk out I heard, "Where are you from?" *This is my moment!* I thought. *He's noticed me, He is going to acknowledge that I come in earlier than most. It's your moment, Jason! Let's go, Jason!*

"I'm from Texas," I said confidently in my twangy southern drawl.

"A little advice," he remarked softly. And in that moment, it was made clear that women with southern accents were intriguing and men with southern accents, uneducated or stupid. He was matter-of-fact about it, and I was stunned. While he didn't say I needed to lose the accent, he basically said I needed to lose the accent.

I instantly became extremely self-conscious. I began paying close attention to the mannerisms and voices of those around me. They seemed to speak a little faster, so I sped up my speech. I mimicked their non-Southern-sounding accents and tried to fix this apparently huge problem. It also became clear I was saying more than a few things wrong, including calling the Los Angeles airport *lax* instead of by its acronym, LAX. And, yes, the common mistake, Rodeo Drive, like the kind with cowboys and bulls, as I mentioned previously. How embarrassing! My wardrobe (or lack thereof) combined with this new accent insecurity made me feel like an ignorant hillbilly for the first time since moving to Hollywood. What made it extra hard to lose the accent was that every time I called friends or family or went back to Texas, I quickly reverted. Like riding a bike, as they say, except I kind of wanted to forget how to ride. I didn't want back on the bike. Eventually I had to give up because it just wasn't going away.

After a couple of months, I'd made a few industry friends and started getting asked to go out to parties. The ethos of Hollywood is work hard, play hard. And some play harder than others. Although I had written off partying with my roommates in favor of focusing on building a career, sometimes after a long day of being bossed around and working for pennies, nothing felt better than a drink and a laugh. I was happy to go out again and be social. I wanted to get ingratiated into another group besides my roommates. A group of accomplished assistants and one moonlighting manager who had navigated their way through the ranks at AMG seemed more my speed. The first night we went out to dinner, the manager yanked out a baggie of cocaine and emptied it onto the booth right beside me. With skilled precision, he made a line with his car key, leaned over, plugged one nostril, and the line vanished. I had never seen anything like this in my life. With a big sniff and a laugh, he looked me in the eye and said, "Now you know the secret of my success."

Now, let me just say, I have never done cocaine. Not just because I don't like hard drugs, but because I don't need the speed. I already operate at an 11 most days, and if I did do drugs, I'd prefer some sort of a depressant to slow me down. That's why I've always liked alcohol. But coke was the drug of choice of everyone at that dinner. They all did it at the table. Shirts unbuttoned and ties loosened more and more as the night progressed. Some did it in the bathroom again before we even left the restaurant, and again multiple times at SkyBar where we went to after. It was a normal Friday night for these guys.

Of course, they offered me some. "Oh, no thanks," I said.

"I thought you wanted to party?" someone said.

"I'm on my friend's airline plan and could be drug tested at any time and lose my flight benefits."

They looked confused at my complex excuse. What I meant was, Mary was a flight attendant for Delta. Each flight attendant got to choose one "companion" to fly free for life, as long as she was employed. Mary and I had remained friends, and are very close even today. And we have had some fun adventures with those flight benefits. Although *she* could get drug tested anytime, I could not. That part was a lie. I remembered Mary told me about how she could be drug tested at any time, and if she failed, she could lose her job and flight privileges.

Quick on my feet, I had lied because I didn't want to do booger sugar (coke slang I had learned that night), but I still wanted to be accepted and I didn't want to tell my new colleagues that I just didn't want to. So, I came up with what I thought was a pretty good excuse. They started calling me Flyboy, and soon after that first night, they stopped inviting me. I wasn't cool anymore, if I'd ever been at all. I had a conservative, simple wardrobe, a slow drawl for an accent, and now I'd refused participation in the primary form of bonding at that company.

The last straw that ended my four-month stint at AMG was actually Kara, the woman whom I was originally so grateful to for getting me a foot in the door. She invited me to a party at her Beverly Hills adjacent condo, and I took one of my roommates. He was excited and thought while I networked, he might "get laid by an older lady." There was no agenda of this sort on my mind. I just liked Kara. She'd really helped me out. She got me in the door. But I was already beginning to doubt whether I should be at AMG at all. It seemed toxic, and I hadn't met anyone there that I connected with. After a few too many drinks, I was standing in the corner of Kara's condo pondering some esoteric questions like *Who am I? What am I doing here? What is my path in life? Should I ditch my job?* when she cornered me between a darker hallway and the dining area.

"It's time for you to pay me back, sir," she said as she moved her hand down my chest and grabbed my crotch. This was my introduction to the concept of favor-swapping in Hollywood. It's a thing. Almost no one does something just out of kindness, or because they care. Most expect the favor granted to be returned at some point and keep an official tally of sorts. It's a nuanced topic. In some ways, it makes sense to me and might be a fair way to operate. Sort of like bartering. And in other regards, it seems insincere and selfish if tallied in the wrong way. Anyway, in this instance, Kara wanted the favor returned in the form of fucking her. I panicked, acted as if I was sick from the drinks, and got out of there as quickly as I could.

It was then that I decided I needed to leave AMG. Although Kara wasn't an employee there, that interaction was the culmination of everything. A realization that I'd have to change to survive in that specific environment, and I wouldn't do that. It wasn't just the unrelated and isolated incidents of coke or Ovitz's advice or Kara's advances, though of course I didn't like any of that. I just wasn't comfortable there. I didn't fit in. And when I did express myself honestly, it was met with rejection. I actually loved my Docker's boat shoes. I liked my accent. And I didn't want to do drugs. It's who I am, and I didn't want to change. I also had this overwhelming desire to deliver on my dreams and not let myself or my parents down. They always provided me unconditional support, encouragement, and trust, and I felt to change myself would have hurt us all.

Look, I don't care if you do coke or favor fuck. Have at it. Your life is your life. You are allowed to lead it any way you choose. We all have our vices, and I certainly have mine. I will admit, though, I still get PTSD when I see a line of coke. I think it stems from the whiplash of going from being so excited to make new friends that night to being completely shunned for not partaking. Anyway, I was still bummed to leave AMG. Working there had been my dream job, I originally thought. I was willing to do the grunt work and grind for little to no money. But I wasn't willing to change who I was.

I also thought of my Gran. It might be cliché, but my mind regularly wondered, *Would she be proud of me?* If she could actually read my emails, or be a fly on my wall, would she be proud of what I was doing and who I was becoming? Whenever I told her about what I was working on in Hollywood, she sure sounded like it. She talked about me like I'd hung the moon, and loved telling everyone in her annual newsletter about her grandson who was chasing his dreams and making it in Hollywood. But would she be proud of this part? The seedy underbelly of the industry I at times felt forced to play along in? Of course she wouldn't. I wanted to be around people who made me better, accepted me for who I was, and didn't make fun of me for driving a clunky Nissan with Aunt Karen's loan (which they did). AMG wasn't it.

I was scared to quit. I wasn't sure what would come next or if I'd get an opportunity like this again. But some things just aren't worth it. I was uncomfortable in my environment. I wanted to be unapologetically me. Not just because it felt true and right, but because I knew I could only achieve my highest potential that way.

Surprisingly, all of this hadn't diminished my infatuation and enthusiasm for the business of Hollywood. My eyes were opened to some things, for sure. But if anything, my drive to accomplish my goals had only strengthened. I was going to do this, and I was going to do it my way. I wouldn't allow this glorious thing I'd built up in my head to be destroyed. It was going to be great; I knew it would. It might be a little Dorothy-somewhere-over-the-rainbow-ish, but I was going to find my place in that town if it was the last thing I did. I'd done it before . . . in high school. I wanted to be part of something important, be where the action was. I just knew I had to find my place again, here in Hollywood. I knew I would figure it out and find exactly where I belonged.

That's when I met Ashlee, who was just a few years away from writing her own story.

CUE: "Autobiography" by Ashlee Simpson

6

Who Are You Wearing?

ONE DAY, BACK at our house, Lane (the guy who forgot to pay the refrigerator bill) walked into the converted garage where all the roommates lounged and asked, "Hey guys, do y'all want to drive down to San Diego on Friday and see my friend Jessica Simpson in concert?" Her father, Joe Simpson, had been Lane's youth pastor back in his Texas high school days, and they had remained close. I'm a little embarrassed to say that I didn't know who Jessica was at the time. I feigned excitement like I knew what a big deal this was, but truly I had no clue and couldn't name a single song of hers. For a guy who loved the entertainment industry and lived in Hollywood, I certainly wasn't fully versed on all things pop culture. But I didn't care who she was. A night out was a night out.

Broke, living with seven actors, and always up for fun, I said yes. So did everyone else, of course. They all wanted a chance to meet a gorgeous, young pop star and her gorgeous, young fans. It was November 14, 1999, and Jessica was at the start of her singing career, opening up for Ricky Martin, playing at what was then the San Diego Sports Arena. I had no idea what I was in for, but a free night out was the best kind of night out. At the risk of sounding cliché, I guess you could say I was livin' la vida loca!

We all piled into whoever's car had gas at the time and drove the couple of hours to San Diego. Lane had gotten us backstage passes and we got there just in time to head back to the dressing room. It was a flurry backstage. Different than backstage at a televised award show like the Victors; this had a different type of energy. A concert energy with an arena of anxious fans. We walked into Jessica's dressing room as she sat having her hair and makeup done by a pack of specialists attending to her. Immediately she stood up, said hi, and gave her old friend Lane a hug, followed by a timid, but genuine wave to the rest of us. She was one part sweet and one part shy, as she rushed back to her chair at the behest of her manager father. For the rest of the time, she was pretty quiet. She was in the zone and focused. Then she started belting a scale of do-re-mi-fa-so-la-ti-do – a practice many artists perform to warm up their vocals before a performance.

All of the guys kept staring at her, swooning. Several lingered awkwardly by her chair, trying to catch her eye in the mirror. Some of them tried to chat with her, and as polite as she was, it was obvious she would rather not. And it was even more obvious from his stare back to the guys that Lane was not going to allow that to happen. I later learned that Lane, like most other guys Jessica grew up with, had a residual crush on her. As beautiful as she was, I wasn't interested in her that way. Plus my roommates were swooning so awkwardly, I didn't want to be associated with that. I wanted to avoid creeping her out.

While everyone was fussing over the blonde pop star, I kept noticing another blonde girl running around, even doing cartwheels. She was laughing and loud and seemed like Miss Personality. *Who's that girl?* I wondered. *She seems really fun.* It was Ashlee Simpson, Jessica's younger sister. At the time, she was a back-up dancer for Jessica, and the bounciest ball of energy. Both of their parents, Joe and Tina, were backstage as well. I loved that they were all so southern. I didn't encounter too many overtly, proudly southern people in Hollywood, but when I did, I felt a kinship. Like a foreigner abroad who hears his native language across a room, when I heard that Texas twang and felt that big, warm, southern hug, I felt like I was home. To some degree, I think I was always searching for that in LA.

Ashlee and I talked a little backstage while everyone else surrounded Jessica. She was a little younger than me, but she seemed wise beyond her years. She wasn't just a cartwheeling charisma. She was quirky, interesting, and thoughtful. She was real. Instantly I felt we could be friends.

We only chatted for a few minutes before they ushered us out of the dressing room and into the audience. As soon as Jessica stepped out and opened her mouth to sing, I was blown away. I had never heard anything like it. She was way better than the other pop stars whose names and songs I knew. And her confidence was palpable as she belted her first single, "I Wanna Love You Forever." I was in awe that she was younger than me, more timid, and could stand on stage and do that in front of thousands of people. And Ashlee turned out to be an incredible dancer as I watched her in her sister's shadow. I loved her energy and confidence as she captured the audience in a different sort of way. She seemed positive, spontaneous, and unapologetically herself, her movements so dramatic and so grand.

After the show, Ashlee and several others from the show went back with my roommates and me to Mary's house. Since we were in San Diego, I knew my way around, and it was only fitting that I showed everyone the town. From there, I continued to hang with Ashlee a lot. She felt like the little sister I never had. She even reminded me so much of my friend Melissa back in Texas.

She became a regular at our house, and I felt protective of her. As a group we regularly went out to eat with her and her family. But as Ashlee and I became closer friends, we started hanging out just the two of us. During the day we'd hit Ventura Boulevard where we ate, shopped, and drove around. And then at night I'd go "over the hill," as they say, to Hollywood, Coldwater, or Laurel Canyon with my roommates, to the club or bar of the night. Ashlee had to stay behind for that, given her age. She would get so irritated with me that she couldn't go along. Sure, I could have likely sourced a fake ID for her, but I felt this unwavering need to shield her from anything that could corrupt her innocence. Specifically, the boners of my roommates. As Jessica's fame and attention increased, I felt more and more that Ashlee deserved that more and more. I felt like her big brother figure. Someone to remind her that she didn't need to live in anyone's shadow and could forge a path of her own. Eventually I slowed the clubs and nightlife to hang back with Ashlee at her family's house watching movies or just driving aimlessly around LA for hours. Fun fact, Ashlee credits me for teaching her how to drive. A running joke to all who know us is that of all the accomplishments we collectively both have, our finest hour was in a Jeep, her as student and I as teacher.

Shortly after I'd left Artist Management Group (AMG), Ashlee, our friend Heather, and I were out driving around one afternoon, seeking sweets. Among the many things that bonded Ashlee and me was our shared love of junk food, candy, and marginal strip mall chain restaurants that remind us of Texas. We were known to pull into convenience stores and just load up on candy in the middle of the day, Ashlee tossing everything from the shelves onto the counter and swiping her card with confidence. I did the driving, and she did the buying. We were a sugar fiend team. On this particular day, we found a convenience store at the edge of a strip mall and decided we must find those Chipwich ice cream sandwiches we were particularly addicted to that week.

As we stood there, I noticed a sign on the wall advertising "Kensington Nannies Placement Agency." It proclaimed that they hire and place nannies and personal assistants, and it listed their phone number and address. I wasn't especially interested in getting back in the nanny biz, but I needed a job, desperately. I still had that pay-by-the-minute phone, and my parents still generously paid for the essentials of car and health insurance. It was very expensive to live in LA, and I wanted to make it on my own, even if that meant nannying again for a while. As I looked at the address, I realized it was in the same center where we were, just above the shop.

"Hey, I'm gonna run upstairs real quick," I said to Ashlee and Heather as I headed toward the stairs. I found the door clearly labeled "Kensington Nannies" on the outside and whipped it open. I remember that because the hinges were loose, and it truly did whip open much easier and wider than you'd expect a door should. This caused me to enter abruptly and surprise the woman sitting behind the desk. The space was small, only a few desks and what looked like a receptionist.

The woman I'd scared was Elise Lewis, and she was not a receptionist. She was the owner. Elise had a New York accent and firmly asked, "Can I help you?" She was polished and refined, and I thought how strange it felt to hear a New York accent in California. Ironically, the only other time I had heard a New York accent was when watching the TV sitcom, *The Nanny*.

"I used to be a nanny," I said, suddenly becoming a little self-conscious because I hadn't prepared for this. "I nannied in San Diego. . . ."

"What part?" she interrupted.

"Del Mar," I replied. She nodded, as if to tell me to continue. I knew I'd just passed a test. Del Mar is fancy and rich. Quickly, I assumed by her nod that Kensington Nannies places nannies for wealthy people. "I nannied for a CEO and his wife. I moved out here from Texas," I went on.

"Do you want to be an actor?" she asked.

"No," I answered honestly.

"Good. Everyone wants to be an actor," she said with a little disdain. "I need commitment. I only place people who can commit. And actors are always quitting."

I told her some more about my experience. I had a good work ethic and had never been fired. She liked me enough to start shuffling through potential openings right there. Meanwhile, Ashlee kept calling my phone. Finally, I answered.

"Hey, where are you?!" she asked.

"Hang on. I'll be right there," I said. I had basically walked into a job interview and potentially even a job offer. Plus, my minutes! I need to conserve those. I couldn't afford to waste them on her when she's right outside.

After a while, Elise looked up and said, "Look, I only have one nanny position. It's for an elementary age boy. His name is Weston. You would have to take him to school, pick him up, help with homework, blah blah blah. His father's an actor, Nicolas Cage, but you'd primarily be working for the mother, Christina. They're not together." On and on she went with details. I was thrilled. I needed work and this sounded like a sure thing and an easy gig. It was perfect, and it was for Nicolas *freaking* Cage.

I reluctantly gave Elise my phone number, again worried about my remaining minutes, and headed out to find my friends plowing through the candy they had just scored. Later that day, Elise called me. She sucked up over five minutes telling me the position had been filled. I was devastated. I thought it was fate that I'd seen the sign on that convenience store door. I thought it had led me to exactly that place so I could get that sweet job. *This sucks*, I thought. Elise could tell how disappointed I was and how much I needed money. I am glad I was honest with her as I bluntly said, "My rent is due in two weeks; I need to figure something out."

"Why don't you swing by again this week," she said. "I'll see what else we have."

I went another few days without any prospects and showed back up at Kensington Nannies the next week. "I think I may have something for you," said Elise. "There's a British director who is looking for someone. She's done some movies and commercials and lives at the top of the hill." What she meant was, she lived between Ventura and Sunset Boulevard, which are divided by the Santa Monica Mountain foothills. One road winds the entire crest – Mulholland Drive. *Oh that's cool,* I thought. I would have worked for anybody at this point, but I was really interested now.

"She owns one of the top commercial production companies in Hollywood," Elise went on, and my heart stopped. I knew it instantly. It was a prolific commercial production company based in the heart of Westside Los Angeles.

"I know it!" I said to Elise before launching into an excited ramble. "I've done a ton of research on production companies because I think I want to produce someday. And I used to work at AMG, and I thought that would be my path in the industry but that turned out to be terrible, despite some eye-opening experiences! Actually, while I worked there, I thought I might want to be an agent or manager but soon decided that wasn't for me and now I definitely think I'm leaning toward production. . . ."

"Relax," she interrupted. "This isn't a job in production. She needs a nanny. You'll pick the kids up from school and likely only work from AJ's home. I doubt you'll ever even go into the production office or be on set." The client was AJ. She was married to another partner in the commercial production company. The fact that this was a nanny position and there was a good chance I wouldn't get anywhere near a movie or commercial set didn't dampen my spirit.

"I'd love an interview," I said. "I have lots of nanny experience and I know what I'm doing." Elise agreed to call AJ and set it up.

She looked me up and down, standing there in my jeans and T-shirt, and said, "She's proper, and British, so make sure you look nice and bring a copy of your résumé."

My *résumé?* I thought, as I walked out the door. I'd heard of a résumé before but they'd seemed like something only older people with skyscraper jobs needed. What would I possibly put on mine?

That I had bagged groceries at Kroger, worked at a One-Hour-Photo, maybe that real estate office job, and the short stints at Mirisch's and Ovitz's companies? I looked like a flake, hopping from one uninspiring job to another. I had a high school diploma but basically dropped out of community college after two years to move up here and do this. This is Hollywood, should I put that I briefly appeared in an episode of *Walker, Texas Ranger*? I wasn't impressed with myself as I pondered the list of non-accomplishments in my head. *Oh well*, I thought, as I drove home, focused on the glass being half full. *You know how to nanny. One step at a time.*

As soon as I got home, I sat down at our shared computer, opened up Word, and began typing out a résumé. In a house full of actors, this was a novelty. None of them had ever had official résumés before, except for a list of what they'd been in. And even then, a manager usually puts that together and sends it out for them.

"Who are you going to work for?" one of them asked.

"I'm trying to get a job with a director," I said. I mean, it wasn't untrue.

"Oh, cool! What will you be doing?" they followed up.

"Uh, I don't know, work on things she directs and stuff," I replied. Now that *was* untrue. I didn't have the heart to tell them I was going to be nannying. They had seemed too excited when I mentioned the director part.

My ruse didn't last long though. "Why are you adding nanny experience to your résumé?" Todd, the nosiest roommate, asked as he leaned over my shoulder.

"Well, there might be some nannying as part of the job," I admitted. Immediately, I became nanny boy. Peaches, fly boy, nanny boy. Why was everyone always making up nicknames for me? And why were they always so degrading? No one else around here seemed to have a dumb nickname that ended in *boy*. Later, the teasing even involved comparing me to Fran Drescher, which frankly I failed to see as an insult because *The Nanny* was a great show and Fran Drescher is hilarious. But in their (politically incorrect) world, this comparison to a woman was supposed to be insulting.

Even though Elise had set up an interview, before she gave me the go-ahead, she made me do a trial run with her son Greg, picking him up and helping with his homework. I passed, and a few days later showed up at AJ's office, résumé in hand. After being forced to recall everything, I had "accomplished" in my last few years as a run-up to applying for yet another nannying job, I wasn't feeling confident at all and had worn a suit to compensate. I believed that to be the respectful thing to wear when you are to meet a "proper British lady." Not that it was a nice suit. It was ill-fitting and cheap, but it was what I had.

When you show up to a successful Los Angeles production company, you're often met with modern design and affluence, like Ovitz's office. If you have an eye for designers, you can spot the latest Air Jordans, Prada hoodie, and $2,000 Noguchi table. At that time, I couldn't tell any of this, of course. I was just surprised by how casual most people looked compared to me. Casual, but also chic and expensive, if that's possible. Somehow, I'd managed to look overdressed and pitiable at the same time.

I approached the front desk. A kind young woman looked up and said, "Hi, I'm Trang, Who are you here to see?"

"I'm here for an interview with AJ," I replied.

Trang clocked me up and down and, no joke, asked, "Who are you wearing?"

I paused. I had no idea what she meant. I'd never heard this question before, and it was long before Joan Rivers popularized it on the red carpet. *Who am I wearing? What kind of question is that?! What does that even mean?* I didn't say anything, and she registered my confusion.

"What brand?" she clarified. *Ah, I see.* I couldn't remember if I'd gotten the suit at Ross Dress for Less or Marshall's but settled on the latter.

"I think it's Marshall," I replied with an earnest smile.

"Never heard of him," she said kindly, as she led me to a waiting area. "Would you like some water or coffee?"

As I looked across at the refrigerator, I noticed that all the beverages were lined up in the most precise, obsessive compulsive disorder way I'd ever seen, by color and height. It was a perfect representation of the dedication and mania of assistants and the creativity and imagination of directors that exists in the production world. It's a creative workspace like no other. They were just drinks, but I was immediately intrigued. It was meticulous, perfect, neurotic, and reminded me of something you'd see in an episode of *Cribs*.

A man who'd been standing around and apparently heard my conversation with Trang leaned over me to get some water. "I'm wearing Helmut Lang," he said with a wink.

"Awesome," I replied. I think I was supposed to be impressed by this, but I had no clue what he meant.

He pointed to another guy passing, "And he's wearing John Varvados." He pointed again, "That's Calvin Klein." *Okay, okay,* I thought. *I guess this is a lesson in designers.* "Who are you wearing?" he asked me.

"Marshall," I repeated.

He literally reached behind my neck and pulled back the collar of my suit. "You're wearing Van Heusen. You bought the suit at Marshall's, right? You're not wearing Marshall." With that, he walked off. I'd just experienced the 20-something version of hazing in LA.

There was a lot to this question, "Who are you wearing?" And I'd be asked many more times in my career, especially at events. It seemed to be a sort of post–high school pecking order designator, meant to either impress or shame the other. In Hollywood, your status and the health of your career is sadly judged by the image you project, who you wear, what you drive, and where you dine. Hollywood is an entertainment industry town and is centered on image making and culture shaping. And, like most industries, it is highly competitive. In that moment, I was sized up, or rather, sized down, with my suit. This is a thing many people feel they need to do to prove (or fake) that they've achieved more than you.

Humiliated, but also a little grateful I now knew how to answer this question appropriately, I settled in and waited for AJ. Like when building my résumé, I was reminded again of how green I was. I thought I'd gotten to a point where I knew some things. I'd been in California for a few years, LA for almost a year. I'd gotten myself and my roommates into a house, had met celebrities, attended some industry parties, and knew pretty much every club door guy I needed to know. I had gained some limited industry knowledge working with Mirisch and AMG, but I was insecure about the collection of short stints on my résumé, not fully reflective of everything I'd learned. I thought, *I'll lean on the skills I've accumulated instead of the jobs I had,* as I sat anxiously there in the lobby, clutching my résumé in my sweaty palm. I was afraid my dream job was even further away than I thought.

Interrupting my self-pity, AJ soon whipped around the corner. She had gorgeous hair, a 1,000-watt smile, and a big, loud personality. She also looked absolutely impeccable. Instantly, I liked her. Since high school I'd had an affinity for women with big personalities, like Melissa, Mary, and Ashlee. They made for the best friends and made me feel comfortable. AJ was warm and genuine, oozing with style. She was clearly accomplished but didn't exude the condescension of many people in Hollywood. We sat across from each other in a little, unassuming office, and she commented on my suit. But not in the way others had. She smiled kindly and in a proper British accent said, "You look brilliant. I like your suit." I could tell she meant it. I'm sure she could tell it wasn't designer, but she recognized I had put in effort.

AJ began to describe the job. "You'll mostly work out of the studio at my house. Pick up and look after the kids, the house, and occasionally ChaCha, the poodle. And you'll help me with personal assistant items from time to time. You'll be replacing Hazel. Those are big shoes to fill." She made me feel comfortable and welcome, the complete opposite of what I'd felt the moment I set foot in AMG. *This is amazing, she's amazing*, I thought. *Of course I want to work for her.* I was excited at the prospect – the opportunity and chance to maybe learn from her. But it was more than that. I wanted to work for someone *like* her. Someone who was successful, but without arrogance. Someone who made me feel the way she made me feel. Plus, her gorgeous British accent just sealed the deal.

I got the job and walked out of there supercharged. We'd made a plan for me to be trained by Hazel, and start picking up the kids by the end of the week. Assuming I passed muster, I'd take over the role full-time by the end of the month. I wasn't working for David Mirisch or Mike Ovitz, trying to climb my way to the top of a prestigious firm. I wasn't passing actors on a studio lot, and I still wasn't making a ton of money. But this just felt right. I'd already had some experience in jumping into something full force because of either the opportunity it seemed to afford, or the people. So far, it'd paid off better to follow the kinds of people I wanted to surround myself with and let the opportunities present themselves. I was finding that staying patient, persistent, and positive presented the right opportunities.

CUE: "I Don't Want to Be" by Gavin DeGraw

7

Read the Tea Leaves

I LEARNED A lot from working with AJ. One of the first things was how to make tea the British way, which she insisted was the only way. You put the milk in first, then the tea. And always ratio the milk to the tea "just right." She taught me how to determine the perfect brown hue of it so the proportions are correct, and, of course, how to serve it properly. I was a quick study, and had that tea ready to meet her beaming smile whenever she asked.

AJ's kids were the quintessential Los Angeles kids of a director. This meant they participated in various music lessons, sports, and extracurriculars. They were scheduled just about every minute of every day. So much so that I had to create a master calendar of sorts for the family to keep track of all of this: a gigantic whiteboard hanging in the hallway between their two bedrooms. I know I did a good job. I grinded like I did with David Mirisch, working hard to prove to AJ that I was valuable and could help, even if it was just in kid and life administration. She liaised smoothly between her job and her kids and family life because I made it as easy as possible. That's the job of a good assistant. I also just managed to make things "work," as she said. AJ loved that I could always figure things out. When there was a problem with the printer, I fixed it. The computer, I fixed it. Some weird charge on the credit card? I investigated it. It wasn't that I actually had knowledge about any of these things, I was just a problem-solver and knew if I kept researching and calling eventually I could figure it out. I could troubleshoot. It wasn't my skills so much as much as my work ethic and attitude that endeared me to her. That, and the fact that we just enjoyed each other.

I didn't have a plan beyond being a responsible, dependable nanny/assistant. I knew how to take care of kids, and people in general. I also knew that many successful people in the entertainment industry began as nannies. Mark Burnett, one of the top reality television show producers, who created shows like *The Apprentice* and *Survivor*, actually started as a nanny. Later on in life I found myself at his annual Christmas party standing in the middle of his $30 million mansion in Malibu overlooking the ocean and meditating on how his first couple of jobs in the industry were just like mine – nannying, babysitting, calendar managing. Now here he was hosting a diverse guest list consisting of Donald Trump and Oprah and everyone in between.

Though, of course, I did always hope I'd get the chance to learn about the industry from AJ, or perhaps just absorb things from being in her presence. I always knew my real job was to take care of the kids and schedule and do that well. Honestly, I just really enjoyed being around her. I enjoyed our conversations and everything she had to teach me; whether it was about tea or directing, I soaked it up like a sponge. She opened my eyes to so many things. I've always responded to and connected with people older than me. My friends say I'm an old soul, and I always seem to soak up everything I can from those older than me. When I was eight years old and living in Virginia, one of my favorite people was our 30-year-old neighbor. It was completely innocent; I just loved asking her a million questions and admired how mature she was – to an eight-year-old anyway.

I loved talking to AJ about music, movies, and food. We had so many conversations about new books or travel destinations. I attribute a lot of this to my parents. They never treated us as kids socially. They never made us sit at a kids' table or disinvited us from interesting conversation. They would ask my brothers and me what we thought of something. AJ and I became close friends, just like Mary and I had.

Eventually, through the natural course of our friendship and close, reliable working relationship, I did share my career ambitions with her, as I would with anyone. I had worked for her for a couple of years when the kids began to have a social life and became more responsible. They didn't need me as much to help them in the day-to-day, so AJ had me take on more personal assistant–type items. I started to be on set more and manage her work and production calendar. I read scripts, and she asked for my thoughts on them. I observed things and learned some of the inner workings of what she did. Just as I had with David Mirisch, I gained so much just by being in her presence, listening to what she said, watching how she worked. It was a dream being on a production set.

This also meant that I was at the office and around her husband/partner a lot more. He was a part owner and ran the company with the third partner. He was always polite to me, in that distinctly British way, but before I started acting as AJ's personal assistant, our main interaction had just been watching him whip out of the driveway in his luxury sports car every morning as I drove up. Beyond that, he didn't pay much attention to me. As I moved into the later years of the job, AJ would confide in me about the distant state of her relationship with the company she had cofounded. And other employees of the company would randomly make comments to me like how AJ "*is not a priority*" or question my loyalty to my boss versus the other partners of the company. While unaware of the specifics, I was starting to feel that there was a power struggle, and I did wonder if any one knew how much I knew. While I won't go into every micro detail, I knew plenty and my loyalty was solely with the woman who had hired me. Unfortunately, this was not the favored approach. I am reminded of a quote by William Raduchel, a former senior executive at Time Warner, turned professor of economics at Harvard: *Don't pick a job, pick a boss. A first boss is the biggest factor in your career success. A boss who doesn't trust you won't support your growth.* AJ trusted me, and I trusted her.

It didn't take long before the partners' power struggle started to affect me personally. I started getting blamed for things I did do. Confused and frustrated, I could feel other employees of the company start to alienate me based solely on false rhetoric and rumor. Given I worked mainly from AJ's guest house, my time spent at her Santa Monica production company had always been limited, but my presence was never unwelcomed. Well, until that one day. The day I got blamed for something that I would never do – using the company credit card and booking a big stretch limo for personal use. AJ and I both received an email questioning this charge "by Jason." I headed straight to AJ's office and explained emphatically how I didn't do it, and thankfully, she believed me. Mere weeks after I had shared with her my concerns about company heresy, it was evident that bigger plans about the power struggle were being architected. I was a threat to the other partners of the company, and they wanted me out. They didn't have a basis to fire me, so I suppose one was created.

Everything unraveled fast after that – AJ's partnership with the company she had started was essentially over through no fault of her own. That fake limo, which was never booked, had become the match on the haystack. And a deeper agenda to force AJ out of the company she had cofounded came to fruition. After all, with one partner pushed out, the economics would get that much more exciting for those remaining.

AJ determined to reframe and forge forward through her own independent projects that she asked me to help her develop. She set up her company in a penthouse loft in Santa Monica and rented the adjacent space next door for me to have my own office. It was quite the downsize, without having an infrastructure of a large production company, but the energy of the new place was inspiring and the force of AJ's newfound creativity was evident. It was pretty much just she and I working together at that point, so I quickly assumed a bigger role, helping her with research for developing scripts and book options. There was never a formal promotion to the role, it was just an understanding given her two kids didn't require a nanny anymore. AJ and I had weathered a lot together, and I was honored she wanted me there in the next phase. I had just assumed with the forced exit, that I would be applying for new jobs. She insisted that would not be the case. She was starting something new, and I was there to help. She negotiated that her (now former) production company continue to pay my salary to her new company as part of her dissolution contract. That's how much she cared about taking care of me and transitioning together. It probably drove her ex-company mad that they had to keep paying my salary during that period, but lies have a price.

Despite the unplanned circumstances that got me there, I suppose I was now officially producing to some extent. Despite what I felt,

I tried to take the high road and kept my opinions about the old company to myself as I settled into my new role. I found myself on more commercial production sets and useful in the early development of AJ's forthcoming feature film a theatrical adaptation from a Carnegie and Whitbread award–winning author.

AJ has a unique way of storytelling, and I learned her way of doing it almost through osmosis, just by being in her orbit. I watched her storyboard and film commercials for companies like Hellman's, Blockbuster Video, and Proctor & Gamble. I sat or listened in on development calls and meetings. I was no longer only the assistant; now she introduced me to her producer, as her associate. I soaked up the knowledge learning how to budget a project, and how to order a light package, camera package, do casting, or location scout for a production. In scouting locations and sitting at casting sessions, AJ asked my opinion and cared about my views. I learned who key vendors were and developed a Rolodex of whom to call for just about anything. It was everything I'd dreamed about in my childhood bedroom back in Texas.

One of the most important elements of production is cost management. If a project goes over the budget, that can be a huge problem. On every production set is something called *craft services*. It's basically catering. They provide food and drinks for everyone on set, paid for by the production company. It usually consists of a couple of tables with a variety of snacks, chips, veggies, and meals when necessary. People graze throughout the day. Craft services is a line item on this all-important budget that producers desperately must keep in check. Everything is accounted for and listed carefully. Some craft services go a little higher end, like shopping at Whole Foods, and some are cheaper and provide more junky food and things from a local value grocery store. Everything is determined based on the budget of the project.

On a shoot one day toward the end of my time with AJ, I had a craving for a particular drink called a Cactus Cooler. I drank them all the time back in Dallas. I'd seen them around LA, too, so I went to a craft services person and asked if they had any. "No, we don't," she said. I thought nothing of it, grabbed another soda, and went about my way. A couple hours later she tapped me on the shoulder and said, "Mr. Felts, here's the Cactus Coolers you were looking for."

"Wow, thanks!" I said. *How nice, what a surprise.* Turns out, she'd sent out for a 12-pack of those Cactus Coolers for me and so I shared them with some of the crew.

A week later, I received a call from our production manager asking, "Hey, did you order some Cactus Coolers from crafty?"

"Well, I didn't *order* them," I replied, "but, yeah, she got me some."

"Well, she thought you did, because there's a line item here that says 'Cactus Coolers for director's assistant' and that put us over budget on catering."

I couldn't believe it. I hadn't realized that just by asking if she had some, she'd assume she needed to go buy them. Later, it was explained to me that she had seen me arrive with AJ and knew who I was. My name was high up on the "call sheet," which is something that goes out right before production, detailing who everyone is, who needs to be there and when, and so on. Call sheet hierarchy is a signal of importance. She knew I was at the top of the sheet, just under the director, and assumed I was her senior, I suppose. It didn't really matter how it happened, just that a budget overage is a big deal. Every penny counts. I ended up offering to pay for it, obviously, but it was a good lesson. Be very specific in how you dialogue in a hierarchical setting. Make the directives clear because the more power others assume you have, the more people bend over backward for you and take your word as gospel.

In this new role, I also realized that the framework for shooting a 30-second commercial was the same for shooting a 30-minute television show, or even a two-hour movie. Although the timetables are extended, the budgets are higher, and there are more zeros on the checks; commercials are essentially just mini TV episodes or mini movies. It was a great place to cut my teeth, the perfect combination of the creative and business sides of content creation. Observing AJ, and working for her during those independent days, outside of a company, was like receiving a bachelor's degree in physical production. I didn't finish my formal college education, but I never needed one. I learned more in that year and a half working side-by-side with her than I ever would in the classroom of the fanciest film school. Working at her big booming company and then in our little development office, I learned much in terms of business communications and dispute management, and even budgeting and project financing, though that was my least favorite part.

I was lucky enough to have the best mentors, coaches, and cheerleaders in AJ and her sales rep Teri, producer Francie, and attorney Linda. And, most important, I had gotten hands-on experience, which was priceless. I still fully endorse formal education, but when I counsel young people trying to break into the industry these days, I always tell them not to underestimate the value of getting their hands dirty and doing the actual job. Nothing compares to that. You can't learn this stuff in a book or even online; you have to get in the game, make mistakes, and just do it, learning as you go. In my case, I'd go as far to say that staying in school would not have been a good use of my time. It would not have been nearly as productive as heading directly where I wanted to go and making things happen.

***

One summer while working for AJ, I received a call from David Mirisch. "The Victor Awards are in a few weeks," he said. "Want to come to Vegas and help out again? I've got a new team, and they could use some training and oversight." I was happy to help, and excited to head to San Diego and see some old friends, so I enthusiastically agreed.

As I was busy backstage making sure everything was running smoothly and that the interns knew what to do, David came up and tapped me on the shoulder. "There's someone you should meet." He steered me toward Shaq and a friendly looking guy who appeared to be about my age. "This is Justin Berfield," he said. "He's an actor on *Malcom in the Middle.*" Justin smiled and shook my hand. While we joked about the height difference between him and Shaq, we quickly hit the subjects of golf, dogs, and the fact that I had not originally grown up in Hollywood, like he had. One of the first things I thought was how wise beyond his years he seemed. And the second was how much he reminded me of my brothers. God, I really missed them. Justin also has a similar sense of humor to my brothers, which I think David sensed as I caught him watching me laugh at something Justin said out of the corner of my eye. His introduction made sense. Meeting Justin made me realize that the biggest thing I was missing in LA was my little brothers. Sure, I had a great job, and great friends, but I missed my family desperately.

My parents knew how much I missed my brothers and had agreed to fly them out each summer to visit me. "My brothers are flying out next month," I said to Justin. "You have to meet them. You'll like them." I was also already secretly planning to invite Ashlee in the shameless hopes that they might find a connection. They were around the same age and seemed to have a lot in common. Plus, because I was protective of Ashlee, Justin felt like someone who would respect her. I left Las Vegas after the Victor Awards and flew back to Los Angeles. I knew I'd see Justin again at one other David event he had invited me to. Following that, we had also made plans for my brothers to meet him and hang during their weekend trip. I didn't tell him until later that Ashlee would join us for one of the outings, hoping that a casual mention wouldn't reveal my initial intentions for them.

That weekend came, and it was just as fun as I'd hoped. We spent the weekend playing Putt-Putt, pranking each other and my roommates, and generally having a good time. I almost felt like a child again. With the stress of my job, it was a welcome relief to be with my brothers. Justin and Ashlee did not end up dating. They hit it off, and her first-ever acting gig ended up being a small part on *Malcolm in the Middle*, but Justin's reserved nature was way too calm for Ashlee, and her wild spirit likely overwhelmed him. Nevertheless, from that weekend forward, Justin and I hung out often. While my little brothers could never be replaced, I did find comfort in having a similar energy in my life.

Justin confided in me that he was exhausted by acting. He'd been doing it since he was five and wanted to try something else. I was beginning to ponder trying something new as well. As happy as I was working for AJ, something still nagged at me. I had moved to Hollywood in search of more. Despite my humble beginnings, I was admittedly after the dream – the mansion, the cars, the beach house, maybe a private jet. I wanted it all. I wanted to shop on Rodeo Drive and not worry about the price of things. In my naive mind, those things defined the good life. Instead, I still found myself periodically cashing in a cup of nickels, dimes, and pennies at Coinstar to supplement my salary. I was doing a lot of the things I'd dreamed of doing – producing and rubbing elbows – and I was even making more money than I ever had before. But California is expensive and I wasn't anywhere near where I was aiming to be.

What's more, I was essentially a company man, and ever since my dad was unceremoniously fired on a whim by his company after a lifetime of loyalty, that worried me. I knew as a company man I could be laid off at any moment. My dad was at the top tier in his job. He was a road warrior who took so much pride in his career and worked harder than anyone I'd ever known to provide for us. While he was there, we had built that brand-new home in Texas and bought new cars. Then, without warning, they had cast him aside, and we had to start over. *Could that happen to me*, I often thought? Early on I learned the lesson to always have as much control of my own career as I could. I never wanted to be a part of corporate America, I never wanted to have the fate of my life in someone else's hands. I didn't want to be remembered as a good employee. I wanted more freedom than that, and to leave a legacy of my own. This is what got me thinking about entrepreneurship.

I already had a little bit of experience in being an entrepreneur through watching David Mirisch and now AJ. David had started and ran his own business from the beginning and AJ, after the unnamed commercial production company, didn't have the crutch of a company and had to start something on her own. Early into our friendship, I shared with Justin my thoughts of becoming an entrepreneur and striking out on my own. He resonated with all of it. He, too, wanted more. He wanted to grow and expand and was ready to jump into something new. We started brainstorming what that could look like. I thought that with my hands-on, practical know-how and his experience as an actor, a creative, a bit of name recognition, and our mutual connections in the industry, we'd be a great team.

Truth be told, we were just two young guys hatching an idea and not knowing what the fuck we were doing. Unsure about how we would make it all happen, the one thing we had going for us was our blind belief and determination, strengthened by our mutual respect and friendship. Like so many of my decisions, both good and bad, going into business with Justin was a gut choice, based on a good feeling. No matter what, I knew I could trust him like a brother; and I reinforced he could trust me the same way.

We called our fledgling production company J2. For Justin and Jason, two Js. Given Justin's direct access and intimate knowledge of his show's characters, we started out experimenting by writing episodes for *Malcolm in the Middle*. Justin would then deliver those to the show's creator, Linwood Boomer. Although none were ultimately used, Linwood always provided us informative feedback, which helped us get better and strengthened our resolve. With that knowledge and experience, we graduated to pitching bigger things.

Given that J2 was a side job at first, my time was really limited. I still worked for AJ, but the remit was slowing. Justin and I used nights and weekends to develop ideas ranging from television concepts to films, usually about themes and topics we felt we related to, like buddy comedies. AJ had met Justin several times by this point and was completely supportive.

One day, a former fellow assistant at the production company called me and said she wanted to make an introduction to a film producer friend of hers who was in town from New York. She had attempted to introduce AJ and others to her friend previously, but this particular time was my opportunity. Over coffee the next weekend, this producer conveyed she had a project that I might find of interest. I immediately asked if it would be a good fit for AJ to direct. While she made it clear that the project had a director already, it was the rest of the financing they were seeking and maybe, just maybe, there could be a small role for Justin.

And just like that I had a movie script land in my inbox. It was presented as an opportunity to "coproduce" a real, bona fide movie called *Romance & Cigarettes*. I'd been asked to do some fundraising, and give our opinion on the script, which was captivating and seemed like it would make for a good film. To proceed with this time-consuming opportunity, it was clear that I'd have to give up my job with AJ. This would require my full attention, and I was feeling really nervous. I wasn't sure if Justin and I were ready, and I was feeling slightly insecure to do anything without AJ. She had become my creative muse to this point. But I also knew that with AJ's production company fully out of the picture, AJ was now footing my salary entirely on her own. She had gone a while without a project, had shifted her priorities to self-discovery (climbing Kilimanjaro, biking Moab, traveling, etc.), and I was sensing that continuing to pay an assistant salary was not ideal for her. *Perhaps I would be doing her a favor*, I determined. Providing her an out to go focus on herself.

As I contemplated my options, I remember pulling out the *Romance & Cigarettes* package and budget and putting it right next to a commercial budget in an attempt to dissect a few things. My eyes scanned back-and-forth, from one to the other. That's when I had a realization. They were essentially the same. Commercials were mini-movies. I knew this already, but seeing it there in black and white, the line items were exactly the same. Not a single difference. *I can do this*, I thought. *I have been doing this. Sort of.* That's when I knew we were going to make this work. Justin and I would take J2 full-time and become our own production company.

It was hard leaving AJ. She is incredible. She lovingly pushed me out of the nest while I relieved her of the expense of an assistant. And with that, I leapt. It was time to go all-in, to finally bet on myself and see if I really had what it took to make it in this industry. There's a phrase you may have heard before: "burning your ships." Spanish explorer Hernán Cortés had to motivate his already exhausted crew to succeed in their new land after their long journey at sea, so he burned their ships. There was no going back, they didn't have that choice anymore. Metaphorically, I had burned my ships. I couldn't go back to a safe, company job with all the associated benefits. Failure wasn't an option. I would find a way to make this work, no matter what. And Justin, plus anyone who had believed in me up until then, was counting on me. As for AJ, I knew we'd be friends forever.

CUE: "Roar" by Katy Perry

PART

II

Take One

8

Meet a Kardashian

JUSTIN AND I made a great team. He was the pragmatic Ying to my confident Yang, so to speak. When we started J2 in 2004, he was in his late teens and I was in my mid-20s. In many ways, we were alike. We were both creative dreamers, and very innocent to the business world. Outside of our upstart company, we bonded over a lot of the same things my brothers and I did – adventure and mischief. Things like paint balling, scuba diving, golfing, and the good solid pranking of a friend or family member. We always sought out a good time, wherever, whenever.

But we were also very different, which contributed to our great partnership. Justin is reserved, slightly introverted, and extremely rational and smart – the polar opposite of the dim-witted character he played on *Malcolm in the Middle*. He's mostly self-educated and did a lot of homeschooling while he was on set filming. Some degree of self-educating really comes with the territory as a child star, and he'd been one for a long time. So long, in fact, that in 2004 he was recognized by Guinness World Records as the youngest actor in history to appear in back-to-back shows. He appeared in over 250 episodes of television before he could drive a car. For a guy who had experienced all of childhood before a live audience (and with much success), he was grounded, modest, and never desired an ounce of fame. In fact, he painfully shied away from any opportunity to promote himself, sign an autograph, or walk a red carpet. Because of this, I learned the self-promoting pitfalls most child actors are pushed into against their will. I realized Justin was different. He didn't desire the attention. In fact, he seemed to require some insulation and protection.

I, however, am extroverted, a bit gregarious, and positive almost to a fault. While Justin and I worked together creatively, I was more of the forward-facing, public part of our partnership. I did most of the outreach and calling, and by default I handled any dealmaking and business partnerships.

Because Justin had a day job that kept him working on set from 7:00 in the morning until late most days, we decided it would be most logical (and fun) to also be roommates. We had become best friends, and we were trying to build a company at the same time. Justin also had a good eye for real estate. After rooming in a few interim condos and makeshift offices for J2, we decided to start investing in property together. The mortgage industry in California in the early 2000s presented a great opportunity for two young, single guys to get a mortgage with little to no due diligence. And we took full advantage. We'd acquire a property, move in, renovate it a little, throw some parties, then flip it for profit. And then we did it again. And again. Then we did it big, in the form of a TV-famous mini-mansion behind big gates in the hills of Calabasas.

Through my friendship with the Simpsons, I learned that Jessica and her then-husband Nick Lachey were looking to sell their house where they lived and shot *The Newlyweds* for MTV. The show had just ended, and they were going through a very public divorce. Jessica had moved out, and Nick was eager to get rid of the house, the furniture, and the memories as quickly he could. I wouldn't call it schadenfreude, but this presented a huge opportunity for us. Justin and I bought 24944 Lorena Drive, which became J2 headquarters, our primary residence, and party central. We had friends and family over all the time and could also be really productive since we'd work out of the property. We could host meetings and dinners and use the house as a networking tool. There were no real lines or boundaries between work time and play time. Everything was everything.

While Justin was finishing his last season of *Malcolm*, I spent the better part of my day doing what I did back in my high school in Texas:

picking up the phone and cold-calling. But this time I wasn't calling celebrity fan clubs or faceless Angelenos, hoping that I would get in touch with somebody who could guide me. I was calling producers, studios, agents, and book authors, trying to assemble a project slate. Justin was also making constant email introductions to those he had worked with, endorsing me and our little company.

The movie I mentioned previously – *Romance & Cigarettes*, the one that helped us take the leap into entrepreneurship – came to us through Jana Edelbaum, the film's executive producer. Early on she insisted, "This is an opportunity for J2. It's a musical comedy. We just need to raise the rest of the money for it." While I loved the script, Justin was busy finishing the last episodes of *Malcolm*, so he didn't have a lot of time to dive into it yet. It was clear I would need to do the heavy lifting on this first one, or we would lose the very opportunity I quit my paying job for.

The movie was an independent film to be directed by John Turturro, produced by the Coen brothers, and had major talent attached to star including Kate Winslet, Susan Sarandon, James Gandolfini, and Christopher Walken. "J2 is fully in," I told Jana. "We'll help with the financing and coproduce." *What had I just signed up for?* I thought, as I hung up the phone. This was my first foray into fundraising. I had never raised money for anything in my entire life before. And I hated it from the start. But it's a necessary part of the business, and one of the less sexy things about the entertainment industry. Basically, it involves a lot of calling fancy people, pitching, and professional begging for people to believe in your project enough to give you money for it. They have to believe that they'll get a big return on their investment, so you're booking meetings with people with deep pockets to try to convince them of exactly that. Not glamorous.

For those who don't know, here's a quick primer. The role of a producer or a production company can vary drastically. Their main function is to oversee all or part of the process of bringing a film or TV show to life, from conceptualization to distribution. They are responsible for financing the project, assembling the rest of the production team, securing locations and permits, managing the budget, and coordinating the logistics. Additionally, production companies often play a significant role in the creative decision-making process.

They work closely with the director, writer, and other key personnel to develop the script, cast the actors, and ensure the overall artistic vision is achieved. They may also provide guidance and support during the editing and postproduction stages.

Furthermore, production companies play a vital role in marketing and distributing the finished product. They collaborate with distributors, negotiate deals with exhibitors, and strategize promotional campaigns to maximize the film's reach and profitability. A production company is responsible for overseeing and managing all aspects of a film or TV show's production from initial idea until you see it on the screen. Depending on the complexity of your specific role, you are granted either a producer, executive producer, coproducer, or associate producer credit. Given that *Romance & Cigarettes* was J2's first project, our role was limited to assisting with financing, providing our creative feedback on the script, and making other strategic introductions that could benefit the film's production and release. But I used this opportunity to dive in deeper and learn as much as I could about everything.

Although I failed in raising all of the requested financing from outside sources, I managed to pull the money together myself, draining my entire savings at the time, with Justin matching me. Jason Felts and Justin Berfield got their first coproducer credits and were off to the races. Truly betting on ourselves, now we had a calling card.

With a little momentum, our names attached to a movie starring Susan Sarandon and Kate Winslet, and our little company off the ground, we knew we needed to become more official. *Romance & Cigarettes* was enough to get us a little clout, and we wanted to step things up. Justin was about to finish *Malcolm*, so as the person with most of the free time, I went to find us a little office space closer to Hollywood. Closer to the action. It just so happened that *Malcolm in the Middle* had been filming on the same CBS lot in Studio City where John Ritter's *Hearts Afire* had filmed decades earlier. I called around and eventually found out that there was a small office available. So I went for a tour.

I arrived and they showed me around the available spaces. It was surreal. *Oh, my God*, I thought, *I've been here before*, as it all came rushing back. It was truly an out of body experience. It had hardly changed since I visited it all those years ago in high school when

I came with my mom to see John Ritter perform. Eventually, we turned the corner and got to the smallest office they said was available. "Here it is," said the kind woman showing me around. "This actually used to be one of the production offices for some shows you may have heard of, *Designing Women, Hearts Afire,* and most recently *Seinfeld,*" she mentioned offhand, without knowing my connection to *Hearts Afire.*

I bit my tongue so as not to spill all about my high school trip and the real moment I was having. I'm not sure how I feel about signs, but this felt like one. Growing our company in the same office where they had produced *Hearts Afire* AND *Seinfeld?* How many times had my childhood idol John Ritter set foot in here? Countless, I imagined. What I felt that day, and many days following when I came into work in that hallowed office, was awestruck. I felt like I was walking in John Ritter's footsteps as a producer. We had to take it. It was too perfect. The universe felt like it was on our side.

We had also picked up enough steam that it was time to make our first hire. I knew exactly who to call. Remember John Ritter's old assistant who had invited my mom and me to the taping to meet my childhood idol those years ago? So did I. I dialed up Susan Wilcox. She was still in business, assisting another actor at the time. Over lunch, I proclaimed in an excited ramble, "My business partner and I need an administrative assistant of sorts. Do you think you could help us with that? We're going to start developing some scripts, and I just found an office space which, weirdly enough, is the old *Hearts Afire* office." Susan, a believer in fate, was just as fascinated as I was. She helped us find and interview my assistant, Rebecca, who has now been with me for over 20 years.

So there we were: we had a movie in the works, an office, a key to that office, parking spots on the lot with our names on them, and one employee. We were stoked. It was time to determine what type of projects we wanted to develop. Until then we had basically taken whatever came our way, grateful for any gig we could get. What did we actually *want* to do?

As Justin and I contemplated what kind of projects we wanted to take on, we realized that movies gave us a lot of credibility, but they were harder to come by. Not to mention they required a lot of work and years to develop and produce. If they ever even got produced at all. I had experience in commercials, so that was an option. But commercials were one-offs, and of course they didn't pay as well nor did they have longevity. We also knew we would not be able to quickly compete with the likes of the big global commercial production company that I had just come from. The sweet spot was something in the middle: 30-minute TV shows. Justin had been on many of these all his life, and I was a self-professed aficionado – er, TV junkie – so it made sense for us to spend our energy there. As I mentioned, we had already concepted and presented a few *Malcolm in the Middle* episode ideas. Those had been fine, as far as ideating goes. But we wanted more of a challenge.

Given Justin was so interested in football, he was excited to develop a back-to-school television concept involving former NFL player Terry Bradshaw. The show centered on Terry and his high school daughter going on college tours, while he is also in the midst of going back to school at the same time. It was essentially a remake of an old Rodney Dangerfield movie, but in TV show form. We wrote up the idea, had the star committed, and sold it to CBS. We were really excited. But ultimately, the show never got made. That is when we were first introduced to something called *development hell*.

This is a common thing in the industry: you sell a show or a movie, go on an emotional high, and then studio executives and network executives get their fingerprints on it. Lots of other things can happen in development hell. There can be contract negotiations that go on forever, or maybe there's a regime change at the network. But the point is, something holds it up or it gets reinvented and turned into something that doesn't even resemble what you set out to make. Worst-case scenario, because of this holdup, it gets canned. That's what happened to the Bradshaw show: it died in development hell. The result is usually that you get a little cash in your pocket from the initial sale, but because nothing ever comes of it, you don't make any more, and even worse, you feel like you wasted a ton of time and energy.

This happened to us many times, as it does to all writers and producers. Shortly after that, we set up another TV show called *The Pet Detective*. Justin and I both liked the movie *Ace Ventura* at the time, and we had discovered a real-life pet detective named Carl Washington.

He claimed that he could find your missing dog, cat, bird, or any lost animal. The show would feature a new missing pet every episode, and Carl was the hero who finds them. We built out the concept and brought in our friend Huntley Ritter (no relation to my idol John Ritter, just a happy coincidence) to produce a first episode teaser that we tried to sell to a network.

Huntley was what the industry refers to as a "physical producer," one who's there on the ground moving the cameras, lights, and equipment around. If a producer is the coach, a physical producer is more like a player. Huntley is a no bullshit guy. Because he's originally from Atlanta, he wasn't very "Hollywood," a trait I connected to. Basically, I felt really comfortable with him because he was just there to do the work, get paid, and make us and the show look good – no hidden agenda, no ulterior motives. He went on to work in a pivotal role with Justin and me at Virgin as well (more on that later). We sold *The Pet Detective* to Animal Planet. How fitting. It was our first J2 production where we had conceived an idea from scratch, sought out the talent, cut a deal with the distributor, scouted the locations, and were on set actually doing what we'd envisioned. Producing! We were making things happen! Then the network executive appointed to our show got let go from the company. Regime change. The new network president didn't like it as much, and so the pilot episode of the show did not get picked to become a full series. More development hell.

The entertainment industry is a roller coaster. Justin took it a lot better than I did. Actors are rejected every single day. They can do a great audition and still not get a callback. But I had never experienced anything like this in my entire life. Justin was such a realist and managed expectations well – again, way better than me. He was able to brush it off and had even been warning me that something like this might happen all along the way. "Why are you being like this?" I would ask. "Stop being so cynical. So negative. We need to be positive." Of course, I came to find out he wasn't being cynical; he was being real. He would say things like, "I'll believe it when I see it" or "there's a good chance it won't happen," and it drove me crazy. But he was great for me in that way. While I tend to have my head in the clouds, shooting for the stars, he kept me grounded. Overall, my positive attitude had served me very well in my career so far. It's why I was able to take some of the crazy leaps that I did and believe things that many people told me were impossible. But also, especially in these early days, it could lead to high highs and low lows.

In those days, we were developing multiple shows at a time. In addition to *The Pet Detective*, we had another in the works designed to star and be coproduced by Courteney Cox. She was married to David Arquette at the time, and they had their own company called Coquette Productions. Our concept was a workplace comedy, which centered on a very diverse group of friends balancing love, life, and work. Courtney had just finished up working on *Friends* and was a new mom and producer. This idea felt like a perfect fit to partner together. It was Justin's name and credits that had gotten us in the door, and it was me who had to go pitch Courteney and her partner, Thea Mann (Lisa Kudrow's cousin) on the concept.

After sitting in the mid-century modern waiting room for what seemed like forever, I was escorted into Courteney's small office. My first encounter with the *Friends* megastar was immediate as she screamed out her office door at David to not ding up her new car as he was driving in the tiny parking lot. I was reminded that I was dealing with a bona fide celebrity who (1) most definitely treasured their Mercedes and (2) still had to do menial tasks on their own when there's a spacing issue in a parking lot. Celebrities, they're just like us!

Courteney was instantly kind and warm as I sat down in a chair across from her, nervous in her flawless office. She had just given birth to her daughter, Coco, whom she was holding in her arms. As I gathered myself to pitch her the show concept when, as if on cue to derail me, she pulled out her breast and started nursing her baby.

"You don't mind if I feed her, do you?" she asked me.

"Um, no," I replied. What was I supposed to say? *No? To Courteney fucking Cox!? Of course, I'll pitch with your boob out. As if I'm not already nervous enough*, I thought. I know that this is a completely normal and natural practice for women, but as an innocent, green, and very nervous young man I was completely thrown. Plus, I was still totally perplexed about my own sexuality, so I didn't quite know how to feel on many levels. I didn't care about boobs, but they also made me nervous.

Anyway, I somehow got through the pitch as she fed her baby. And, Courteney loved it. Her company wanted to move forward and agreed to produce it with us. "Who do you want to write it?" she asked me. I said I had a writer named Jeff in mind who could be great. We set up a second meeting that went equally well. No nipples involved in that one. We were ready to take it to studio.

Courteney wanted to take it to Warner Bros. because they had produced *Friends*, and she had a first look deal there. *This will be a slam dunk*, I thought. No-brainer. Because Jeff had written out the concept, all three of us would attend the meeting, with him pitching it. If you have an experienced writer involved at the pitch stage, it's customary that they take the lead. That's just how it works. With other hit shows under his belt, Jeff was clearly more experienced than me and more than qualified to pitch.

As we were escorted into that posh Warner Bros. conference room on pitch day, we all sat, awaiting the arrival of the network development executives to hear us out. But before that, the formality goes a little like this: "Coffee, tea, water? Can I get you anything?" That's the part where the assistant to the executives attempts to make you feel comfortable while taking an extra-long glance at whatever celebrity talent may be in the room. In walked the Warner Bros. execs, ready for the pitch from Courteney Cox and her newbie partners. As I glanced over at Jeff, he didn't look okay. I couldn't tell if he was nervous or sick, but I began to worry. He didn't look well. His face was completely white, and he hardly said a word. We sat around a gorgeous, huge marble conference table, and as the executives settled themselves, we turned our attention to Jeff to begin. When he opened his mouth to pitch our show, what came out instead was, "I have a terrible migraine. I can't do this. Jason, can you take over?"

You have to be kidding me, I thought. I immediately thought he was lying. Justin's eyes widened as he looked at me in disbelief. And Courteney looked confused and gave me an intense stare begging me with her stare to not to screw this up. My heart sank. This was our first pitch for a huge network or studio. I don't think Courteney knew that. Even though I made lots of calls and had meetings with plenty of industry professionals, I had never been asked to pitch in front of decision-making executives before. And if I had known what I would be doing that day, of course I would have prepared. I did my best and gave a truncated version of the pitch that probably could have been worse, but certainly wasn't compelling. Long story short, they didn't buy the show. Another disappointment.

And this time, it really weighed on me. The meeting ended a bit abruptly, though cordial, and we certainly didn't get a cheery goodbye from Courteney. I knew that show was dead before it even really started. I was devasted and really beat myself up for not having a contingency plan in place. Trying to be positive, I knew we could take the project to other studios. My realistic and more seasoned partner, Justin, was as pragmatic as ever. "It's dead. Courtney wants no part of this show now that Warner Bros. has passed. She needs to be loyal to her home studio." Yep, Justin was right. He really had an instinct for these things.

With no series order of *The Pet Detective* and our botched Warner Bros. pitch thanks to Jeff, I struggled with where to go from there. I was still convinced that 30-minute TV shows were where we should focus. But it was getting harder and harder, even for me, to stay positive. I felt a sense that I was failing both myself and Justin. J2 desperately needed a win.

About three months later, on a flight to Cabo, I was watching the movie *City Slickers* on the seat back while I slurped down a ginger ale and munched on a standard issued mini package of pretzels. Justin and I were with some friends headed to an all-inclusive weekend away. Only $399 each for a two-night stay and all you can eat. I was really watching my pennies at this point, but needed the getaway. Our friend Haley, Pat Benatar's daughter, was with us. As I sat there, my eyes panned between the movie and watching Haley interact with a flight attendant. Haley is fun and bubbly, and, as most famous children tend to be, she was a tad unaware and entitled. It wasn't her fault; she was born into it. She was after something from the flight attendant and kept asking, but the flight attendant was busy and ignored her. Haley kept looking at me, rolling her eyes, and putting her fist jokingly in the air, frustrated.

Oh my God, I thought, *she's such a TV character*. I had never seen this side of her. Then I turned and went back to watching *City Slickers*. My mind began to wander. I started imagining Haley on the horse driving cattle like Billy Crystal in the movie. *That would be hilarious*, I thought to myself. I even mentioned it to Justin in passing after we landed. "How funny would it be to see Haley on the back of a horse?" We laughed about it, basically blew it off, and went about our vacation. But the idea stuck with me. I just couldn't let it go. *There's something to this* . . .

While in Cabo, as luck would have it, we ran into Michael, one of the writers from *Malcolm in the Middle*. We got to chatting, and he was interested in what we were working on. "What do you have going on now?" Michael asked. "Oh, just a few projects here and there," I said vaguely, "but on the flight over I had this funny thought about taking celebrity kids and putting them on a working ranch, *City Slickers*–style. A fish-out-of-water thing." He laughed and agreed that it was a funny concept. *Wow*, I thought. *If one of the head writers from* Malcolm in the Middle *thinks this is funny, maybe I really am onto something.* Justin agreed.

Reality TV was just beginning to be "a thing" in 2005. There were only a few breakout shows on – *The Osbournes, The Newlyweds, The Simple Life* – and they were all huge hits. My idea had a very similar premise to *The Simple Life*. The word around town was that networks were looking to capitalize on this trend and everyone wanted the next big one. With our connections, demographic, and interests, it seemed right up our alley.

When we got back from vacation, I reached out to Joe Simpson. Because of my friendship with Ashlee, I was close with the whole Simpson clan including "Papa Joe," as he called himself. Always a good sounding board at that time, when I mentioned my idea him, he instantly felt this could work. In fact, he shared a similar idea he had based on his time in Texas. I felt validated; my instincts were right. Joe strategically invited me to a dinner with some people who could possibly help get the project off the ground. He did this occasionally to make connections and build business, coordinating meals with a variety of new and established industry types. I always appreciated the invite. This was when he was at the height of his power as the manager of one of the biggest pop stars in the world.

We went to Mr. Chow in Beverly Hills. It was a very fancy restaurant at the time. Fancier than most places I had ever been. I was already nervous being introduced to possible power players who had the ability to make things a reality with a single phone call. And meeting those types at this kind of place really put me out of my comfort zone. Maybe it was the posttraumatic stress disorder from Ovitz and Artist Management Group. I'm not really sure what it was, but what I did know was a white tablecloth signaled me to channel my Gran and *mind my manners*.

At the beginning of the meal, the waitress brought some bowls out filled with what just looked like normal clear soup to me. I knew enough to know that fancy restaurants have many courses within a meal, this must be the first. The amuse-bouche. I picked mine up and took a little sip. *Gross!* It tasted awful. But I tried to keep it together as everyone looked at me with confusion. It tasted just like warm, soap water. It was the worst soup I'd ever had. My dinner table began to titter a little. "That's not soup," one said to me. "It's a bowl for your fingers." Apparently, at Mr. Chow they do this thing where you put your fingers in a bowl to wash them off before you eat. I had no idea, and was mortified. It was just warm lemon water. We were off to a great start.

Despite drinking the finger bowl water, the meeting did go really well. Well enough that it led to another meeting. In less than a week, I found myself sitting down with Ted Harbert, the then-president of the E! network, and Joe. The biggest shows they had at the time were *Talk Soup* and *The Chelsea Handler Show*. Ted revealed that it just so happened he was looking for their version of *The Simple Life*, which at the time was on the FOX network. The industry chatter was true. And we were there to pitch almost exactly that. Celebrity kids on a cattle drive. "They will all get filthy. It will be hilarious," I proclaimed.

"*Filthy Rich Cattle Drive*," Joe said with a laugh.

Ted replied, "If you can cast it before summer, you've got a show."

They're in! The E! network wants to produce a reality show I conceived on a flight to Cabo! Joe got me in the room, and we had a real commitment from E! My head was spinning. I had to call Justin. "My daydreaming is finally going to pay off," I told Justin on the other line. I was trying not to get ahead of myself because I'd gotten my hopes up plenty of times already, only for nothing to come of it. But I couldn't help it. I was psyched. This one felt different.

"Sweet! Now we need to cast it," Justin proclaimed with cautious optimism.

There was one small thing that nagged at me in the weeks right after the meeting, though. Joe was taking full credit for the idea around town. But it didn't bother me for long. We got traction so quickly that there was too much else to think about soon and it didn't matter. After all, his manager clout had gotten a meeting for us at E! And for that we were grateful. Later in my career, I adopted the philosophy of "There is no limit to what a person can do or where they can go if they don't mind who gets the credit." It's served me very well in life, including in that meeting. I believe living by this credo will get you far.

Immediately, we started watching casting tapes from every kid of a celebrity you can imagine. We cast George Foreman's son, (the Incredible Hulk) Lou Ferrigno's daughter, and Robert Blake's son (six months after Robert Blake was convicted for killing his wife). And we considered a whole host of others we didn't end up choosing, like the young (now *Beverly Hills Housewife* alum) Teddy Mellencamp. It took a bit of persuading with her mother, but I even got our friend Haley, the one who had inspired the original idea, to sign on. We were assembling a unique cast at rapid speed.

But we still had a few more slots to fill and were having a little trouble picking the remaining few. It was clear the network was on the hunt for a somewhat big name to add to the roster. One day, the physical producers showed us a casting tape from a then-unknown young woman named Kim Kardashian. She was described (somewhat oddly) as Paris Hilton's closet organizer. Basically, no one had heard of her. She was confident and compelling on tape (as the rest of the world would come to learn), but most of the people in the room still looked unconvinced. At the very end of the tape, the last question the interviewer asked was, "What's the one thing you would never leave home without?" Kim answered without missing a beat, "My nose hair tweezers." I burst out laughing. There was something so raw and real and funny about that. *What kind of gorgeous young woman would claim nose hair tweezers as the ONE thing she must have?* I thought to myself.

No one seemed to enjoy her casting tape as much as I did. Focused on casting famous last names, our network executive remarked, "Kardashian is not a big name." She was right, at the time *Kardashian* wasn't a household name and they certainly were not *Filthy Rich*. Her dad was one of several attorneys on the O. J. Simpson trial more than 10 years prior, and to most people, that didn't make them famous. "That's not a rich celebrity kid," the president said. "We need bigger."

I actually did sort of know of the Kardashians already, not because of the O. J. trial, but because they lived a few doors up from me in my Calabasas neighborhood. I saw some of them around the area and stepparent Caitlyn Jenner seemed to recall me from David Mirisch events years prior. I knew they owned a small children's store called Smooch, which was right next to Blue Table, a small café where Justin and I lunched a lot. We were not friends, but we were friendly. I figured that as a family, they were not camera shy. Caitlyn and her wife Kris had been doing infomercials for years. I had seen something in Kim's tape, something funny and honest. I was convinced that big personality ran in the family. But I had to convince the president of the network the same.

Nose hair tweezers aside, I felt we needed a Kardashian on the show to add character, sex appeal, and a sense of diversity to our mainly vanilla white cast. The stars seemed to align one day as I sat outside of Blue Table and ran into Caitlyn, who was barking on the phone something about their pool and filming something. I saw my entry point. As she hung up and was just about to enter their store, I proclaimed presumptuously that our "little mansion" just down the street from them was available for a shoot if they ever needed it. It seemed she had a problem on the phone, and this felt like a kind offer, because we did own the most famous house in town. We had been asked by plenty of people before to use "*The Newlyweds* House" for something or another. Offering it up seemed like a good, neighborly gesture, right? I must admit, I did have an ulterior motive. I wanted to gauge their interest on the show and see if my hunch about being reality TV material was right.

"Kourtney and her mom run the shop; you can talk to them," Caitlyn replied. As everyone now knows, Kourtney is, of course, Kim's older sister.

Long story made short: I was introduced to Kourtney, loved her blunt personality, and went to work lobbying to cast her for the show. Kim was great, and had made me laugh out loud. But Kourtney had this stoic, no-bullshit demeanor that I really found compelling, and I was convinced audiences would as well. She didn't come across as entitled in her casting tape. And although that was the directive by the network, I truly felt Kourtney had an innate authenticity that would give us an unfiltered window into her life and her family. I knew she would be great. We just had to convince the network. The physical producers were on board instantly, her mom Kris was supportive, and other cast members were lobbying, but it was the network that was still not quite convinced she had a big enough last name to round out the cast. I will never forget an email that was circulated from the network insisting "We want a household last name like Jagger, Brosnan, Stewart, Kravitz, or Willis. The UK and Middle America doesn't know Kardashian." Lots of phone calls and pitching later, eventually we were successful in getting Kourtney signed off by E! and cast in *Filthy Rich Cattle Drive*. And on August 7, 2005, the world was introduced to the Kardashians via our show, which aired every single Sunday night for the rest of the year.

We ended up shooting and producing one whole season. It did rate well, but not well enough by E!'s standards to renew it. One of the things that worked the best was Kourtney. She was a breakout character. And her mom knew it. Next to Richard Branson, Kris Jenner is the best strategic brand builder I have ever studied, though I didn't yet know it back then. No one did but her. Kris was and is an incredible force of entrepreneurial nature. Though she's had famous partners, she's never in the shadow of anyone. In any room, she casts her own shadow.

Following the airing of *Filthy Rich*, it didn't take long for the Kardashian name to hit the media again. This time in conjunction with Kim's infamous sex tape with Ray J. After that, the door opened to create an entire show all about their family. They were all like Kourtney, but dialed up to 11, each in their own way. Imagine a show about a gradually rich, extremely ambitious, raw, funny, glamourous family that (seemingly) had no filter. They would let you in on every facet of their lives: love, marriage, babies, fights, divorce, successes and mistakes, and everything in between. They would air all of their laundry, unapologetically. It was an irresistible idea. But it was not mine. The network had just signed a multi-million-dollar deal with Ryan Seacrest's new company for him to produce content for the network. And when that happens, networks tend to feel a sense of urgency to greenlight projects immediately so they can start to recoup their investment. Especially if it's 2007 and you are Ryan Seacrest. As you all know by now, E! launched the show, *Keeping Up with the Kardashians*, and Ryan Seacrest produced it.

At first, I was annoyed to not have even been asked to coproduce. Despite a continued friendship with Kourtney and us having several discussions about future show ideas, I knew this didn't entitle me to a producer credit. What I didn't understand was why the very network who had resisted casting a Kardashian previously was betting on the family to carry an entire show. Did they not remember me begging to cast a Kardashian in our show? Did they not remember sending me an email that said, word-for-word, "Jason, it's a no on Kardashian. We need a household name." Was the friendship with Kourtney an illusion I had? We had become friends during and following *Filthy Rich*'s airing. Countless meals, hangs at each other's houses, calls, texts, and Blackberry messages. And in true Southern fashion, I had even introduced her to her first NASCAR race. For the first time I felt like I not only made a real business mistake but also had misjudged a new friend. In our contract, I hadn't ensured that we retained the derivative rights for anything that came from *Filthy Rich Cattle Drive*. And *Keeping Up* was exactly that. But we didn't have a claim on it, and with naivety, we hadn't known to establish that in our deal. And that stung, at first.

Over time, as the show evolved, I realized it would not have been a good creative fit anyway. As much as I was excited for Kourtney, *Keeping Up* did not become a show that aligned with the mandate of the globally recognized company I would end up running shortly thereafter. In that way, it was for the best. But financially, at the time, it was frustrating. Especially for our fledgling J2.

Ironically, in 2022, E! posted on one of their social media accounts a throwback picture of Kourtney on *Filthy Rich Cattle Drive*. It got an overwhelming reaction, as many had no idea that show was how she got her start in reality television and was the catalyst for everything to follow at E! The thought of a now 45-year-old, really famous and rich, mother, wife, and entrepreneur being tossed around on the back of a horse was intriguing to people as it garnered tens of thousands of comments immediately. "Bring back the show" was the common theme in the comments. It sparked a lot of demand to distribute the 2005 era episodes again, which E! streamed online, and gained much traction.

As it happens in Hollywood, old shows and movies get remade. And they came knocking on our door, asking us to remake this. Because we do still retain the format rights to the original show concept, Justin, Joe, and I agreed. They greenlit it fast, and decades later, we produced the updated version of *Filthy Rich Cattle Drive*. This time it was called *Relatively Famous Ranch Rules* and featured a whole new cast of characters, more celebrity kids. Although this time around it wasn't a priority project, it was a full circle moment.

It was very validating, after having the original show only run for one season, and then have a gigantic hit come out of it that didn't involve us, to have the network come back saying they wanted to do it again. This all happened at the same time *Keeping Up with the Kardashians* ended at E! and Kris cut a new deal for the family at Hulu. "We would love for you to discover new talent," is how the network presented it to us. We were in, but this time we knew better. We negotiated our deal differently and secured the derivative rights from any character that could break out as a star from *Relatively Famous*. Don't make the same mistake twice.

As for the Kardashian-Jenners, we all know their story. Like I said, there is no better personal brand architect or media strategist than Kris Jenner. She is a master, and I have tremendous respect and admiration for her, and I've told her as much. Nobody holds a candle to her ambition to empire build. And while I don't chat with Kourtney as often as we did, I did recently catch her in a rerun episode of *Keeping Up with the Kardashians* (now in its 16th year!) saying, "If it wasn't for my personality and being funny, then our show wouldn't exist." I completely agree. She is underestimated by audiences and fans and is, in my opinion, the funniest, most centered, and grounded Kardashian. Caitlyn and I have stayed in touch the most, and I appreciate her supporting my various projects and nonprofit initiatives over the years.

All in all, that short-lived series we produced for E! did provide J2 enough profit for Justin and me to continue building our business and project slate. While we continued developing our television concepts, we now had a firm foundation to expand J2 into developing films.

While Justin was still acting on *Malcolm in the Middle*, he was always getting invited to red carpet events, and often I'd come along. At one of them, we had both met *American Idol* runner up Diana DeGarmo, and the two of them developed a short-lived connection. Justin was even her date to the Grammy Awards the year she was on *American Idol*. Anyway, during this time, she invited Justin and me to a charity event in Florida. I didn't really have any idea what it was for, but as two guys trying to get our production company off the ground, we said yes to just about everything back then. It was important to network and connect with as many people as possible.

The promoter of the event was a guy named Jonathan Jaxon. He was a Perez Hilton type who had a blog and was early to social media. He created rumors and wrote clickbait with scandalous headlines just to stir things up. He was an instigator and, more bluntly, a liar. Diana, Justin, and I, along with some other celebrity guests, went to an afterparty following the event and then later ended up all hanging out in Diana's suite. Jonathan wasn't around for any of that. He attended the event he worked and had not been invited to hang out after the event.

But that didn't stop him from writing a blog headline the next day that said, Malcolm in the Middle's *Justin Barfield Snuggles Next to His Boyfriend Jason Phelps*. I was mortified. Justin was mortified. That never happened. We went to the charity event and nobody was snuggling. It didn't it happen, and it would never happen. The audacity of someone to claim that it did infuriated me. I have no idea where he even got this impression. Maybe he just wanted revenge for not being invited to the suite for the afterparty hang. I hadn't snuggled with anyone and Justin is straight. We had to fix this.

I looked up more about Jonathan Jaxon and realized he'd had plenty of issues for coming after celebrities before. He'd create rumors and public figures would go after him. I read that someone else he'd done this to was Kim Kardashian. *Perfect*, I thought. *Someone with experience with this guy*. So I called Kourtney and asked her to connect me with

Kim to see how she handled a similar situation. She obliged and passed along her phone number and email address, which, I'm delighted to inform you, was PrincessKim@____. Of course it was. This is exactly the email address I would hope and expect that Kim was using.

We ended up chatting on the phone, and she gave me some great advice. Even in her 20s, Kim thought and acted like an attorney. "It's just a blatant lie," I told her.

"I know," she said. "You need to have your lawyer send a cease-and-desist letter. He'll take it down and won't do it again." That was my first time ever hiring a lawyer. I did exactly as Kim instructed, and Jaxon eventually took it off his blog. It was a little bit of fight as he originally wanted us to pay him to remove it. But without giving him a dime, it was removed. That advice came in handy a few times throughout my career when others have attempted to publish nonsense about me or my business.

Though the blog post didn't exist anymore, much of the damage was already done. Unfortunately, at the time the clickbaiter's site was a marginally popular rumor mill. Despite Jaxon taking the story off his blog, it had already been syndicated to other sites and was making the rounds elsewhere. In fact, it spurred more misleading tabloid headlines like Malcolm's *Justin Berfield lives in* Newlyweds *love nest mansion w/ producer Jason Felts*. Plenty of people we knew had read it and wondered about Justin and me, which made us both extremely upset. Yes, we lived and worked together, but we weren't snuggling, dating, or whatever else was driving views online. Justin was still a public figure on TV. He was on a hit television show airing in over 100 countries, so stories that included his name spread fast at the time. I know when I showed up at the *Malcolm in the Middle* wrap party, people were whispering.

It really sucked that with one click, someone could publish a complete lie, and there was little to nothing much we could do to stop the rumors. We were best friends, business partners, and roommates who had just essentially been called gay lovers. We discussed the post together the morning it was published, but after that day, we never addressed it again. Justin, who was younger, single, and interested in women, was visibly upset at what Jaxon had done. Although he wasn't homophobic, he did not want to be misrepresented. And I mostly just cared that Justin was hurt. I was still truly unsure of my own sexuality. More than anything, I felt I was asexual and attracted to no one. I didn't want a girlfriend, and I didn't want a boyfriend. I was angry, protective, and vowed I would handle the situation on our behalf. Legally, I did. But personally, we just pushed it aside and acted like it never happened. We moved on. Plus, we had a business to run together. The topic of my sexuality wouldn't come up again for a long time.

CUE: "Popular" by The Weeknd and Madonna

9

Searching for Greenlight

ALL THINGS CONSIDERED, Justin and I had created a nice little company. There were deep disappointments and some big wins. We had some major achievements and learned some big lessons in our few short years. Finally, business was cruising along nicely. In the same vein as reality TV, Justin and I were both deeply interested in true-life stories. I've always loved documentaries, and Justin was drawn to biographical and history-oriented films that portrayed the lives of interesting characters or fundamental moments in history. So when writer/producer Eunetta Boone called me up one day and said, "You need to hear about Doris Payne," I was immediately intrigued.

Doris is a Black woman and one of the most notorious jewel thieves in history. You read that right. Born in the 1930s in West Virginia, she used to play a game called "Miss Lady," where she would envision herself with an affluent lifestyle, far removed from the impoverished one she was actually living in the still mostly segregated South. She'd stroll around in a fancy store like she belonged, trying on different pieces of jewelry, casually slipping them on and off as she charmed the sales associates with her manners and good looks. Many police accounts even mention how gorgeous she was, "like a model." She learned that dressing the part, carrying a designer handbag, and wearing couture clothes was just about all she needed to fly under the radar and disarm sales associates surprised to see a woman of color in their store. After a few minutes of browsing, she'd slip something into her tissue or purse and make a quick getaway before anyone noticed. She had a gift for sleight-of-hand and was a master at the getaway.

As Doris told it, it all started as a way to help her mother escape her abusive father. One day, after a particularly abusive episode, Doris became determined to get away and help her mother do the same. She boarded a bus to Pittsburgh, stole her first diamond, immediately turned around and pawned it, and gave the money to her mother to start a new life. She was officially hooked and empowered. This kicked off a nearly 40-year career in which she stole over $2 million worth of jewelry. She had been arrested five times and even escaped prison more than once. Over the years, she'd had 32 aliases and nine fake passports. She traveled the world and had committed crimes in Milan, Paris, New York, London, and Tokyo. What I'm saying is: she had an absolutely movie-worthy story. It was begging to be turned into a feature film.

That's what Eunetta called to tell me, and I completely agreed. At the time, a then-80-something-year-old Doris was incarcerated in Las Vegas. We managed to track down her daughter and set up a meeting with Doris in prison. Eunetta, Justin, and I flew out to Las Vegas to look Doris in the eyes and assess how she would feel about us developing a movie about her.

As I sat across from the feeble, lovely looking literal grandmother, even I couldn't believe she was a completely unrepentant criminal. (She once said that she doesn't regret a single thing except being caught! I'd never endorse crime, but there's something to be said for her gumption.) Small in stature, big in bravado, she'd clearly won the awe and respect of her fellow prisoners passing by.

"We want to tell your story," Eunetta said to her. Justin and I chimed in, reinforcing that we felt her story had merit and would be attractive to both actors and directors. In exchange for her life rights, we told her that, in addition to making her story known, we'd help her out financially while she was incarcerated. We promised to keep her commissary money stocked and make sure she got the medical care she needed. This was the only way she could actually benefit, given the Son of Sam law that would prevent her from profiting from the film. Doris's eyes lit up as she readily agreed. She wanted the world to know what she'd done and why. And she wanted to become famous, so the lead actor portraying her had to be a bona fide movie star. "No B-lister, you hear me," she said several times. She was unapologetic and proud, insistent an A-list, top-tier movie star play Doris Payne. Proving again she was a perfect character inspiration for the big screen. She was excited about the arrangement, and we were pumped to get started. After her power of attorney (her daughter) reviewed the agreement and signed on the dotted line, we had Doris's life rights, and were out the door. Actually, three or four doors later, we reached the hot Vegas sun that awaited us outside the Clark County Prison.

As we walked to our rental car, Eunetta looked at Justin and me and said, "It's time to celebrate!"

"Okay, what are we doing?" we asked enthusiastically.

Pointing to the Las Vegas strip in the distance, "I'm taking you to see Prince," she replied casually.

Justin and I looked at each other, "Wait, what?" we said almost in unison. As it turned out, Prince was doing a private show and, of course, being the charismatic and magnetic producer that she was, Eunetta had a connection. Eunetta (who later passed from a heart attack) was the type that always lived large. Big houses, luxury cars – she never failed to find a reason to celebrate. Always tossing her hard-earned money around ensuring everyone knew how much she had. Given we had just signed our very first life rights document with one of the most fascinating characters nobody had heard of, it only made sense to Eunetta that we all go sing "Let's Go Crazy" at the top of our lungs. In a lot of ways, Eunetta acted as a mentor and mother figure to Justin and me. She was proud of us. There were only 80 other people in the room, but Prince put on a full concert with the same energy as if he was entertaining a stadium. It was a once-in-a-lifetime thing and an incredibly special moment. I felt everything we'd accomplished thus far was truly worth celebrating. We felt triumphant and great excitement for the road ahead.

The next day we flew back to Los Angeles and got to work on the script outline. We tried to allow Doris as much influence in the process as possible, so early on we asked her, "Doris, if you could pick anyone, who would you favor to play you in the movie?" "Halle Berry," she said without missing a beat. She'd clearly already thought about it. Honestly, the resemblance wasn't too far off from younger Doris. So I got to work on prepping for the most important cold-call of my career (so far) to Halle Berry's manager, Vincent Cirrincione, a self-made, straight-shooting New Yorker who was not known for his gentle demeanor. Fortunately, I had some experience now, friends in common, and more excitement than nervousness. On the other end of the line, Vincent said in his raspy voice, "That sounds interesting," after I'd pitched him the idea. "Go write the script, and then I will take a look."

This wasn't my first rodeo, and I said back, "We've got it already." In just a few shorts weeks following our Vegas trip, Eunetta had already written the first draft of *Who Is Doris Payne?*

He chuckled. "Alright, you buried the lead. Send it to me."

After a quick call to Justin and Eunetta to let them know, we sent him the script, and he passed it on to Halle. It took about three months, and God only knows how many follow-up emails from me, but he called us back and said that Halle was interested and wanted to meet. Eunetta, being the strategist that she was, suggested we do it at her house for home court advantage. In retrospect, I think it was important to Eunetta to show Halle that she, too, was successful in her own right. Welcoming Halle into her grand home and serving her lunch by a personal chef would put Eunetta on somewhat equal footing. Waiting to meet Halle Berry at Eunetta's kitchen table is something that in all of my years of dreaming about Hollywood, I never imagined. We waited and waited and waited. Finally, the phone rang to let us know she was coming around the back. To avoid paparazzi, she had been dropped by her driver in the alley so she could slip in through the backyard gate. An A-list talent meeting to pitch a movie was new terrain for me, but I was there for it and happy to comply with whatever door Halle Berry wanted to enter through.

A few moments later, a sliding glass door slid open, and in she walked. Fresh-faced with no makeup on, the most angelic person I'd ever seen in my entire life. "Hey, guys," she said sweetly. Still to this day, she is the most beautiful woman I've ever sat across from. For the first time in my life, I was starstruck, speechless. By this time, I had met many celebrities, and had several friends who were considered famous. And of course, living in LA, I'd seen many at restaurants and around town.

But Halle was different. I've always been extremely relaxed and level-headed in the presence of entertainers and celebrities, despite my nerdy, unwavering desire to get out to Hollywood as a high schooler. Someone's clout and power weren't ever as intoxicating to me as you'd think. But something about being in the presence of Halle Berry that day threw me off. Justin was speechless as well. We just sat like two knots on a log watching Eunetta hold court.

Halle and Eunetta began to talk about Doris and her weaving story around the world. Every now and then, Halle looked over to Justin and me and tossed a question, prompting us to weigh in. One of the ways you assess the character of someone is how often they make contact and address everyone at the table, not just whom they consider to be the power players. Justin and I were not the power players at that table. But that didn't matter to Halle. She was inclusive and wanted our input. She felt we were the target demographic audience. We did the best we could fielding Halle's questions, embarrassingly starstruck as we were. In the end, she said, simply, "I'm in." *She's in! Halle Berry was in!* I couldn't believe it.

Not to spoil the ending for you, but this was my first lesson in the fact that you can have a concept, you can have the script, and you can have the star, but if you don't have the money, you don't have a movie. We began contract negotiation for Halle's salary. Which, as you can imagine, was not small. We had mostly been doing TV shows up until this point except for *Romance & Cigarettes* and *Blonde Ambition*. But those were independent movies, and we didn't have nearly as large of a role as we had here. I had never negotiated a salary for an A-list movie star before. I got plenty of practice later in my career, but this was my first time. Through the process, it became clear that J2 and Eunetta didn't have nearly enough money to pay Halle what she required. Not that she didn't deserve it, of course. Vincent definitely leveraged his power and experience over us and demanded a deal far richer for Halle than this project could sustain. He wanted $10 million for Halle to play Doris Payne. Plus a producer fee for himself. It was way too much.

In the meantime, Doris Payne had become increasingly difficult. We were constantly sending her money to prison, but she was always somehow running out. We were buying her glasses, food, eye drops, underwear, basically anything that she asked for. But she kept running out . . . fast. Justin and I were asking each other, "How much money could she possibly need?! What is she even doing with it?" *Things in prison couldn't be that expensive*, I thought. Eventually, it came out that she was bartering her money away and had developed her own little business within the prison walls that we were funding. Old habits die hard, I guess. She was a hustler at heart. And we were bankrolling it.

Her gumption was part of the character we were trying to bring to the screen, but it was beginning to be a problem. Every day, there were new demands. Eunetta was in charge of the script; we were put in charge of Doris. We were having trouble getting money together quickly enough to replenish her commissary account. It wasn't like this project was funded yet, so it was coming out of our company account. We started pushing back some and told her she had to cool it. We were happy to provide for her, as promised, but we couldn't be the financial backers of a prison black market for toiletries. She disagreed and seemed to relish her role as the new unofficial boss of her state penitentiary. She started holding her life rights extension hostage until she got exactly what she wanted. Though she had signed an option contract for the first year, we still had to renew the option every six months until the film went into production or the purchase price was paid to her daughter's charity of choice.

To make matters worse, we were running out of time on the Halle Barry salary negotiation. Eventually, the whole thing crumbled. We couldn't just pull it off money-wise, and we really had to do a cost-benefit analysis on our time at that point. We were a small company, and we couldn't put all of our eggs into one basket. It was a blow, but when word got around town and in the media that Halle Berry was attached to star in one of our projects, a lot of other things started coming our way pretty quickly.

One of them was the potential to option a book about the life of Jerry Garcia, lead guitarist and front person for the infamous rock band the Grateful Dead. *Captain Trips* by Sandy Troy was the first biography released after Jerry's death. Sandy, although an affable guy, was merciless in his pursuit to get *Captain Trips* turned into a movie. He was close with Jerry's circle and was well connected in the Grateful

Dead world. He could put us in the room with people like Carolyn "Mountain Girl" Garcia (Jerry Garcia and Ken Kesey's former wife), Bob Weir (another Grateful Dead band member), Mark Pinkus (Rhino Records executive), Stanley Mouse (creator of the recognizable logo for the Grateful Dead), and Tim Jorstad (the Grateful Dead's long-time accountant). The list went on. The bottom line is Sandy had connections to many friends and family of the band, but he desired a young producer to help him create relevance for a story that had a very niche demographic. Basically, he promised access to anyone we wanted, a dream for someone trying to produce a biographical movie. He just desired our ability to package a star into the deal and help make it young and fresh in the eyes of Hollywood. *How could we not do this project?* I thought.

But Justin wasn't really into it from day one. Though we liked true stories, neither of us were Grateful Dead fans. There wasn't much about it that interested us, personally. But it was timely in some regard (rock biopics *Walk the Line* and *Ray* had recently been released with success) and seemed like it would be of interest to the public if cast with the right star and an interesting take on a more modern soundtrack – an idea we had was to create modern relevance by featuring current rock artists remaking old Grateful Dead songs. Sometimes you just have to make a business decision, and it felt like a good one. Especially when you're at the start of your career and just trying to make something substantial work, to some degree. I knew enough to know by this point that nothing was guaranteed. Finding projects that aligned with our passions was great, but we weren't in a position yet to turn much down. Like a lot of things, this was a numbers game. We had to keep taking shots to eventually make one. If we were putting all of our eggs in separate baskets, this egg had a real shot.

Plus, Sandy was persistent and bullish on getting this thing made. He was very persuasive and convinced me with all of his promises of access. He called me constantly, borderline desperate to get the film made. I related to the passion and so I understood his pursuit. Another one of those people he had access to was a guy named Jeff Robinov. At the time, Jeff was the president of Warner Bros. and apparently a huge Grateful Dead fan. Rumor had it, Robinov used to sell "Dead Dogs" (hotdogs) in the parking lot of Grateful Dead concerts. As such a big fan, I agreed with Sandy that Jeff would likely be personally interested, which makes a considerable difference in getting projects sold and made. *Worst case scenario, we'll just sell it to Warner Bros.*, I thought in the back of my mind.

So I started the process, first optioning the book and then meeting everyone whom Sandy had promised to introduce me to. It was research and development at its core, and a lot of it. When the process started, I didn't know anything about Jerry Garcia or the Grateful Dead. I had not heard one song, I did not know who American novelist Ken Kesey was, what the Merry Pranksters were, and I certainly had not been to Haight-Ashbury, the center of the counterculture movement. Most of that happened before I was even born. All the while, Justin didn't really seem to care and was frankly uninterested. "That's your project," he would say. I can't blame him; it wasn't going to be an easy one with the subject matter requiring deep study.

So there I was, once again, on the bumpy gravel road attempting to steer a project toward pavement and out the other end of a development hell tunnel. Why I kept getting inspired by period pieces, stories that took place decades and decades ago, is beyond me. It was obvious that the movie was going to be expensive to make, being that it mainly took place in the 1960s and 1970s. Period films must use older cars, costumes of the time, and locations that are of the time period. Often these have to be sourced, which adds significant cost to the production. Although I had been successful in getting actor Paul Giamatti attached to the film to play Jerry, it wasn't exactly easy getting a director to sign on. The 1960s and 1970s had a very distinct look and feel in many respects, and required a skilled visionary director who both had a point of view and understood the importance of authenticity that was vital in telling this cultural story. This was a large part of American culture and needed to be done right, or not at all. It was becoming clear that the movie couldn't be made independently. Just about every independent financier and director had passed on it for various reasons, all stemming from the fear that if the budget wasn't big enough, the movie wouldn't be good enough and the Deadheads would come for them. Beloved figures and movements are tricky to make in that way. Fandoms can destroy a career if you portray the object of that fandom inaccurately. It had to be made with a studio, which limited our options given the subject matter.

Though Sandy often treated me like a child and became really difficult to work with, he made good on his connections, and we got a meeting on the books with Jeff Robinov. It was our last hope to keep the project alive. If Jeff and Warner Bros. passed, I felt it would be a sign that we should hang it up and move on. By this time, I had spent two years in development hell. The line between persistence and stupidity can be thin sometimes. We were scheduled to sit with the president of Warner Bros., and Sandy had the idea to bring "Mountain Girl" Garcia to the meeting to help entice Jeff.

It worked to the extent that he was enamored with her. She is an icon of the 1960s and famous in her own right. But it was clear he was way more interested in her stories than the actual movie. He was a fan. Eventually, even "Mountain Girl" herself couldn't convince Jeff to get on board with the film and so Warner Bros. passed, too. Another thing that plagued me during the process was there was always an underpinning worry that Jerry's widow, Deborah, was going to shut down the project. She was apparently the love of Jerry's life, and mostly controlled his estate. She never seemed supportive of the movie, and so a dark cloud hovered above it as we waited for her to pull the plug any moment.

It was a good lesson for me in understanding the importance of a clear chain of title to story rights. Who controls what is in the public domain? Who really has the ability to tell a *true story*? We had optioned underlying source material (the book), and Jerry's story was public domain, but the widow who never returned a phone call did pose a problem that lingered in the back of my mind. It was another great lesson for a green producer. Justin was definitely not upset that the project fell apart. He didn't like that I was disappointed, but he knew it wasn't meant for us. I think deep down I probably knew that, as well. It is so hard to walk that line between what your gut knows and persevering in the name of hard work and good business. Looking back, it wasn't a good sign that my partner wasn't on board. Usually, I trusted Justin's instincts. That's what a strong partnership is all about. And when on the rare occasion that I went against them, I often regretted it.

In the midst of all of this, I got another intriguing call. This time from a guy who wanted to make a film about Pablo Escobar's life based on a book his brother wrote called *My Brother Pablo*. If this sounds familiar to you, it's probably because there is a show on Netflix called

Narcos, which is pretty much exactly what this was meant to be. This writer, let's call him Harry, told me he already had an option for the book. He even had a script. Immediately I replied, "Wait, you mean the *real* Pablo Escobar, the most notorious drug lord in the world? You have an option for his brother's book, one of the closest guys to him, *and* you have a script?" It seemed too good to be true. He really had it all prepackaged. This time Justin and I were both equally intrigued. I was glad he was on board this time. Once again, it was time to put together our team, but first we felt it best to make the press announcement about our new project.

Despite still being new and making many mistakes, word was getting around town about us and our ability to attract interesting projects and attach strong talent. We seemed to be getting pitched timely story after timely story, and the scripts were rolling in from the agencies. New projects would get a hit in the media, and agents called to pitch us actors, or suggest writers and directors we should partner with. We wanted to capitalize on our little bit of attention, and a press announcement that we had the rights to the Escobar book and a script would surely keep the phone ringing. Our Halle Berry project, then Jerry Garcia, and now Pablo Escobar helped raise our profile drastically, even though none of these had even been made! Our company was looking great on the outside but I was starting to feel a bit of imposter syndrome on the inside. I was anxious. By most standards, we were successful. But I wasn't experiencing the joy of any of it. I still felt like I was falling short of all I'd hoped to accomplish. Everything else I'd done didn't matter. I needed and wanted more. The projects that had fallen through still haunted me. I wanted to prove that J2 (read: I) could do this. That we were as great as everyone thought we were. Better, even.

I received a call from an agent at Creative Artists Agency about the Escobar project. Oliver Stone wanted to meet with us. THE Oliver Stone, the king of biopics. He made movies like *Wall Street, Born on the Fourth of July, World Trade Center, W.*, the new *Wall Street, Snowden*, and, most important to my dad, *JFK*. The JFK movie came out when we were living in Dallas, and my first call after I heard Oliver wanted to meet us was to my dad to tell him. He grew up in the Kennedy era, and loved the film and all things Oliver Stone. He was so excited for me. Sometimes it was hard to connect with my parents about my work;

they were so far removed from it all. But whenever I got the chance to impress them with a connection to someone they found interesting, like I did with Yogi Berra or Oliver Stone, it was so much fun.

Justin and I arrived to meet with Oliver. We were there to pitch him the Escobar project, but it turned out he already knew almost everything about it and was ready to produce it with us. He even already had a director in mind and wanted to introduce us. I was a little surprised, as originally I'd hoped he would want to direct it. But he was in the middle of directing *W.* (the movie with Josh Brolin about George W. Bush) and felt more comfortable as producer on this one given his bandwidth. That was still great by me, and I was hoping he'd mentor me through the experience. Act as a producer Yoda, if you will. I was enamored, not just because of his interest in the project, which was flattering, but of his general warmth and kindness. He loved the story of J2, of Justin's and my real-life friendship turned business partners where we focused on true stories in the film space and situational comedies on TV. He was sincere and authentic. And he did go on to be a significant mentor to me for a while.

The guy he wanted to direct the movie turned out to be Antoine Fuqua. He's a major film director probably most famous for the movie *American Gangster*. There it was in *Variety*'s headline on October 8, 2007: *Stone to Produce Escobar with J2. Fuqua to Direct.* Antoine was accomplished for sure, but he was also intimidating and scared me a bit. "You're going to get this done my way, right, Jason?" he would ask me all the time. I wasn't sure what to make of him, but I knew with his name and *American Gangster* credit attached to the project, it would go a long way.

With Oliver and Antoine on board, the project moved along, but once again got hung up in financing. No, even with Oliver Stone and a major director, a project isn't an instant greenlight. It also became complicated because the rights to the book were controlled under a Colombian-drafted agreement, which meant we needed an attorney who was licensed in Colombia. Despite having a strong script, we had to navigate many moving parts to ensure a clear chain of title, a mistake I would not ever make again. In many ways, we were still winging it and figuring it out as we went along as every project brought a new set of unique circumstances with it. I've come to believe that one of most universal truths in life is that no one really knows everything. No matter how accomplished or confident someone appears, most of us are just making it up as we go along. No matter how much experienced we gained, each project always had new challenges that we hadn't faced before. And in that respect, we just took our best guess and moved forward.

After a lot of effort and persistence, the money eventually did come together, hallelujah. We decided to shoot in Puerto Rico instead of Columbia, not only because it was much safer, but because the Puerto Rican government was granting us a 40% rebate. That meant we were getting 40% of our money back, essentially. No-brainer. Hundreds of films had shot there and taken advantage of the same financing structure.

We all flew down to Puerto Rico to scout locations, and when we landed in San Juan, we were appointed bodyguards. It was described to us more like these were Antoine's bodyguards, there primarily for him. The whole thing was a little odd. *Why does Antoine need bodyguards? A lot of pomp and circumstance*, I thought. Puerto Rico didn't seem unsafe in a large group, and we were only there for two days, scouting most of the day and night. The last night in Puerto Rico, after a long, professional dinner with government officials, it was off to a "nice bar for a drink," they proclaimed. As we approached the bar doors and went through a beaded curtain, I instantly felt out of place. We had reached the interior of a strip club, to put it mildly. Not exactly where I expected we would end up with my work colleagues and our government liaison. My lack of enthusiasm was evident, driven in part by my desire to maintain professionalism mixed with my uneasy, internal confusion about my lack of interest in naked women. They had their fun, and I awkwardly sat and had a drink, solo. This attracted some weird looks and whispers behind my back, but more or less everyone just left me alone and got on with it. Sadly, I was getting used to being the one guy who was never interested in a hookup and others thinking that I was abnormal for it.

The final day, as we were leaving the hotel to go back to the States, one of the bodyguards came up and joined me in the elevator.

"I've told to deliver you message," he said in fractured English.

"What's up?" I said. *What could he possibly have to say to me? Maybe our taxi to the airport is delayed?*

"You will not film your movie here in Puerto Rico. You will film it in Colombia," he said.

"Huh? Who asked you to tell me this?" I asked, confused.

Staring straight ahead with no eye contact, he replied, "Make sure you listen." And with that the elevator door opened and he was out.

I was so confused. *What does that mean? Was that a threat? If so, from who?* I couldn't tell if it was a bad joke or if my life was in danger. Momentarily, I blew it off and walked to the front desk to check out. I was supposed to be getting in the taxi van with Antoine and the rest of the group to go to the airport when I saw Antoine get in a separate van. I asked the translator on our team what was going on, and he said that Antoine was heading straight from here to Columbia, where Escobar is from. "To do what?" I asked. "To scout for the movie," they replied. But . . . I was the producer of the movie. I should be informed and included in every part of the scouting process. I'm the one who optioned the book and the script. I was the one who arranged the financing and brought in Oliver Stone. I was the reason Antoine was even there. Plus, all the rebate incentives had been lined up for us to do it in Puerto Rico. On the heels of the message the bodyguard had just delivered to me, this just couldn't be a coincidence. "What do you mean?" I asked back. "What I understand is the movie is going to need to shoot in Columbia. If it happens at all," the translator replied. The others piled into the taxi van, and we were off to the airport. I was confused, but I didn't know what to do about it.

The problem was the financiers whom I had lined up were not going to support shooting in Columbia. There was no safety guarantee and, most important to them, no tax rebate. We had just scouted Puerto Rico and everyone seemed happy with the locations we picked. Puerto Rico was simply the best jurisdiction to shoot this film, plain and simple. We couldn't afford to make the movie in Columbia, nor was it safe to do so at that time. I got back to California and tried to reach Antoine several times to understand why he was in Columbia, what he knew, and what was happening. *Had he received a similar warning?* I asked up and down the chain of command why this was happening. Oliver Stone said he was equally as confused and didn't support the change of venue. Although he was a producer on the film, he also had little knowledge as to the apparent change, of course. Being the visionary filmmaker that he is, all he could offer to me was, "Maybe it would be more authentic if it was shot in Columbia. Let's see if it's even a possibility, before shunning the idea."

A possibility? I knew it wasn't, that he was just being optimistic. Although Oliver was sympathetic to the situation, his head was neck deep in the reshoots for his other film; the planning and coordinating for this one was all me. I was in the deep end, and he wanted me to swim. Tough love. It was just all so strange to me and more than a little scary. Maybe it was actually a threat. Maybe Escobar's brother had gotten involved. I don't know. I'll never know. And eventually, I gave up trying to know. The financing was based on Puerto Rico, and that was that. When Antoine returned from Columbia, after many heated arguments with his agent, I fired him as director of the project. It was my first firing and, although hard, it felt really good. He had been condescending and not a team player from the start, defying the better good of the production and our financiers. Oliver Stone stayed attached to the film as our producing partner and was supportive to the end.

We began the effort of meeting with replacement directors. Oliver set a meeting with director José Padiha, who was essentially unknown in Hollywood at the time. He did not have the same credit pedigree as Antoine, but he was clearly educated on the subject matter, a visionary, and would have made an aligned team player. Oliver saw something in him and was insistent he be the one to now direct *Escobar*. Justin and I liked him a lot, too. Unfortunately for us, the timing was early, as Padiha had directed only one independent foreign film (*Elite Squad*) to date and was not considered "bankable" by studios or financiers. He's gone on to produce some large films such as *RoboCop* and fittingly, season one of *Narcos* for Netflix. It was critically acclaimed and went on to win several Emmy and BAFTA awards. It's my belief that everything does happen for a reason. If I had pushed harder and somehow convinced the financial backers to allow us to shoot the movie in Columbia, because of the lack of infrastructure and threats, the film likely would have still never been completed anyway. And even worse, maybe something bad would have happened to us or the crew.

All in all, the subject matter was best suited as a streaming show rather than a two-hour movie. I see that now and commend Padiha for his work. As much satisfaction as I found in standing up for myself and following my gut, the movie fell apart and it was a huge blow to our company. We had been taking the profits we made on *Filthy Rich Cattle Drive* and a few other projects we had set up, and put them into developing this movie. We had basically put it all on the line for this. We weren't diversified like my dad had been telling me to be for years. As much as we were trying to put those eggs in different baskets, somehow most of them still ended up in the *Escobar* one. As soon as someone pulled the rug out from under us, it was over – the basket tipped and the eggs broke.

I was beginning to wonder when we would actually make this Hollywood thing work in a big way. We had some marginal success – a lot, some may say – for two young guys who had little experience producing. But having so many things fall through after putting so much effort into it, it was beating us down. Even with my usually unbridled positive attitude, I was worried. I became desperate, both personally and professionally. And bad things come from desperation.

CUE: "I'm Still Standing" by Elton John

10

Scarf or Noose?

AFTER THE PABLO Escobar project fell apart, we were in real trouble. We hadn't had a win in a while. Remember how our phone was ringing off the hook there for a while because of the big names associated with us and exciting projects we worked on? Yeah, that was wearing off. Word was now getting around about our projects falling apart. Hollywood is a big town, but it's a small industry. People in our personal lives began telling us that forming J2 might have been a mistake. *What if you don't recover? Should Justin have just stuck with acting? Maybe you should go back to assisting someone else. Or go in a different direction and try something else.* Even some well-meaning people who cared for us told us it looked like it was time to change course.

When I had lunch with friends or ran into people around town, I saw that look of pity in their eyes as they asked me, "How are things going?" Those unaware friends outside of Hollywood would ask, "When's that Garcia movie coming out?" or say "Can't wait to see Halle in that jewel thief film." It felt like a gut punch every time. Even for a person with a naturally sunny disposition, it was embarrassing and hard to cover the disappointment. I tried to remind myself that we were both still young, and we were working hard; there was still time to achieve our dreams. But it didn't help. The imposter syndrome feeling was weighing on me. Maybe I wasn't cut out for this.

To make a bad situation worse, J2 wasn't bringing in much revenue, and it was the height of the economic and housing market crash of 2009. Justin and I also had a mini real estate portfolio by now, which, in a good market, was appreciating and even renting well. But by mid-2009, without enough paying film or TV projects, we struggled to cover all of the mortgages. Everyone was short-selling real estate left and right in LA with over 140,000 short sales and 90,000 foreclosures in 2009 alone. We were losing money, a lot of it. We had to cash out of one property just to make ends meet and keep things afloat. During this period, we also made the difficult but prudent decision to sell our coveted J2 headquarters and home in Calabasas. Owning that *Newlyweds* mansion cost many thousands a month to maintain, and that certainly was not something we could continue doing in a down market with no projects on the horizon.

That financial and business stress inevitably turned into personal stress. It started to tax Justin's and my personal relationship. Justin and I have always been great friends. Best friends, actually. Minus similar DNA, we are truly brothers and treat each other like it. We have a strong bond and a trust that has survived many hard things. But there were tense moments when we were both tempted to blame each other in different ways for where we found ourselves. He was ready to blame me for choosing the wrong projects, focusing too much time or money on them and not diversifying enough. He also blamed me for not raising outside capital to support our business, instead relying on him and our production fees to support the overhead. And I blamed him for all the water I was carrying, trying to learn as we went with what I felt was little to no support at times.

I admit, maybe I did laser focus too long on certain projects and should have let them go faster, but I was too naive to know it. Maybe I should have attempted to raise outside capital for our company, but I wasn't convinced we had enough on the résumé to garner interest. I also wasn't experienced enough to know how to raise capital well yet. And, yes, I was resentful that I felt I carried the responsibility of running the company. But this was my role, and I had to own that. Really, we were novices, and nobody was to blame. We were doing the best we could do. I was constantly reassuring him that it was all going to be okay. Though I had moments of doubt, deep down I truly did believe that. I wasn't sure how things were going to work out, but I knew we would find a way.

One thing was for sure, I was grateful for the continued loyalty and support of our assistant, Rebecca. She was still with us, and rallied to every daunting task ahead of her. She was in that trench with us, less as an assistant and more like a strategist. The loyalty went both ways. Maybe we wouldn't be the most successful production company in Hollywood, but we were never going to be homeless, or lose Rebecca. We weren't going to miss payroll, and no one was even going to miss as much as one meal. I wasn't above getting three side jobs, working a graveyard shift at FedEx, or selling my sperm. Well, maybe not the last one. But I'd do what I had to do. The point is, it might sound silly or simple, but we are good people with strong values and we were willing to do the work. I believed if we kept moving forward honestly and with good intention, we could figure this out. And I was going to continue to lead us toward the light at the end of the tunnel, even if it was just a glimmer in the distance.

I believe in solutions. I have always believed I have the power to manifest positive things and solutions to problems. Lots of people throughout my life have mocked this as naive and childish. There are plenty of times in my life, some of which you've heard about already, when that might even be a fair assessment. I've been taken advantage of and seen things through rose-colored glasses when perhaps I should have been more cautious. But more often than not, it's served as a superpower. I'd rather go through life betting that things will work out and sometimes be wrong than assume we're screwed. I could need $1,000 tomorrow and have no idea where to get it from, but figure it out within hours. Somehow, whether from my innate personality or the way my parents raised me, I never let my mind get too far into a negative place. I've always felt that if you remain positive, you will find solutions. Negative thinking triggers your body's immune response. This means, negative thinking will literally affect your immune system and make you sicker. No matter how childish it made me look, a positive attitude is always the way to go.

That's why, when a man named Omar Amanat walked into our lives, I believed he was exactly one of these solutions that I manifested. We first met Amanat on a trip with some friends to the Caribbean. He was gregarious, fun, nice, polished, and a self-proclaimed financial wizard. He also always had a designer scarf draped around his neck. Amanat was married with three kids and resided at the Alfred in Manhattan, in the largest penthouse complete with six terraces. His home had its own Hollywood claim to fame. It was the former residence of character Gordon Gekko in the film *Wall Street*. A few years prior to meeting him, Omar founded and grew the company Tradescape, eventually selling it to E*Trade for $276 million. Before that, he created an online trading system called Cyber-Block, which was acquired by Charles Schwab for $488 million in 2000. By all measures, he was a successful guy and clearly knew how to make money.

He also had an affinity for movies and entertainment. Especially the kind that we liked and were desperately hoping to make more of, assuming J2 survived Hollywood. We were still primarily focused on realistic, nonfictional films or biopics about real people and events. Amanat had recently invested in a film called *Darfur Now* and was a board member of Human Rights Watch and Malaria No More. Those credentials alone gave us the impression that he was a values-driven guy who cared about larger issues. We were impressed by him, and as luck would have it, he was enamored with us. Like many people, he thought Justin's and my story of two loyal friends who didn't come from money, worked hard, and did what we loved, was a good one. Despite our recent project setbacks, he was quite complimentary of us and thought we were extraordinarily successful for how young we were. I'll admit, that felt good to hear.

He showed an interest in us personally, and in J2. On several back-to-back visits to Los Angeles, he emailed to meet up. At each meeting, he asked a lot of questions, and we gave him more information on our company goals and the types of projects we were drawn to. He was seemingly so impressed by us, in fact, that on the Fourth of July, at his rented Malibu beach house, he told us he wanted to invest in our company. I hadn't told him about our dire situation or made it sound like we needed assistance; he just was genuinely interested. As the fireworks shot through the sky, we all waved our sparklers, looked out at the ocean, and sipped our champagne as he toasted, "To J2!" We felt like he was a savior, the answer we had been looking for, the way forward and our path to grow. It had been a long time since I had been in a church, and I'd come a long way from my Southern Baptist roots, but this seemed like an answer to prayer. It could not have come at a better time.

Amanat shared our positive outlook for the future and believed in us as founders. He had already made investments in other Hollywood companies (including big studios like Summit and production companies including Groundswell), and he expressed that he saw us as another great investment. He told us he wanted to help take J2 to the next level. Put us on the map. Always adjusting that damn designer scarf as he talked. He was a great salesman. We felt honored to be in the company of a successful financial wizard who had made investments in companies much larger and more successful than ours. In fact, Summit had just produced the famed tween film *Twilight*, which Hollywood was all abuzz about at the time. *We have the same investor as the owner of the* Twilight *studio*, we thought. *That has to be a good sign.*

He asked for a 25% equity grant of the company, which our attorney informed us was quite fair and normal for an investor of this caliber. We'd retain control of the company in every meaningful way. All he asked in return was for us to invest $350,000 into his venture fund, which would pay dividends out monthly to aid our business in covering overhead, bridging the company as it gained revenue traction. These dividends would cover the hiring of an experienced development executive and the very basic nuts and bolts of our expenses to get us to our next big project. The capital was protected. It sounded fantastic, and coming from the founder of Tradescape, made sense to us financial novices. We trusted him.

At the time, I had almost exactly $71,000 in my bank account. Justin had more, and we agreed that I would put all $71,000 toward Amanat's fund and Justin would cover the rest. He would put in almost $300,000 to keep J2 going because he trusted Amanat as much as I did, and because I felt it was a good idea. Our attorneys had put in our agreements that after 12 months we could recall the funds we had invested and pull them if we wanted. It felt like we couldn't lose.

In the short term, this whole thing worked out great. For the first six months, Amanat's fund paid out exactly like he said it would. The money came in predictably, and it did keep us afloat, enabling us to continue developing and selling our projects. It was exactly the lifeline we needed. And it wasn't long until we sold another big TV show exactly because we were able to keep going. Justin, our new-hire Harvey, and I developed the show *Sons of Tucson*, which we sold to FOX. It was basically a reunion of the behind-the-scenes people from *Malcolm in the Middle*. It had the same director, a lot of the same writers, and Justin as the executive producer also set to act in a few episodes. We brought the band back together and created a hilarious 30-minute comedy that got picked up for 12 episodes. It felt like a resurgence. J2 was back!

We had everything lined up to begin shooting the show, when all of a sudden, the dividends from Amanat stopped coming in. No phone call, no warning, no discussion. They just stopped being deposited into J2's bank account. Justin and I were both frustrated and thinking how out-of-character this seemed for our new, wonderful business partner. It was very fortunate we had just sold a TV show and had some cash on hand because something was seriously wrong here with the Amanat deal. I began calling him every day. But, just like his money, he seemed to have disappeared. I left messages everywhere and talked to his assistant Sabrina whenever I could reach her. She, by the way, was just as perplexed as I was. She couldn't seem to get a hold of him either and often didn't know where he was.

The funny thing was, because Amanat was a social-climbing man about town, he was walking red carpets and being photographed at popular events. I couldn't get a hold of this man, his investment had dried up, and now he was living the life in the media. I still saw him in the trades and on the internet constantly. Sabrina and I didn't know where he was at any given moment, but I could find out the next day in Page Six in the *New York Post*. He and his scarf of the day were on red carpets at the premieres of movies he had funded, in pictures with celebrities at openings for bars and restaurants, on the back of yachts in Cannes, and whatever else. It was also rumored that his wife had left him and he was with a younger woman with a baby on the way. I knew he wasn't dead, but he wouldn't pick up his phone. Justin and I were furious.

Fortunately, that clause in our contract said if we wanted our money back we just had to give 30 days' notice and we got it. I had learned enough about contracts by this point to cover our asses legally. So on the first day of the 12th month, we gave notice, and asked for our money back out of the fund. But the thing about a contract is, it doesn't really matter what it means or says if the other side doesn't honor the deal. We asked in voicemails, emails, registered mail letters, and all manner of communication to no avail. We called his ex-wife, his business partners, and anyone we could get a hold of to track him. Amanat was in the wind and our deposit into his fund was gone. Yet, he still retained 25% of J2 and technically his pro rata share of any profits of the company. Finally, after months of no contact, no distribution, and no return of our money, Justin and I found ourselves swallowed in overstuffed and uncomfortable leather chairs in a lawyer's office in downtown Santa Monica. We looked across the lawyer's big mahogany desk and told him everything that happened in the last few months. We weren't sure what to do next.

Our lawyer, Phil, looked up from a stack of papers and made eye contact, first with me and then with Justin. He furrowed his brow a little and said, "Guys, I'm afraid you have been the victims of a Ponzi scheme." We both looked at each other, puzzled. *What the fuck is that?* I thought and then asked out loud minus the *fuck*. He explained to us how a Ponzi scheme worked. My mind seemed to catch only every few sentences of what he was saying. "A form of fraud . . . quick returns from the first investors from money from past investors . . . illegal . . . doesn't actually earn any money." I'm not sure what I expected to hear, but it certainly wasn't that.

The whole thing had been Amanat's idea to invest in us. He saw us as Ponzi prey. I was the one who thought Amanat was the way to go, the solution to our problems. Justin believed the same, but only because he trusted me. This was supposed to be our big comeback. The thing that was going to take us to the next level. I could barely even look at Justin. I was humiliated and ashamed. The depression set in fast. I was literally sick to my stomach. For the very first time, maybe ever, I let myself wonder if we could really do this. If *I* could really do this. *How dumb does one need to be to fall for a Ponzi scheme*, I thought. *What kind of good business partner loses his friend's money like that? Or my own savings?* And even after I'd already learned so much. How did I not see the signs?

It turned out, the answer is because there were no signs to see. Bernie Madoff, the mastermind of the biggest Ponzi scheme in history and one-time chairman of the Nasdaq stock exchange, managed to scam some of the richest investors over a 50-year run. Madoff's scheme made global headlines way after Amanat's, introducing the layperson to Ponzi schemes. The point is, the best criminals are smooth. Very smooth. Justin held his head in his hands, so Phil looked at me with empathy, "You need to sue this guy," he said.

I knew he was right, but in my mind, suing someone was just horrible. No matter what this guy had done to us, I didn't want to sue him. I didn't want to sue anybody. I value relationships above everything and just wanted to find a way to make this right. Did things have to get so aggressive? Suing someone felt combative and not in line with my personality or my values. Call me childish, but I had always been able to talk out issues with others. I wished this could be the same. One night, troubled by all of this and scared of what would come next, I rang up an acquaintance and now dear friend and mentor named Suhail Rizvi. Suhail is one of the most successful private venture capitalists in the world. He was a seed founder behind Twitter, Facebook, Square, and was once one of the largest shareholders in SpaceX.

"Suhail," I said, "I can't believe it's come to this." That night, he told me many things that I did not want to hear at the time, but have since turned out to be absolutely true. "You're going to get through this," he said. "I know it's stressful, but these kinds of situations are how you grow and position you to handle the future even better. You're going to have a better business and an even brighter future because of this. But it will get worse before it gets better. The important thing to remember though is that it *will* get better."

At the time, those words made me feel sick. I didn't want to hear that it was going to get worse or that this would make our business stronger in the long run. All I wanted was Justin's money back. Sure, I wanted my money back and our TV shows to work and our business to succeed. But mostly I wanted Justin's money back. I felt like I had failed my best friend and that the writing was on the wall for the little company we had been so proud to form years prior. Suhail ended with, "Your lawyer is right; you need to sue Omar. You need to do that in order to move through this." After seeking advice from a few others I respect, I realized that Suhail was right. Business disputes are inevitable, and every truly successful entrepreneur in America has been to court at least once. Maybe it's a rite of passage.

I still felt like a small fish in many ways. Who cared about us and what we did? We weren't trying to make some big statement or declaration about what was right and wrong. But I did understand that you can't let people get away with things like this. If we didn't help try and stop him, Amanat was going to keep doing this to other unassuming entrepreneurs and businesses and could go on to hurt more people.

And so we did. Shortly after that, we filed a lawsuit against him. I'll never forget seeing "J2 Inc. versus Omar Amanat, an individual and the Crescendo Constellation Fund, LP" on that depressing, complicated legal paperwork. The whole thing was taxing and stressful. I hated just about every minute of it. After a few weeks of chasing Amanat to have him served, and a couple of years later waiting our turn in the judicial system, a judge did decide in our favor. We prevailed with a settlement of $1 million dollars against Amanat. We weren't the only ones he had screwed over. Later, in 2016 he was arrested and sentenced to five years of jail time. And then again on August 19, 2021, the Department of Justice issued a press release stating that Amanat had been sentenced to prison for multiple fraud schemes after conviction at trial.

Apparently, we were one of the smallest victims in Amanat's overall scheme. According to a statement by US Attorney Audrey Strauss, "Omar Amanat defrauded investors of millions of dollars through years of lies and deceit. Among his many fraudulent tactics, Amanat teamed up with others to manipulate stock prices and hide investment losses through years of false account statements. When he was finally caught, Amanat doubled down on his lies by introducing fake emails into the trial record as 'exculpatory' evidence. Neither the Government nor the jury was fooled. Amanat was convicted on all counts and remanded by the court into federal custody, where he will remain until his sentence is fully served."

It turned out he was running a multicountry scheme that spanned continents. Articles at the time called it a "striking fall from power" as he had once been "the most powerful man in Hollywood you've never heard of." In his opening statement, the prosecutor accused him of "lies upon lies."

In the end, we were only able to collect a tiny fraction of the million dollars that Amanat owed us. As these Ponzi schemes usually go, he filed for bankruptcy and couldn't afford to repay hardly any of what his victims were owed. He ruined the lives of many people, including his own, and he sits in federal prison. Though it was one of the hardest times in my life, I'm confident that we did do the right thing. Our judgment was the first major, unsealed judgment against him and was reported to the Department of Justice, putting him squarely on their radar as he continued the scheme.

Still, through it all, the worst part of it was the strain on my relationship with Justin. I felt responsible for the loss of that money, more of his than mine. Because what we eventually got back from the Amanat settlement didn't cover the whole amount, minus legal fees of course, over time I have paid Justin the equivalent of that $300,000, out of my own pocket just because it was the right thing to do. I was so grateful for his trust in me and partnership in everything we've done together. It was important for him to know that. Money isn't everything, but it's a representation of what we value. And I value his friendship, partnership, and brotherhood over everything else in business. To this day, neither he, his wife, nor I ever utter the name Omar Amanat. We can't stand to speak it aloud. Like Voldemort.

Though Amanat wasn't the investor that we thought he was, we survived and moved on, though maybe a little worse for the wear. We were headed into 2009 having learned valuable business lessons, just finished producing a fun primetime sitcom for FOX, and grown significantly both personally and professionally. We had also seasoned a bit and weren't so green in the production business anymore. Though still young, in many ways we felt like battled-scarred professionals who were still in the game. Omar had put us through hell, and we had given it right back. And, we hadn't lost our sense of humor; we still liked to have fun. We were also ready for a vacation. Fortunately, one day around this time we received an exclusive invitation to a paradise called Necker Island. We were about to head to one of the most gorgeous places on the planet and meet one of the rowdiest, most fun-loving businessmen of our generation.

CUE: "Gives You Hell" by All American Rejects

PART

III

Take Two

11

Necker Island

ONE DAY IN 2007, I got a call from a producer friend out of New York. She was putting together a group of "interesting people" to go down to Sir Richard Branson's 74-acre private home, Necker Island, for "a week involving like-minded people and a bit of sport and adventure." As I understood it, she and her husband were friends of this Richard guy and had been assembling annual summer sojourns like this for the past few years. I had no idea who Richard was at the time, much less that he was a knighted "Sir." I'd heard of Virgin Records, sort of, and had once been in one to peruse music shortly after arriving in Los Angeles. Yes, kids, we used to actually go to a store, place headphones on our ears, and listen to music before we bought it. I feel old even typing that last sentence. I'd also been to Jessica Simpson's new record signing at a Virgin store, but those two experiences were so far my only interactions with the brand at all.

It was a well-known fact (to everyone but me) that Virgin Records was THE holy grail of music stores. Those stores are long gone now, and I was clueless to the facts that Richard had founded the company and that he'd gone on to start many businesses in many industries, making him a certified billionaire and arguably one of the most successful entrepreneurs in the last 100 years. My friend told me that Sir Richard (or SRB as she called him) regularly hosted these "celebration weeks" on his island where people who'd likely never met before vacationed together. These trips served not only as a vacation but also as networking think tanks of sorts – a small gathering of individuals and families to initiate thought leadership, idea incubation, and mutually beneficial connections. At the very least, I was told it'd be a lot of fun and a good disconnect from Los Angeles. A disconnect was exactly what I needed, so it was a no-brainer for me. I invited Justin, who was more up for the sport and adventure than I was, while I focused on recentering myself and the future of J2. We were still reeling a bit after the Omar experience, but firmly back on our feet with our new prime-time television series, *Sons of Tucson*, about to air on FOX.

Let me pause and say here that often when I tell this story, people can't believe it actually happened that way. *You just randomly got invited to Necker Island?* Basically . . . yes. I cannot ignore the amount of sheer luck it was that Richard was looking to put together a think tank of up-and-comers in the entertainment world and Justin and I happened to come to the mind of the guy who was putting it together. Of course, we also worked hard to get where we were. Despite our setbacks, we had a good reputation, and you know by now that one of my superpowers is networking, which is how I met my producer friend. But this absolutely seismic shift that was about to happen in my life is certainly also due to luck – being in the right place at the right time. Maybe much of my life can be chalked up to that. It was lucky that David Mirisch spoke to my class that day. Lucky that the woman I happened to nanny for turned out to be an esteemed producer. Lucky that I met Justin and lucky that one of my roommates was personal friends with the Simpsons. I acknowledge all of that. I also acknowledge that if you work hard enough and are positive enough, when luck eventually comes your way . . . you'll be ready. I didn't know it yet, but I was about to get the luckiest opportunity of my life. And I was going to dive in head first.

Necker itself was unlike anything I'd ever experienced, and I consider myself an island guy. I grew up going to the Cayman Islands. They've always felt like my second home. I had dreams of building a house there to live permanently for parts of the year. But Necker was private and next level. It's located in the British Virgin Islands surrounded by coral reefs, warm turquoise waters, tropical verdant foliage, and stretches of white sandy beaches – an eco-luxury experience on steroids, with enough champagne to serve the population of a small country. For a week away, I packed a huge suitcase, not realizing that on Necker, your dirty clothes don't stay on the floor for more than a few hours. By the next they are washed and folded and ready to wear again. I could have shown up with just the clothes on my back and been perfectly fine. This was a level of service I had never quite experienced, and oddly I felt right at home without any sense of reservation or a feeling of being out of place.

That first trip was exactly as advertised. It was full of amazing, spirited people, both guests and staff alike. To understate it, we had a great time. Justin and I did make lots of interesting new friends, but we mostly just ate and drank our way through the week. While all of the other guests' attention was focused on talking with our hosts, Richard and his wife Joan, I ended up enjoying much discussion with a guy called Sam who was, unbeknownst to me until the last day, Richard and Joan's son. Sam and I hit it off the first night, and when he put his contact info into my phone it was as "Sam Rastafarian Brother." For days I knew nothing else except that. When I finally found out he was a Branson (from someone else!), I felt a little ridiculous. Especially when I began to notice there were pictures of him up all over the place.

We hung out with his girlfriend (now wife), Bella, and a small group of friends. With Sam and his pals, there was no business talk, only fun. And that's exactly what I wanted as well. Justin and I ended up enjoying the week with this smaller group, versus with the larger group who seemed more interested in networking with Richard. The trip was filled with hiking, boating, adventure, and bonding with new friends. I did meet Richard briefly, but just in a cordial, passing moment. I expressed my gratitude for being included in the week. It was my new friendship with Sam and the others that filled me with such wonderful memories. My conversations with Sam had inspired me. While on Necker, we had a few deep discussions about purpose. We talked about his dreams and goals of being a musician and advocacy work for the environment. I shared my goals for living a life more inspired by my creative pursuits, while balancing that with business.

When the vacation was over, Justin and I returned to LA and continued on with our new television series and building J2. I stayed in touch with Sam and was appreciative that he and his friends didn't treat the holiday meet as a moment in time, but rather the start of a friendship.

Despite the geographic distance between us, he invited me to parties and events. A highlight was his birthday bash at his family home in England – a Mad Hatter Tea Party. Sam's friends and family were so different than the usual people I hung out with. I found that I really enjoyed the comradery and being in the presence of studied and thoughtful peers, free of judgment, bias, and expectation. It was a different culture than I was living in in Hollywood, which was image-driven and résumé-focused. I felt a freedom to be unapologetically myself and share my views on life, having fun, and not being judged based on what I had or had not accomplished yet. I figured if that was the only thing to come out of the Necker trip, it was well worth it.

A few months later, I received a call from Sam that he was looking to attend music school in LA. He was following his dream and looking to venture out to LA solo. He crashed at my Calabasas house for a few days, and then I helped him move into his rented apartment closer to Hollywood. Sam in Hollywood felt out of place to me. It's a cold town. Not literally, of course, but rather one where it's hard to make real friends. However, as Sam does, he did LA his way. He didn't sling his last name around to get in somewhere. He was fine waiting in line, and demonstrated real class. We spent a lot of time that summer with mutual friends and hung out everywhere from coffee shops to parties at the Playboy Mansion.

One night, Sam's parents were in town, and he invited me to dinner at Yamashiro with them. A small group of us had an intimate, simple sushi dinner and meaningful conversation. After all of our time together that summer, I'd just about forgotten that Sam was Richard's son until he was back in front of me across the table. It struck me again how incredibly normal and warm this accomplished family is. It never felt like dinner with a billionaire brimming with business opportunities. It was simply a dinner with my friend and his parents. As crazy as that may seem, it's the truth. Though it may sound overly simplified, many good things come when you just act like a normal person and treat everyone equally no matter what they have to "offer" you. People can sniff out insincerity, ulterior motive, or a personal agenda. From the beginning, Richard treated me with as much respect as he did any world leader, and I never engaged with him because I was trying to gain something.

At dinner, Sam, Justin, Richard, Joan, and I were all chatting when Richard looked over at me and said, "Jason, how's the production company going?" This was the first time I became aware that he really had any idea of what I did for a living. I knew he knew I was "Jason who had come to Necker and was now Sam's friend." But on our trip down there, he was so busy being the consummate host, we hadn't spoken much. I answered and we had a lengthy conversation about J2, our accomplishments so far, and our vision for it in the future, including some music-related projects. "I know a thing or two about music," he said with a smile.

"Oh yeah, do tell," my sake-influenced brain and mouth courageously replied.

"Virgin" – Richard replied as his chopsticks took the last sushi role off my plate – "RECORDS!" he finished with a laugh. These cheeky subtleties are a fine art that only Richard can deliver, and this was my first encounter. Okay Virgin Records, I did know that much. He recalled some details and stories about the founding of Virgin Records, and I noted a little nostalgia in his voice, maybe even sadness. Toward the end of dinner I asked him if he had a significant goal that he desired to achieve in life beyond business. He replied simply, "I'm going to space." Not "I want to go to space." But definitively, "I'm going to space." *Noted!* I thought.

We continued on, talking about how music school was going for Sam and what we were all up to that summer. Then Sam asked, "Necker soon?" Richard mentioned that our mutual friend, Suhail Rizvi (who advised us out so heroically during the Omar debacle), was to be there later in the summer and Justin and I should come along. Because we had so much fun last time, of course, Justin and I readily agreed again. Serendipitously, Suhail also reached out and extended the invite to join for the week.

A few weeks later, we were back on the island again. This time around, I'd done my research on Virgin, so I knew much more about Richard and his businesses. His grab of my sushi roll was a playful gesture, but it also suggested to me that I should get educated and know who my host was and respect his accomplishments. I noticed the group on this trip was a slightly different kind of crowd than last time. In general, they were a little older and a bit more diverse. But more than that, the air about them seemed more distinguished, refined, maybe even a little more serious. The group on our last trip had been mostly entertainment folks; casual and loose and ready to party. I wasn't sure what this crowd did for a living, but they were definitely into something different than entertainment. It was vital on this

British soil that I didn't come across like a young, ignorant American who didn't know anything. I could have a good time, but I must be aware of my surroundings and actively contribute to group discussions versus being lazily naive to current news and hot topic policies that were being discussed at every table. This was a different kind of trip, and more intellectually rewarding. Most people just introduced themselves by their first names on Necker, so I had to listen intently to every conversation to try and piece together information and context clues to identify them. I was quickly learning that the company Richard kept lived in the highest echelon of success and had the ability to effectuate significant commercial deal flow as well as drive awareness for environmental issues and social movements. I was excited to be there, but I sure was out of my depth this time.

Sergey Brin, cofounder of Google, was the first one I identified. There aren't many Sergeys in the world, so that one was easy. Later, when my laundry was delivered to my room on the second day, right on top there was underwear I didn't recognize. More specifically, a lace thong. I take fashion risks but a lace thong has never been one of them. It definitely was not mine. I knew there was a lovely woman staying in the room beside me, so I assumed it was hers and went over to deliver it back to her. As she snatched it out of my hand with an awkward laugh, she introduced herself as Noor. "Beautiful name, how do you spell that?" I asked. After she replied, I hurried back to my suite to Google her. That's when I learned she was Queen Noor of Jordan. *Wow*, I thought.

Now, we were both understandably a little embarrassed by that situation. So later that night at dinner, a few glasses of champagne in, I suggested she could knight me in exchange for me returning her "royal goods." She laughed, and the elephant in the room was gone. She jokingly knighted me Sir Jason of Necker Island. That's exactly the kind of unbelievable and surreal thing that happens on the island. And for me it continued for almost two decades to follow. Necker is a special place where unique and interesting people come together to share ideas and have a ton of fun. I can't even tell you how many times I've been yanked off my Hobie cat – a racing boat – by Richard Branson because I was beating him. The man loves to win. Fun, adventure, friendship, ideas, conversation. It's part of the magical alchemy of Necker.

On the third night, we were all sitting around at dinner down at the beach pool. The table is enormous and carved in the shape of an alligator.

It seats about forty people. Communal dinners are a huge part of the experience, and they are important to Richard. It's where so much of the magic happens. The table overlooks the ocean and is surrounded by hammocks for an after-dinner lounge. The epitome of tropical. More than once I've sat there or laid in those hammocks and wondered how in the world my life had brought me there. Sometimes I'm still not sure, but I'm so incredibly grateful.

That particular night, the conversation and vibe were impeccable. It was diverse. It was loud. And it was jubilant. Topics ranged from kids and schools to multi-million-dollar business deals and building third houses in the Hamptons. And, of course, the champagne was flowing. Every time I turned my head my glass was refilled. I couldn't even keep track how many I'd had. Though I'd warmed up to everyone and was definitely chattier than the first two days (when I was uncharacteristically quiet), I was still acutely aware that besides Justin, I was the youngest and most certainly the poorest at that table. By a lot. By many millions. And to some by billions. As much as I pride myself in being comfortable in most situations and with anyone no matter who they are, I have to admit, I was still intimidated and a little uncomfortable. And I was trying to drink myself comfortable.

I felt Richard sensed this and out of nowhere he said, "Jason, why don't you tell everybody about yourself." I wasn't sure if he'd plotted it or if it was just another cheeky idea that crossed his mind in the moment.

A little shocked but empowered by the champagne, I said "Okay," and started to introduce myself. "I'm Jason and I run a production company . . ."

I began when someone from way down on the other end shouted, "We can't hear you!"

I felt my face flush with red and was about to repeat myself louder when Richard gestured with his hand, "Get up. Get up on the table."

I stared at him for a second like a deer in headlights. Then I backed up my chair and gingerly stepped up onto the huge alligator table top. You don't say no to Richard Branson. Especially in his house. This much I had learned already. Richard raised his finger in the air, swiping it. I took this to mean he wanted me to walk back-and-forth on the table so everyone could hear. As I did, I started again and told everyone my name and that, with Justin (pointing to him), I ran a company called J2. With all the faces staring up at me, suddenly I felt a little lame.

I was so proud of what we'd accomplished at J2, but in the company of these people, it didn't feel impressive at all. So, instead of using my time on the "catwalk" to go into all of our TV shows and experience to date, I veered left and shared a somewhat philosophical vision I had that I hadn't talked about in public yet. "I'm an entrepreneur and run a production company, and I think content consumption behavior is shifting. People are already going to movie theaters less and less. They get their DVDs sent to them in the mail from Netflix. Blockbuster is a thing of the past, theaters will be too at some point. Soon everyone will watch everything on their phones. I know that's how I already prefer to do it."

Then I heard someone from behind me say, "He must agree. That's why he just bought YouTube." The voice was coming from one of Sam's friends who was pointing at the man at the end of the table. It was a guy who had attempted to teach me how to kite surf earlier that day down on the beach. Turns out, it was Larry Page, the other cofounder of Google. I smiled, and with that, stumbled down off of the table, careful of the glassware. That moment changed my life forever. Because of that experience, I no longer feel nervousness, anxiety, or fear around anyone. No matter who they are or what they have accomplished. And I no longer worry about public speaking. Once you've had to explain your career and philosophical predictions of the future to a table full of some of the richest visionaries in the entire world, nothing much scares you anymore. Plus, having Larry Page agree with you is a boost of confidence like no other. When I look back at when the second act of my Hollywood career officially began, I think it's here. I stepped off of that table a different man. I had catwalked in front of world leaders and not faltered, but more important, I had shared my ideas, and they had validated them. I was on the right track – my instincts were good. My vision for the future of entertainment was clear, and I was more inspired than ever to create it.

My brief speech led to a lively discussion about the future of content and how Justin and I desired J2 to be a part of it. Afterwards, I was pretty ready for bed and slightly drunk. The last thing I wanted was a vulnerability hangover after revealing my deep thoughts in front of some of the world's most powerful people. But first, Suhail reminded me that we made a bet earlier on who could beat the other in sumo wrestling. I couldn't renege. Sumo on! So we headed down to the beach and put on ridiculous oversized blow-up sumo costumes and wrestled each other in front of the entire group. Yep, just me and one of the most polished and reserved businessman I had ever met sumo wrestling for all to watch. Thanks to the champagne and pinot noir, I wasn't nearly as embarrassed as I probably should have been. Afterwards, Richard walked up with a massive grin and high-fived me. I felt he was grateful I humored him and was a good sport when he put me on the spot.

At different points during the rest of the week, whether it be on the boat or around the breakfast table, he asked me more questions about myself and about J2. I didn't have a lot to say except that we were a small company forging our way. We were currently looking to reinvent ourselves and grow further. We valued supporting artists, writers, and directors, and investing in projects that were interesting and meaningful. Sam, an artist and now documentary producer himself, shared this same "art before commerce" approach to the business. On the last day, I questioned Richard a little more on his history in the entertainment industry. He shared about his start in the business and the various initiatives the brand had taken over the years. He was also quick to point out that there was no Virgin-branded film or television production company.

"I like what you're doing, Jason," he said, "and I think maybe we could help." By *we* he meant Virgin. By *we* he meant him. "Why don't you draw up a business plan for what you think a partnership between Virgin and J2 could look like and set up a discussion with our guys in London when you get back home? Imagine the Virgin brand in film and TV. What do you think of that?"

What did I think of that?! I thought, *Hell yes to you, sir; one of the greatest entrepreneurs who's ever lived is interested in partnering up, this might be the best day of my life!* I also thought, *I've never drawn up a business plan before, I better Google that.* On the plane ride home, Justin and I discussed what Richard had said. He was looking out the window and as soon as I said *business plan* he darted his eyes at me. I knew exactly what he was thinking. "No, Justin, this guy is for real, I promise. He's serious." He'd just been through the pain of the Omar situation and couldn't handle another disappointment and financial upheaval. And I couldn't either, honestly. But I knew this was different. We had just gotten J2 to a point where it was profitable and neither one of us wanted to take a step backwards. This wasn't a joke; it was a once-in-a-lifetime opportunity. I needed Justin to trust me on this. And fortunately, he did. I also wanted to run it by Sam and make sure I had his blessing to potentially go into business with his dad. Of course he said I did.

When we got back I put together a business plan for the company I called Virgin Produced. Another thing I'd done immediately on return was read Richard's memoir *Losing My Virginity*. In it he explains that the day he sold Virgin Records was both the happiest and saddest day of his life. The happiest because it made him $1 billion. Hard to be sad about that. But it was sad because it was his life's work, and he loves entertainment. After that, of course, Virgin ventured into airlines, trains, mobile phone services, gyms, hotels, cruises, even space, and so on. Sure, a sale of Virgin Records must have been sad, but likely necessary to launch and achieve brand growth in the other industries. I thought it must have pained Richard personally to be out of entertainment. I believed he saw this as a return of some kind. It was really important to me that I show him I understood that. So my business plan reflected this sentiment and was mostly pictures and a lot of words about the big picture idea of what I imagined this company could be. I spent about a week on it and proudly sent it off to Richard. Pretty quickly I heard back, and Richard said it looked good but he'd copied his right-hand man, Gordon McCallum, to weigh in.

Mr. McCallum took a look and called me almost immediately. He said, "Jason, this looks good in theory, but we need a business plan." I was silent for a moment as I thought, *Well, this is the business plan.* I wasn't really sure what to do beyond what I'd already done. Maybe he sensed I was confused because he followed that up with, "You know, with a financial model." *Ah, financial model, right.* I felt so inept. "I'm going to put you in touch with Gabriel Baldinucci and he can help." Gabriel Baldinucci was the closest Virgin had at the time to an "entertainment guy" as he'd been involved with the short-lived FOX TV show featuring Richard called *Rebel Billionaire*. He and I fostered a relationship, and he was instrumental in building the first *real* Virgin Produced business plan with me. As part of that process, I had to get to know some of the CEOs and CMOs at all of the other Virgin companies to understand the brand standards, markets, and customers. I spent four weeks getting a crash course in all things Virgin. It was during this time that I had my real light bulb moment about everything Virgin Produced could be.

After Gabriel and I had a solid plan, I set up a call with Richard. "Richard," I said, "Thanks so much for the introduction to Gordon. He's introduced me to Gabriel and I've spent the last four weeks immersed and learning about all of the different Virgin companies." I took a deep breath and started again, stuttering slightly over my words, "What I believe is that there are a lot of 'kids' in this family that all share the same father but have different mothers. They share the same name and many characteristics, and they most definitely all want Dad's attention. But because they have different mothers, they aren't incentivized to play and work together consistently." As I nervously delivered my analogy, I didn't want to offend him. What he'd built is extraordinary, and I still wanted to be part of it, but I meant what I said.

My view was that the different "mothers" – the CEOs, investors, and shareholders – maybe kept things from being as cohesive as they could be. They were 100% focused on the bottom line, not necessarily 100% focused on the brand. And that in some instances, they didn't truly appreciate the brand behind the iconic red logo. I was pitching Virgin Produced as some form of a solution that could tie them all together. The way I saw it, planes have screens, phones have screens, gyms have screens, and the eventual hotels and cruise lines would all have screens. Screens that could captivate an audience! Virgin Produced could create content that would be shown on millions of screens within Virgin companies worldwide, and we could also use those screens to market and promote our movies. In my mind, everything would be emblematic of the brand and the kind of entertaining and purpose-driven content Richard himself would be proud to deliver. We could bring in other like-minded content partners like iHeartRadio, Vevo, Funny or Die, and Vice to help us do it.

"Yes, we'll be making movies," I said. "But we could do so much more than that. Eventually we could even have our own channel. What unites all of the Virgin companies is that they are entirely focused on elevating the consumer experience. And that's what we'd do with interesting and innovative content. This is about being more than making Hollywood movies; this is about reminding the consumer, irrespective of the sector, that the Virgin brand is entertaining.

Bringing the brand back full circle to its roots. To its original DNA strand." And with that I finished talking.

"Yes," Richard said simply. "Let's do it." I let out a huge sigh of relief. This initiated a lot of conversations, negotiations, contract drafting, and contract signing that needed to happen. Because we were creating a new entity, on one call a Virgin attorney asked me if we were creating an LLC or a corporation, and during the writing of this book I found a note in an old notebook that said, "LLC or Inc – research the difference." That's how new I was to all of this.

Another big decision to make after we entered into our brand license contract with Richard was how we wanted to structure financing and ownership. I was told I had two options: either Virgin could finance the company and own 100% of it, essentially making Justin and me employees, or J2 could not take any investment from Virgin, own the majority of Virgin Produced, and become a licensed partner of the brand. In the end, we decided on the latter. We were entrepreneurs at heart and no matter how much we admired Richard and the brand, neither of us were interested in working on salary for anyone else. That was instilled in me from my dad from a young age. It was a bigger risk, of course, but there were also much, much bigger upsides and potential rewards. Plus, there was also the satisfaction of being in control of your business. I didn't want them to write a check. I wanted to prove myself. I saw myself as an "intrapreneur," someone who could disrupt and be creative within someone else's brand, helping take it to the next level. Besides, I have always believed that a salary is what someone else pays you when they want you to build their vision. And this was ours; albeit with a legacy and well-respected logo on the door. The perfect partnership.

In those early days we assembled our first people. Rebecca, our trusty assistant who had been with us since the beginning; Michael Forman and Barrick Prince, both seasoned television development pros; and the brilliant Rene Rigal, who added a few other amazing creatives to our team along the way. We rented out a beautiful starter office at 315 South Beverly Drive in Beverly Hills. We were officially in business. This was the age of Virgin Produced.

CUE: "You Make My Dreams Come True" by Hall and Oates

12

Becoming Limitless

VIRGIN HADN'T CREATED any of the industries that it had ventured into, but it was improving on them all. With over 40 companies operating in over 35 countries with an estimated 60,000 employees, the Virgin brand is incredibly people-focused, both externally with consumers and internally with its employees. Virgin embodies a culture that strongly emphasizes treating people right and elevating experiences in everything they do. All of this stems, of course, from "Dr. Yes" (Richard's nickname internally at Virgin) himself.

Virgin Produced had to be the same. We never set out to be the largest production company, but we did want to change ways in which it was done. We wanted to invent a whole new methodology. It centered on artist and talent collaboration as the priority. It did not revolve around getting a remit from a studio or a network and reverse engineering a concept. It focused on creatives. Again, people first. I know that may sound like cheesy industry speak, but we meant it. Hollywood is cutthroat. And it certainly is not people first. Unless you are a person who is making another person a lot of money, you are disposable. That's it, plain and simple. The cliché phrase "You are only as good as your last hit" is reality, and everyone who ends up in Hollywood with any level of success learns this lesson at some point. All of the different stakeholders in a project have their own motivations and incentives. Actors and directors quickly find out after they sign onto a project that the studio and financiers always get the last say, regardless of what the contract says or anyone's creative vision. And most disappointingly, the producer or production company that developed the project, at the end of the day, will always side with the studio or financier.

So we wanted to create an environment of true collaboration when we aligned with the writers, actors, and directors who worked with us and gave them creative liberty to do what they do best. From there, our vision was simple: protect the artist by always voting with them versus the studio. Yes, we might have to sometimes bite the hand that feeds us, but so be it. In this way, we put people first and in that regard became contrarians in the business, which fit right into the larger Virgin brand. We were intent on our employees and collaborators alike having healthy, creative, balanced lives in which we didn't exert too much control over them and the process. Richard has always advocated that if you take care of your people, they'll take care of your business. This is the philosophy I agreed with and adopted.

We officially launched to great fanfare, as is the Virgin way. To mark our debut, we shot an iconic video of Richard on the runway of an airport getting left behind by his production crew. We had billboards, international media announcements, and ads in *Variety*, *Hollywood Reporter*, and *Billboard* proclaiming our arrival. This was all done with one simple yet remarkable image of Richard, hair perfectly quaffed, on a plane looking out the window at the famous Hollywood sign. A few words emblazoned across the top of the billboard: "There's a new Dick in town." So yeah, we were trying to have a little fun. Shake it up a bit.

The first big move we made was striking a deal with an independent studio called Relativity. They were attractive to us not only because they were independent (i.e. not owned by a conglomerate like NewsCorp), but because they had financed and released 89 of the most successful and well-known Hollywood films from 2006 to 2010. That is substantial success and at this time, they were the only ones with the foresight of having a distribution deal with Netflix. Recall what I proclaimed walking on that table on Necker half a year prior. We were all just understanding how consumer content consumption behavior was about to shift. People were watching movies at home and on their phones, and Netflix was the biggest player in that arena at the time. As soon as a Relativity-financed film left theaters it streamed exclusively on Netflix. Not many people realized it at the time, but that was a big fucking deal. We had deep discussions with a few large studios like Universal and Paramount, but Relativity was the only one doing things differently and moving in the same direction as us. They weren't bogged down with big corporate politics, so they were able to shift quickly with the changing distribution landscape. And they wanted to be in business with Virgin Produced.

Once we signed our seven-figure (pinching myself) multiyear deal with Relativity, the first movie that came our way was a then little-known script called *Limitless*. Relativity came to us early on and pitched the idea of a movie starring Bradley Cooper as a down-on-his-luck protagonist who discovers a secret drug that allows him to access 100% of his brain and turn his life around, but, of course, not without complications. The story and script were a cautionary tale to be careful what you wish for. It was also set to costar Robert De Niro and Abbie Cornish. As soon as I heard the concept, my mind started racing with ideas. Instantly, I felt the marketing itself was, well, limitless. The idea of being limitless could extend through so many of the Virgin companies. We could promote a Limitless vacation on Virgin Atlantic or a Limitless calling plan on Virgin Mobile. A Limitless lifestyle membership at Virgin Active or even a Limitless drink on Virgin America. I was ready to brand the airline's napkins and take over all the screens at every airport gate and terminal. It seemed like the perfect way to showcase exactly what I'd meant when I told Richard I wanted Virgin Produced to be *the thread that unites them all*. Needless to say, we agreed to produce the movie and did all of the above.

The film was shot beautifully by director Neil Burger and our promotions launched. To drum up added excitement, we made another video, a fake infomercial starring Richard taking that fictional NZT-48 pill from the movie and claiming that the secret to his success was that very pill. Soon enough, it was time to fly off to New York for the fancy red carpet premiere.

It was my first big event as the CEO of a Virgin company, and the pressure I put on myself was intense. I had a lot to prove: I was the youngest CEO of a Virgin company and trying to shake up the industry.

Richard flew in and was scheduled to walk the red carpet with me to incite even more press attention. I was excited and nervous for him to see what we'd been working on, the result of everything we'd promised since we first met nearly two years earlier. Ryan Kavanaugh, the polarizing founder and CEO of Relativity studio, was also going to be in attendance and had specifically requested a picture on the red carpet with Richard. As part of this plan, the event planners insisted that Richard be exactly on time to a certain spot to make it happen. *Not a problem*, I thought.

Richard and I arrived on the red carpet in time, despite even stopping for some medicine because he felt a little ill. I had nearly chewed my nails to stubs hoping we'd still make it on time, but we both knew how important this was, so we hustled. But Kavanaugh was nowhere to be found. Five minutes went by, then 10, then 15, and 20. Richard and I were making small talk and looking around, trying to act like this was fine and that he didn't have plenty of other places to be during this all-important event. Eventually, the movie was about to start and the handlers started ushering us into the theater without Kavanaugh. Richard was visibly annoyed as he knew Kavanaugh's office had insisted we be on time. Up until then I'd only seen Richard as my jovial, hard-working, and easygoing founder. He clearly was not happy that Kavanaugh hadn't showed and saw it as a sign of disrespect. Richard deeply believes and has taught me that no one's time is worth any more than anyone else's. It doesn't matter if you're the studio boss or the high schooler sweeping the theater floor.

I felt bad that this experience wasn't going as perfectly as I'd hoped, but there was nothing I could do. Seeing his irritation with Kavanaugh, I was silently grateful that I'd never been late to a call or meeting with Richard myself. As we took our seats, he noticed that Kavanaugh was tagged to sit between us. But instead, Richard swapped their name cards and put himself in the middle and moved Abbie Cornish up to Kavanaugh's seat. This put Kavanaugh behind us and the beautiful star of the film next to Richard and me. I was a little panicked at this maneuver in the moment, but now I see what it was: a gentle, harmless gesture to remind someone else to be respectful. It was a subtle jab. A classic Richard thing to do, with a figurative wink.

We took our seats and the opening credits began to roll. That's when Kavanaugh finally entered the dark theater. He shuffled down the aisle and got to our row. With a puzzled look at Abbie's empty seat, he switched the name tags back and took the seat next to Richard. He turned to us and offered a quick whisper of an apology. Because Richard is kind, he smiled and offered a few pleasantries, but I could tell he was still annoyed. *Damn it, this is really not going how I wanted it to. I wanted these guys to be friends!* Branson was my new boss and Kavanaugh was one of the most powerful studio heads in town. We were all in business together, and this should have been an amazing day of celebration of all we'd accomplished together. Instead, I worried that we were sitting there stewing on what had just happened, all of us uncomfortable for different reasons.

Anyway, the movie was incredible in every way. It was met with a standing ovation, and the whole audience loved it, including Richard. Toward the end, as the Virgin Produced logo appeared on screen, he looked over at me with a simple affirmative nod. In Richard language that meant "Good work." I had never been prouder. Because Richard had to catch a flight, he was going to sneak out a few minutes before the credits ended. He leaned over and told me he had to head out, so I texted Kavanaugh (not wanting to interrupt the end of the movie) on the other side of him that Richard needed to catch a flight. Ryan saw his phone buzz, looked at it, and immediately texted back, "He can just take my jet, have him stay!" I read it and awkwardly showed Richard the text, to which he shook his head, "No." With that, Richard hopped up and headed to the exit to meet his driver.

As we walked out of the building, Kavanaugh followed us. He stopped beside at the door to the theater and said, "Richard, thank you so much for coming. Really, you can take my plane, it's no problem. It'll take you wherever you want to go." Richard politely replied, "No, no it's fine. Thank you." Now, of course, Richard has his own private plane. He could have easily taken that if he wanted and stayed through the entire event. However, he is very carbon footprint conscious and has strict rules about when he uses it. One of those rules is that he never takes it if he's traveling alone. It's not worth the emissions for only one person. Besides, if he's traveling alone he can easily fly commercial on a Virgin Atlantic flight, which was the case that day. He did not give Kavanaugh any explanation. He simply declined.

"Okay, okay," Kavanaugh said, relenting. As Richard walked away he said, "Congratulations on the film. I know you're going to have a fantastic relationship with Virgin Produced. I'm supportive of Jason and can't wait to see what you do next." As the driver pulled up outside Kavanaugh asked, "Could we still get that picture really quick?"

I caught a fleeting look of exasperation on Richard's face at the request, but he nodded and said, "Sure." I pulled out my phone and backed up a few paces to take the picture as the two men came together and smiled. Just as I went to push the button, Richard lifted the open, half-drunk water bottle he'd been holding throughout the movie into the air and dumped it on Kavanaugh's head. Kavanaugh, understandably shocked, looked at Richard awkwardly in disbelief. "You mustn't be late," Richard said with his enormous signature smile. "It's rude." *Holy fuck.* Then Richard and I walked toward the waiting car without saying anything about what had just happened. As he went to get in he paused, looked at me, and said, "Don't ever borrow anybody's plane. You'll owe them something." Then he jumped in the car and was off.

I hurried back over to Kavanaugh, whose assistant had brought napkins in an attempt to dry him off. "What happened?!" the assistant asked me.

"I don't really know. We waited for a long time on the red carpet and Richard was kinda irritated and . . . honestly I'm not sure how to explain it to you. It just happened. I'm sorry." Kavanaugh headed back into the theater . . . soggy. I don't recall him ever being late to our premieres or Virgin-related meetings again.

We knew the movie was well received. It was getting great reviews and it seemed like everyone was loving it, not only around town but also throughout the world. But none of that really matters unless audiences go see it and it makes a bunch of money, right? You don't get to keep making movies if your movies aren't profitable. And since this was our first one, it felt like the stakes were even higher. Once we were back in Los Angeles, about a week after the *Limitless* release, Justin and I were at a dinner event only half paying attention to anyone there because we were expecting the weekly box office results to roll in any minute. We kept refreshing a website called Box Office Mojo on our phones to see how much the movie had made so far. It had cost about $25 million to make, but the true total was closer to $40 million when you include the money our studio spent in advertising. Eventually, the results populated, and there it was. *Limitless* had done over $18 million in its first week. To say we lost our shit then and there in the middle of dinner would be an understatement. We knew based on those results that over the next few weeks the movie was going to easily make everyone way more money than was spent on it. And it did. In the following months it grossed over $161 million worldwide, and in the process made Virgin Produced a bona fide success. All of our hard work had paid off. This crazy ride Justin and I had been on for so many years together, through all the ups and downs, had finally led us here. There was just nothing like it. I had my name listed as a producer next to Bradley Cooper in the credits of what would become one of the highest-grossing films of the year. It was everything I'd ever dreamed about since my high school days and everything I'd ever wanted for as long as I can remember.

As things go in Hollywood, because of that success, people came calling. We got calls from agents and directors from Sony, Universal, and Lionsgate asking us to come work on their movies, not only because of the success of *Limitless* but also because of the massive marketing ecosystem we'd created to promote films globally. They wanted us to give creative notes and create similar buzz campaigns for them. After *Limitless*, Relativity touted us around town and at the Cannes Film Festival market as their secret creative weapon. We got our pick of projects, and it was exhilarating (and financially rewarding). For several years, we were locked into our lucrative deal with Relativity, but eventually, we were able to take those calls with others and teamed up with more prestigious studios. Our filmography quickly became a who's who with *Immortals* starring Henry Cavill and Luke Evans; *The Impossible* with Naomi Watts, Ewan McGregor, and Tom Holland; *Movie 43* starring Hugh Jackman, Kate Winslet, Richard Gere, Halle Berry, Chloë Moretz, and Emma Stone; *21 & Over* starring Miles Teller; *Jobs* with Ashton Kutcher; *That Awkward Moment* with Zach Efron; *Bad Moms* with Mila Kunis and Kristen Bell; *After Earth* starring Will and Jaden Smith; and many others. We also eventually launched an office in Mumbai, India. Virgin Produced India made Bollywood remakes of popular Hollywood films. These films in total had collectively generated billions at the global box office. I could go on and on about how exciting all of this was. Not only were we proving out our business model but also we were driving significant awareness for the Virgin brand in Hollywood, in North America, and anywhere films with our logo were being released.

Out of all of these projects, perhaps surprisingly, none were more rewarding to me than the groundbreaking airline safety video we concepted and shot for Virgin America. From the beginning, Justin and I had a vision for Virgin Produced that was bigger than just movies. A few years into running the company, I re-approached Richard and said, "All of your companies are using different ad agencies and production companies for their internal videos and content. Shouldn't they just be using Virgin Produced? We know the brand better than an agency. We are the brand!" I proclaimed. He was on board, and that led to us contracting with the heads of other Virgin companies to produce their commercials, content, and other marketing to further aid in the cohesiveness between Virgin-branded companies. This also led to the official creation of the Virgin Produced channel, our own digital network, on which we had short-form original lifestyle, comedy, music, and technology content that played onboard all three Virgin airlines, in Virgin Hotel rooms, and on over 30,000 airport terminal screens throughout airports nationwide.

The idea for the Virgin America *Safety Dance* video came during a classic late-night (sometimes slightly buzzed) brainstorming session I hosted at my house. These were common back then. All credit goes to Justin who came up with the idea, a music video format, and I knew immediately he was onto something. Airline safety videos are classically and famously boring. But they didn't need to be. And Virgin America was anything but a boring airline. What if we could spice it up? What if instead of people staring out the window and tuning out during the safety instructions, they were entertained with a musical version and actually paid attention? Maybe they'd even remember the song and tell their friends about it after they landed. So our in-house team of Rene Rigal and Huntley Ritter, along with film director Jon Chu, got to work. And boy did they execute!

The video starred Todrick Hall, an American choreographer and well-known YouTuber. He had gained national attention on the ninth season of the televised singing competition *American Idol*. After that, he amassed a huge following on social media with viral videos including original songs, parodies, and skits. We also enlisted a whole host of other widely followed social media influencers. The idea for the safety video was simple, unique, and, quite frankly, ahead of its time. Todrick and his fellow young, attractive influencers sang and danced to an original, absolute bop of a song that delivered all of the classic safety information you've heard a zillion times before, but in a fun way so that you can't stop watching. Like an actual music video. The song was an ear worm and the choreography was mind-blowing. Every now and then there was a joke, a kid rapped about halfway through, and it finished with a music switch-up to some robotic techno beats. It had it all. If you haven't seen it, join the other 12.2 million viewers and take a minute to go watch it. It's worth your time. Of course, we also had to abide by FAA regulations, so we made sure every piece of necessary information was delivered clearly.

I took the production of the video as seriously as I had any movie we worked on. I knew it was groundbreaking and could generate some amazing PR if we handled it right. We launched the video to insane fanfare. It helped that we implored all of those influencers involved to post about it and create organic traction among their followings. It got those millions and millions of views within its first 24 hours online and was covered by publications and news stations around the world. An airline safety video! I've been lucky enough to work on some huge movies in my tenure, and still this five-minute video is one of my proudest accomplishments. Everybody in the world was talking about it. It went onto win Cleo, Webby, and Shorty awards. And it further cemented us as an advertising powerhouse. It also firmly solidified my business thesis for Virgin Produced, and happened to generate a $727 million ad equivalency value for Virgin America. That meant that our little $300,000 video created almost $75 million in earned media value for the airline. I don't know what that ended up converting to in actual revenue for Richard and the airline, but when he gifted my team and me companywide Platinum status – meaning we could all fly for free – I assumed we had done something *really* right.

Other brands took notice. That video led to us producing a tri-brand film called *Departure Date*, shot entirely in flight at 30,000 feet on all three Virgin airlines, as well as commercials for companies like

Coca Cola and Uber, just to name a few. Meanwhile, we were also licensing and churning out up to 50 pieces of original content per year for our Virgin Channel that Justin and Rebecca now headed up. We were dialed in on what we did best, and we were a force.

I had done it. I was the CEO of a known and respected Virgin-branded company: a major production company with offices in Los Angeles and Mumbai and plenty of awards, respect, and money to show for it. I was flying high and life was in excess. This was as Hollywood as one could get.

CUE: "Glamorous" by Fergie, featuring Ludacris

13

Glad Expression, Wrong Impression

ONE THING ABOUT me is, I never do anything halfway. And back then, I didn't even do anything at 100%, I did everything full throttle at 150%. Once after a successful Virgin event late one night followed by an early morning event the next day where I didn't miss a beat, Richard emailed me that I was "the epitome of work hard, play hard." I took that as a compliment as it's the ethos of Hollywood! I owned it, and felt pride. After the success of a dozens of movies, our safety video, and the Virgin Channel, my main pursuit had become to turn Virgin Produced into a full-fledged studio. We were a production company, which meant we could make content: movies, TV shows, and commercials. But studios were the holy grail, the top of the food chain. That's what Relativity, Universal, Sony, Paramount, FOX, and now Netflix are. They not only produce but they also distribute the content. To be in a position where we could work with artists, writers, and directors to create films, and also be able to finance and distribute them, would be substantial. By this time, we had gained international respect and were well positioned to expand. I was convinced this was the direction we needed to go to keep growing. And I was doing everything I could to architect a plan and sell this organic growth plan. We had been approached by several major private equity players in the industry, as well as engaged in long talks with significant capital secured to accomplish this next growth phase. All we needed was Virgin Group approval out of London.

Unfortunately, these efforts coincided with the appointment of a new board member by the brand to my board of directors. The person was appointed to be supportive and ensure I stayed within compliance of the brand. Well, this particular new board member was not supportive of my studio idea at all. To make a long story short, after sharing my vision, it quickly became clear that he was going to railroad me at every turn. I learned that he had contacted several other Virgin Group executives and spread the word about what a bad idea he thought it was to become a studio. He thought my "vision was too grand" and began his sabotage early. Isn't that the whole point of visions to be grand and almost slightly out of reach, to encourage you to stretch and grow?! That's what I believe, anyway. Plus, look at what we'd already been able to accomplish? I knew it'd take hard work and fortitude, but I thought we could definitely do it.

Anyway, he wasn't my biggest fan. And because of the power he held, soon it became clear that my dream of becoming a studio was pretty unlikely. That's when I learned the difference between the brand and the bankers. This guy was a banker. Some Virgin companies move the needle more for the bank. They have a bigger impact on the bottom line. And some of them, like Virgin Produced, move the needle for the brand. We were definitely profitable, but for a Virgin company, we were still relatively new compared to the others. Certain executives, like the one who poison-pilled my idea, didn't care much about the Virgin companies that did the most for the brand if they weren't also doing the most for the bottom line. Sometimes, the brand and the bankers were at odds with each other, especially when it came to Virgin Produced. I think it's fair to say that not everyone at Virgin corporate believed in me and our company. Early on, there were a lot of naysayers who considered me too young and inexperienced, or that Virgin Produced was just Richard's pet project. This couldn't be further from the truth. I had an idea and a promise that Richard believed in and I delivered, quite successfully. I believe Richard knew I'd always protect the brand and that doing something that is great for the Virgin legacy wouldn't always be profit-driven but would pay off in the long run.

Some executives saw the concept of Virgin Studios as a pipe dream, one that wasn't worth the effort and money it would take to achieve. And although Richard had supported the incubation and growth of Virgin Produced thus far, I was not about to go whine to him that his banker team just didn't get it.

I was incredibly frustrated by this. I was frustrated in many ways, if you catch my drift. With the dream of having our own studio practically dead, I ramped up my drinking. I'd done the "work hard," and it wasn't going my way right now. Enter the "play hard." Everything in Hollywood revolves around drinking and eating and drinking some more. Every meeting is a lunch or dinner or drinks or after-dinner thing, all of which involve alcohol. I'd been drinking and using our events and premieres to party for a long time. I started back in the earlier days with my crazy roommates. But during this frustrating era, it went into overdrive. You know those parties I used to uncomfortably attend in my Artist Management Group days? Now, with money, tons of film credits, and a CEO title, I was hosting them. Many of those late-night brainstorming sessions at my house with our team involved drinking, too. There was just no line between work and play. It was all everything. It all blurs together.

I was unhappy, but at the time I couldn't put a finger on why. Of course, the work roadblocks made some sense. I'd always buried myself in work and found my identity there, so when it wasn't going my way, I really struggled. And my striver syndrome compelled me to keep going and keep pushing no matter what. I had success, admiration, and money. I had a beautiful home of my own in LA and was finally building my beach house compound in the Cayman Islands (which a friend of mine jokingly calls "the house that *Limitless* built"), and it still wasn't enough. I was beginning to understand that my unhappiness was deeper than just work troubles.

I was lonely. I had never been in an actual relationship. I had never had sex. I still felt like I had never even been really attracted to anyone. If you're wondering why that hasn't come up again until now, it's because it just wasn't a factor in my life. When I decided years earlier to bury my tiny peak of curiosity about being interested in men for the sake of social acceptance and my career, I meant it. I had successfully buried it. Maybe that was an unhealthy coping mechanism, but it was how I'd survived thus far. I still wondered if maybe I was created to never be attracted to anyone. For the first time in a long time, I was living on my own, which is what I thought I wanted. But coming home to an empty house and waving goodnight to my housekeeper or assistant was bleak. The silence was deafening. I was almost debilitatingly lonely and chased away the pain with more work, alcohol, and even more alcohol. I didn't think I had a serious problem because my productivity was still extremely high. But in hindsight, there is no doubt about it. I was depressed and repressed, though I didn't quite have that insight yet.

I started hanging out with a couple of friends who liked to drink hard and bounce from bar to club any night of the week. This group was generally not a great influence on me. The least toxic was Jenn. Jenn and I had a special bond that involved anything intoxicating and fun, but the next day hangover typically made me feel even worse than I did before. One night we were at a concert and a good-looking guy started flirting with me. I had met him before but didn't remember his name so I just introduced him by his job title, Sophia Vergara's assistant. He leaned in, kissed my cheek, and whispered, "I have a name." I flirted back a little, perhaps even subconsciously, and I remember, for the first time ever, enjoying the attention from a man. It had been so long since I'd let my guard down in that way. So for just a moment, I opened up that part of myself again as something stirred in me.

Later that night, Jenn and I were having a night cap at a hotel rooftop bar when she looked over and said to me, "You were flirting with that guy."

"I was?" I replied, as I thought about it for a moment. "Yeah, maybe, I dunno. . . ." I trailed off. And then I finally let myself wonder aloud, "Maybe I'm bi . . ."

Jenn's eyes lit up and she looked at me with such happiness and empathy. "Oh, my God!" she said. "I've known this whole time! I'm so proud of you for saying that," and she gave me a big hug.

To this, I was actually somewhat put off. *Now hold on, wait a minute,* I thought. *I didn't just come out to you, this isn't an official declaration or anything, I'm just thinking out loud.* I just kept saying, "I don't know, maybe," as Jenn kept telling me how amazing it was like we'd had a huge breakthrough. But I wasn't ready for that yet. I didn't know what

I *was*, but I was finally ready to find out. The loneliness had gotten to me, and I was desperate and aware enough now to understand that this was no way to live. I wanted companionship and attraction. There had to be someone out there for me.

When I got home later that night, I downloaded Tinder for the first time. The app was still pretty new, and I figured it was time to start exploring. But as I registered, I still chose "interested in females." I was willing to drunkenly admit to Jenn at 2:00 in the morning that I wondered if I was bi, but I wasn't ready to look for men to date on the internet yet. I cannot overstate how much homophobia I grew up with in rural Texas in the 1990s with a Southern Baptist preacher grandfather. Learning that being gay was "bad" was like learning how to tie your shoes down there. "You're either a steer or a queer" was something I'd heard way more times than I'd like to admit. So, no, I couldn't go on a date with a man yet. But maybe I could try to actually date women and see if anything came of it. I figured at least I needed to get some practice trying to be in a relationship and figure out how meaningful sex even works. I'd never really dated in my entire life and I was in my 30s.

So, I swiped right on a few women and ended up going on some first dates. Inevitably, when I got to chatting with these women, the conversation at some point always turned to their thoughts on marriage and children. And that just freaked me out. I was terrified at the thought of being committed to someone for life, especially a woman. (If you're thinking that this should have been a huge giveaway to most people in my life, you'd be right. And many told me as much later.) The white picket fence, soccer carpool with the kids, and taking the trash out . . . no thank you.

After a few weeks of this, I went to sign into the app again when it made me update. Through some kind of technological quirk, during this update it asked me to reenter all of my information. I was peeved, but started going through the motions. Then, once again, it asked what gender I was interested in. I hesitated. Dating women wasn't going so well. I didn't click with them, and the fact that they often wanted to talk about the "future" was a turnoff. *Well, I bet at least guys won't ask me if I want kids and try to put a timeline on marriage*, I thought. And with that, I selected "male."

So I started swiping and messaging with guys. Instantly, I found it more fun. I also enjoyed the attention, as I had that night in the club weeks earlier. Before I had the confidence to ever meet anyone in person, I flirted without inhibition in the messages and allowed myself to practice engaging with someone I found attractive. I was such a novice, though; I made some incredibly embarrassing mistakes. Like sending one guy a snap of myself cooking pasta when he requested a "pic." "Um, cute, but no," he replied back. "Of your dick." And thus I learned the art of the dick pic. It was all so nerve-wracking, but exciting. Something in me was finally starting to unlock.

Eventually, I did meet up with a guy in person. His name I will not mention, but he was my first of many things. He was my first real relationship and my first real sexual experience. Hollywood Virgin no more! He was younger than me, and we were in much different places in our lives. All in all, it didn't last long. But it was real enough that I felt like I needed to tell all of the important people in my life. Which meant that I had to come out. At least to my family.

I decided to tell Justin first. In addition to being business partners, Justin has always been my best friend. There was also the complication of the fact that we'd been roommates for many years. I was worried that Justin would think I'd been keeping a secret from him for so long. But in reality, I was just coming to this realization myself. I never wanted him to think I'd lied or been inauthentic. I just genuinely didn't know.

I asked him to lunch one day to tell him, and I was terrified. As much as I knew he loved me, I also had no idea what would happen. Besides my accidental (and inaccurate) coming out as bi to Jenn on that rooftop a few months earlier, I had never come out to anyone before. By now Barack Obama was president, and I knew our culture and country had made a lot of progress on the issue of equality in the last few years. But I knew, even in California, there was still somewhat of a stigma associated with being gay. And though I knew Justin to be one of the most liberal, open-minded people in my life, I worried what this would do to our friendship – and our business.

As we sat at a sandwich shop in Santa Monica I took a deep breath, looked across the table and said out of the blue (because there's no good segue for this one), "Justin, I'm seeing someone. His name is X. And I'm bi or gay or whatever. I am still figuring it out."

Immediately and without a word, he got up, walked around the table, and hugged me. If you knew Justin, you'd understand this was a rare gesture. He is not a super affectionate person and a hug from him means a lot. A weight came off of me like I've never experienced. It was the biggest relief of my life. Unless you've hidden something from people your entire life, whether you meant to or not, it's hard to explain what it feels like to finally be loved and known for who you truly and authentically are. "I'm really happy for you," he said.

The second person I wanted to tell was Liza, Justin's fiancé at the time and now wife. I took her to lunch shortly after, and she had the same reaction. She hugged me and said, "Dupree, you deserve the very best." She's always called me Dupree after the movie, *You, Me, and Dupree* because I third-wheeled with her and Justin so often, just like Dupree does in the movie.

From there, I started arranging to meet others or calling those who I couldn't meet in person that same week. I told my brothers, and all of them embraced me and couldn't have cared less, in the best way. I told my brother Joe, who was unfazed and, like most people, already assumed. My brother Logan was also living in LA at the time and I actually got to tell him in person after I said I had something important to share. He was just relieved to find out I wasn't dying or something. (Hot tip if you need to come out: make it sound like something worse first!) After he let out a sigh of relief that I didn't have cancer, he let me know that if I told anyone and they didn't like what I had to say, just let him know and he'd kick their ass. Noted. So far, so good. My news hadn't changed my relationship with anyone important in my life. It was business as usual. Now, I just had to tell my parents.

As I've said before, I have been blessed with the best and most accepting and supportive parents in the entire world. They've never showed me anything but unconditional love, so you'd think I'd have nothing to worry about when it came to telling them. But I think maybe it was precisely because our relationship was the most important in the entire world that there was more pressure about it. There was so much I wanted to explain to them about how confused I'd been and how I'd gotten here. Similar to Justin, I desperately didn't want them to feel misled or like I was living a lie. It was such a hard thing to explain that I didn't understand my own orientation until now. It just felt like for so much of my life, I didn't know which way was up. And now I finally did.

I decided to take them to the Cayman Islands, my second home, and tell them there. More accurately, I felt like I had so much to say and was so worried I was going to trip over my words that I wrote them a letter and would deliver it to them there. My half-baked plan was to slip it under their bedroom door at some point. I know, I know. Not the best idea. And on our last full day there, I realized that. It felt like a cop-out. My parents and I have always been able to talk about everything. I knew they'd be disappointed in me for slipping them a letter. They'd probably even be hurt. No, I needed to tell them in person. But I still didn't know how or when.

On that last day on the island, Mom, Dad, and I were down on the beach, drinking rosé and wading in the ocean. It was a perfectly gorgeous night and it was dusk. Golden hour. We'd had a great trip and were recalling how much fun we'd had. All the while in the back of my head a voice was screaming, *Just do it already! You have to tell them!* "Anybody want another round?" I asked. "Sure!" they both replied, so I ran back up the beach bar and grabbed another wine for myself and Mom, and a beer for my dad.

As I walked back down to the where they sat, draping a napkin over my arm, I carried the drinks on a tray like a waiter. I looked at my parents chatting and laughing together as the ocean lapped up onto the shore. I just love their love. The sun was setting in front of me and I could see it sparkle through the rosé in the glasses. The sky was almost the same color pink. It was a perfect night. My dad noticed me approaching and said, "Hey, stop, I wanna get a picture!" He's great about snapping pics of Mom and his boys in moments he wants to remember.

He got up off of his lounge chair, phone in hand. "Hold still," he said as he took a picture of me with our drinks, silhouetted by the setting sun behind me. "That's perfect," he proclaimed, and looked from his phone to me. "Would you still think it's perfect if I told you I was gay?" I blurted out.

He looked a little surprised at my blunt delivery but simply smiled and defiantly said, "Yes. Now hand me my drink." My mom had seen and heard the whole interaction and walked up to give me a huge hug. That turned into a group hug, and one of the best moments of my life.

When we released, I noticed a cute guy jogging down the beach, glistening in tanning oil and said, half-joking, "I think that's my type."

My mom looked at me and said, "Mine, too."

"Hey, I can hear you guys," my dad said. And the whole thing was perfection. It was not the first time in my life when I realized how lucky I am to be raised by this uncommon couple.

We finished our drinks and headed back up to our condo. As we passed by the bar, my mom stopped and said to the bartender, "Can we get a bottle of that Whispering Angel, please?" This is not normally something she does, order a whole bottle of wine. But that night was a celebration. We toasted and danced in our condo. I still have the best photos of the three of us from that night, which I will treasure forever. And as we watched the remaining sun set over the island that I love so much, my parents told me how proud they were of me and reminded me, both with their words and actions, how much they loved me. My "gayness" wasn't something I needed to be ashamed of or explain. And it didn't mean I was all of a sudden going to become anyone different than I already was. It did not define me, but rather is just a part of who I am, and they have always made me feel like every part of me should be celebrated. The next day we packed up and went back to the States as if nothing had changed. I still had a long journey of self-discovery ahead of me, but I had the support of everyone that mattered, and I finally understood why I'd felt so empty for so long. I hadn't been truly living as my whole self, and thus I couldn't be loved as my whole self. But now I could. And that's the best thing in the world.

CUE: "The Tears of a Clown" by Smokey Robinson

14

One Pulse

SHORTLY AFTER I was out to my friends, things with my first boyfriend ended and I started dating again. I also started to have some misgivings about the countries Virgin Produced was doing business with. Now that I understood my sexual orientation better, I started to feel conflicted about partnering with companies in the Middle East, where homosexuality is still highly stigmatized and even illegal in some places. I wasn't out publicly, so I never discussed this with my coworkers, I just started seeing my entire life and work differently as I came to terms with being part of the LGBTQ+ community. It was all too fresh for me to take a stand on anything in a public manner. I was still in a headspace where I was nervous about what people would think and wanted to ease into my new identity.

Eventually, I started officially dating another guy. He was closer to my age and was a professional dancer. He had just finished up a tour with Ricky Martin when we met. A few years prior he had worked at Walt Disney World in Orlando and spent a lot of time at the Pulse nightclub, an LGBTQ+ social scene. He was the first boyfriend to move in with me, and we were playing house.

After a couple of years, our relationship started to fall apart. I was still struggling with living a life of excess. I thought reaping the financial rewards of being a workaholic justified my putting our company projects before my relationships. I was still drinking way too much, and my boyfriend's lifestyle of staying out until 3:00 in the morning bartending or partying wasn't helping. It certainly wasn't his fault. I take responsibility for my own choices and was happy to partake in everything. But I was entering a place in my life where I wanted to settle down a little, and he did not. I had a wake-up call one morning when the alarm went off and, still drunk from the night before, I hopped into my sports car and drove to a meeting with Jeff Robinov (the Warner Bros. studio boss) who we'd pitched the Garcia movie to years earlier. He was the head of a new studio and considering partnering with us on a slate of projects. I went to the early breakfast meeting, came back home, and fell right back to sleep. When I woke up, I couldn't remember a thing. I couldn't remember the route I drove to the meeting, much of the breakfast, or a single thing I had said. Needless to say, I am confident I wasn't on my usual A game. A quick follow-up note that Jeff returned said that he was going to pass on working with us. Although he was polite in his email to me, I knew deep down I had been reckless and had acted in total disregard for my business, not to mention my own personal health and safety. My striving had turned into sinking. In that very moment, I realized that I needed – and *wanted* – to make a change. But it was hard to move in the right direction while I lived with someone who lived so differently than me.

Toward the end of our relationship, I returned to Texas with my best friend Melissa for our high school reunion. It was the first time in 20 years that I heard the name Peaches again. It was also the first time in Texas, among these people of my past, that I felt popular. Like *really* popular. I had become the "Hollywood guy." I had become rich, and to them, well, famous. But mostly, I had become the boy that had gotten out of town and succeeded. I'd accomplished what I always said I would, and it had garnered me some respect that I never had in high school. I'd be lying if I didn't admit that was mildly satisfying. Peaches was somebody!

After the ego-stroke reunion, Melissa and I were walking back into the hotel when I got a call from the boyfriend. He was in hysterics. I could hardly understand him. He kept saying there'd been a shooting somewhere but I couldn't make out much as I entered the elevator. He told me to turn on the news and hung up. Like the rest of the world,

I watched in horror as every outlet covered one of the deadliest shootings in American history at the Pulse nightclub. A man had walked in, killed 49 people, and injured 53. I had never been there myself, but I knew from my boyfriend that Pulse was a very special place. It was more than a gay bar; it was a place where the LGBTQ+ community and their allies gathered to drink, dine, and dance. For many Central Florida–based gay, bi, or trans people who'd been rejected by their families or lost their livelihood because of their sexual orientation, Pulse was their chosen home and family. It was a safe place where they could be themselves and not ashamed. And some bigot had just walked in and destroyed it.

"You have to do something!" he cried to me when I called him back later.

"What do you mean, what could I do?" I replied.

"I don't know. Use your influence! You have connections! You have to help somehow."

With a simple "Okay," I agreed.

But seriously, what the heck could I possibly do? I thought again as we hung up. I wasn't an activist. It was never my intention to make a big impact in the gay community. I was never going to march or be a flag waver. I wanted to keep that part of my life private. Plus, selfishly, I was trying to work through my vice with alcohol, probably breaking up with the boyfriend, and had a huge career that was fulfilling but really hard. I was in no place to add anything else to my plate.

But as I crawled into bed that night, I thought more about it. "You need to use your influence for good," he had said. Really, he was right. Why did I have all of these resources and these relationships for if it weren't to help people? I may not be able to heal this but I certainly could do my small part to help. Falling asleep wasn't an option, so I called him back. "Do you know the owner of the club?" I asked.

"Yes," he said, "Barbara Poma."

"Okay, contact her and set up a call for us. I'll come home tomorrow." And with that, our slowly ending relationship was put aside as we both focused on a common cause. I was on the first flight out of Texas the next morning and landed in LA for barely 24 hours before we were on a flight out to Orlando. We met with the Pomas the next day. I learned about the origin of Pulse, a place she created in honor of her long since passed gay brother. She shared heartwarming stories of the community and of brighter days there. I shared that although I knew this would never make up for the harm that was done, if she wanted, I could create a nonprofit foundation that would likely have significant impact in the community. "The onePULSE Foundation," I suggested. It just felt natural. She had created a place with the Pulse nightclub that unified people. It could raise funds to build a memorial on the very site of the tragedy and the foundation could provide scholarships for the victims and their families and other vulnerable members of the local LGBTQ+ community. With my entertainment resources, I believed we could kick all of this off with an impactful event to raise the needed seed money. Barbara beamed with relief. She was still reeling, of course, but she readily agreed. She shared that she felt the course of her life had changed that week and she wanted to devote the rest of her life to "not letting hate win."

We headed back home and I got to work calling in every contact and favor I'd ever earned in my nearly 20 years in Hollywood. I called producers, executives, assistants, assistant's assistants, and every single famous actor, singer, or influencer I had ever met. I pulled every last string because I couldn't think of a more worthy cause. With the help of a few friends, we architected a concert livestreamed around the world from Hollywood. It included performances and appearances by many recognizable faces. I implored them to share with their large fan bases, and they did. A huge list of allies performed including Jesse J, will.i.am, Melissa Etheridge, Cindy Lauper, and more. We hustled and pulled it off in just a few weeks.

In between the tragic shooting and the benefit concert, I was scheduled to fly out to Washington, DC, for the birthday party of President Obama at the White House. Through a series of events in the last year, I'd become part of the president's Arts and Entertainment Council and had become friendly with his senior advisor, Valerie Jarrett. Every few months she'd round up a few of us from various entertainment companies (like iHeart Radio, Sony, Funny or Die, etc.) and caucus for a cause. The most recent centered on Obamacare. Valerie had gathered us a few months prior to use our entertainment and marketing brains to pitch nonpartisan ways we could encourage signups for Obamacare during the next enrollment period. It was through opportunities like this that I'd had the honor to meet President Obama a couple of times and lend my expertise in certain ways.

I was delighted to be invited to his birthday celebration, and my invite included a plus one. I had officially become single, as I assumed I would. So I rang up Richard Branson and asked if he wanted to go with me. I knew he hadn't yet met President Obama, and I believed they'd hit it off instantly. I also let President Obama's assistant know that Richard was coming and to see if I could arrange a private lunch with just the two of them before the party. I figured they'd have plenty to talk about, and it'd be a great opportunity for two thought leaders to mind-meld. While Richard was otherwise preoccupied with lunch, I had hoped I could arrange my own meet-and-greet with *someone* I admired – White House photographer, Pete Souza. I was a fanboy of his and really loved his work.

As he landed in DC, Richard texted asking what I was wearing to the White House. "I'm just wearing jeans and a blazer," I said. "Just be yourself, not fancy." He's a jeans and blazer guy anyway, and I figured Obama would appreciate that Richard was being his authentic self. I mean, you don't tell a basketball player not to wear his high tops or Lady Gaga to be conservative. Richard is renowned for "saying goodbye to the tie," a corporate initiative he led personally that Virgin launched years prior. But when we showed up, of course, everyone else was in full suits and ties. I did get to meet Pete Souza, and he took a picture of the three of us in the Oval Office before their lunch.

When Richard saw it he shook his head and said, "Just look at our jeans. . . ." He still gives me shit about that to this day. But I regret nothing. We were ourselves and you can't fault that.

After Richard went off to have lunch, I sat outside the Oval Office to wait for Obama's right hand, Joe Paulsen, to give me a quick walk around and grab a bite at the Navy grog in the basement of the White House. As I sat, I noticed an older gentlemen also waiting out of the corner of my eye. When I looked up, I saw it was none other than Stevie Wonder. THE Stevie Wonder. He was set to perform that night at the birthday party and I guess was waiting for some kind of briefing. As I sat there, I had an idea. It was a long shot, but I couldn't squander this opportunity. I struck up a brief conversation and before someone could come in and swoop either of us away, I asked, "Mr. Wonder, I'm putting on a benefit concert in a few weeks for the victims of the Pulse shooting and to raise awareness and contributions for a new foundation. Would you consider performing?"

He turned in my direction and said, "That sounds just lovely. Yeah, I might be able to make that happen. You can get my number from him." He placed his hand on the arm of his assistant and suggested we converse. *Whoa*, I thought. *Did that just happen, and in, like, 45 seconds?* He wasn't officially committed yet, but I'd gotten a soft yes from Stevie Wonder. Let that be a lesson to anyone, including myself. Closed mouths don't get fed. You can't get something if you don't ask. Never be afraid to ask. No matter the circumstances.

Unsurprisingly, the birthday party was absolutely mind-blowing. The Obamas sure can throw a party, and the venue wasn't bad either. At a certain point, I found myself chatting with Michelle (you know, the First Lady) when her favorite song came on and I learned quickly that she *loves* to dance. As that song started, she jumped up on that dance floor and motioned with her finger for us to join her. I looked over at Richard and mouthed, "Come on, let's go!" He shook his head slightly, but I still ushered/pushed him out there anyway and we proceeded to join the Michelle Obama dance party. That memory really makes me smile.

It was the perfect celebration for the only living president I had ever admired. It went on for another three or four hours, but Richard and I left shortly after that dance. We had had a great time, talked to just about everyone, weren't overserved, and could still get a good night's sleep. One of the many lessons I learned from Richard was the art of the perfect French (or sometimes called Irish) exit and how to know exactly when it's time to leave. You can't be the last group to leave, overstay your welcome, or have so much "fun" you are remembered for exactly that. But of course, you must arrive on time, stay long enough to enjoy meaningful conversation, have enough fun, make a memory or two, and then gracefully exit. It really is an art to know when it's time to pull the rip cord and shut it down. In short, the goal is to ensure the host doesn't view your invite as a regret – and to get your ass to bed. Besides, by that stage of my life, I could use a little more bed time and less party time.

Lest you think us too cool after our smooth exit, as we walked through the gates of the White House, Richard looked over and gave me a mischievous grin. Then he pulled out a wad full of napkins with the White House emblem on them from his pocket. I laughed hysterically as I pulled out a stack from my own pockets. Unbeknownst to each other, we had done the exact same thing – swiped a handful of napkins on our way out as a souvenir. I have a picture of that moment and it is pure joy. We are smiling so hard and laughing so hard you can just about see our molars while we each hold the napkins in our hands. Sometimes I really can't believe this is my life.

In the couple of weeks left until the onePULSE Foundation benefit concert, I was persistent about messaging Stevie Wonder's assistant. We had some big names ready to perform for the cause, but Stevie would definitely be the most iconic. With the blessing of his performance, I felt like we would really drive a well-rounded viewership. The day before the event, his assistant texted and finally confirmed, but also with a disclaimer that Stevie doesn't really arrive early or hang around long at events. He usually just shows up whenever and performs. I guess when you get to be at that level, you can do whatever you want and people are just grateful you're there. All of that was fine by me, though I wasn't quite sure what I was going to do or where I would slot him if I had no idea when he'd show up.

The day of the event was highly intense. We were running around stressed, doing everything necessary to get ready. The pressure of it being livestreamed amplified everything. If anything went wrong, everyone would know in real time. The Pulse shooting had been a global news story just a month before, and the world was watching. Thankfully, it all did go off without a hitch, though I was stressed all night wondering when Stevie Wonder would show up. As promised, right in the middle of the event, I got a text from Stevie's assistant. "We'll meet you out back in 20 minutes at the loading dock." *Stevie Fucking Wonder*. I think a part of me questioned if he really would show until that moment. I looked out into the audience at my parents. I knew my dad, a Motown cinephile, was going to be giddy. Similar to the Yogi Berra and Oliver Stone connections, I treasured those times when my career intersected my dad's interests and I got to bring a little joy to his life.

Twenty minutes later I was out back as instructed, opening up the door to an arriving SUV with Stevie Wonder inside. The first thing I said was, "Stevie, thank you so much for coming tonight. It really means a lot." He put his arm on me as we entered backstage, squeezing it slightly, and said, "Boy, you need to eat more."

"Hah!" I laughed. "Well, I've been so busy I haven't had a chance to eat today, but I'll make sure I go after this." He smiled and said, "Good, take me where we need to be." I led Stevie backstage, adjacent to the waiting grand piano I had positioned for his hopeful appearance. Jessie J had just finished on stage as I prepped Stevie. But that didn't last long, because it quickly became clear that Stevie Wonder needs no preparation. I guided him to the bench, he placed his hands on the keys, and he did his thing. Not surprisingly, he absolutely knocked it out of the park as he shared stories of injustice, his hope for a more inclusive tomorrow, and interweaved his catalog of hit songs into the final act of the evening. The event was a huge success, though it was a small consolation in light of the tragedy that necessitated it. We raised a sizeable amount that evening, and the foundation was officially launched. And in honor of Stevie, I did have an entire pizza later that night. I'm a man of my word.

A year later, we were set to dedicate a temporary memorial at the Pulse site and unveil plans for the permanent memorial. Barbara Poma had been running the foundation as her full-time job and assembled an impressive board of trustees and team. In advance of the ceremony, she'd asked me to come and give a speech. In the months that followed the concert and initiation of the foundation, I'd struggled with what to tell people about my connection to Pulse and why it meant so much to me. Still no one in my work life knew I was gay. I never really even wanted to be publicly "out." I mean, none of my straight friends had ever had an "I'm straight" proclamation, waved hetero flags, or marched in parades. I just didn't understand why I needed to announce anything officially. It wasn't that I wasn't proud of who I was, but the last thing I wanted to do was act as if I was part of a minority group that needed respect and consideration when my primary identity was an incredibly privileged white guy.

Also, despite how far our culture has come, I'll admit I was a little afraid of what it might do to my career if everyone knew. It wasn't that long ago that my old roommates hazed me because they could tell I was different and how important it was to them that I slept with a woman. Or that I remembered how they started seeing me differently after that kind girl slept in my bed one night and let everyone believe we'd had sex. It mattered to them. They treated me differently after they thought I was straight. There was also the fact that Virgin Produced films were being released internationally and many countries were not LGBTQ+ friendly. How would they feel about doing business with a gay guy? In short, I worried that many of the things and people who were important to me could go away if everyone knew the truth.

But as I engaged deeper with onePULSE and the LGBTQ+ community, I began to feel dishonest in not sharing that part of me. It didn't feel right to be a founding trustee and not let everyone know that I was not only an ally of the community but also a part of it. It felt misaligned to keep hiding that. Inauthentic. Plus, hiding is exhausting. And, as they say, the truth will set you free. So I decided to finally speak the truth. Not just to my loved ones, but to the world at large.

When I traveled down to Orlando for the memorial dedication, I publicly came out. I didn't make a big show of it as I wanted to keep the focus on onePULSE, the victims, and the good work the foundation intended to do. I simply added in a line to my speech that said, "As a part of this community myself, it is our job to ensure that hate does not win." And that was that. From that day forward, I was out to everyone. No more hiding. I'm not a celebrity, but I was sure interested parties and assuming minds would hear about it and spread the word. Which was fine by me. Despite my fears, I was ready for everyone to know. I was ready for the entertainment industry to know, and for my colleagues, investors, hometown friends, and extended family to know, no matter the repercussions. It was liberating and 99% of people in my life couldn't care less, including my Virgin colleagues and industry associates. I think my extended family and acquaintances found validation of their decades-long assumption that I was gay.

There was only one business associate who wasn't accepting. This particular individual decided that my being gay was not aligned with his values and pulled out of an investment he had promised Virgin. For a bit, I was ashamed my authenticity might have let the company down and potentially even derailed our latest project. I voiced my sadness innocently to my friend Dr. Bill Dorfman over lunch one day. At the end of lunch, Bill looked at me and said, "I'll replace that investor. His loss." I was incredibly moved. The people who truly cared about me stuck around, supported me, and were proud. All in all, authenticity won and good people align with good intention.

A few months later, Richard and I got invited back to the White House for the president and First Lady's annual Christmas party. Helen Clarke (Richard's longtime assistant), Justin, and Joan came along this time. The party was grand, just like the birthday party. But there was a noticeable mood shift this time. The month before, Donald Trump had won the 2016 presidential election. It felt like a dark cloud hung in the air as we all held our breath to find out what the future held. Barack Obama had been a very meaningful president to me, and I imagine to many. Among his administration's many accomplishments, he made gay marriage legal and helped normalize it. Now as an engaged man (previously a self-proclaimed lifelong bachelor), I'm incredibly grateful for that. The thought of Donald Trump, a reality TV star, filling Obama's seat made many of us nervous.

I consider myself an independent and have never been a registered Democrat or Republican. In general I try not to pick a political side, but rather a candidate. But there was no doubt within the LGBTQ+ community that Obama was and is seen as an ally, and Trump was a terrifying unknown. Whenever I thought of Donald Trump, I could not help but recall how Richard told me he'd once shared a short meal with Trump decades prior. At that meal, Trump shared with Richard that he had a list. This so-called list included names of people he desired to destroy if and when he got the opportunity. Suggesting that this was normal, he quizzed Richard on who was on *his* list. Richard made it clear that he doesn't have a list. Needless to say, the meal started and ended quickly. The thought of the "list keeper" sitting at the most powerful desk in America terrified me.

At the Christmas party, one of Obama's aides asked if Richard, Joan, and I would like to come up to the private residence after the party. That was one of the easiest affirmative nods of my life. Perhaps another serendipitous, fortunate stroke of luck. A small group of us, including Valerie and her daughter, headed up to the Obamas' private living room and sat by a crackling fire having martinis with the president and First Lady. We stood on the Truman balcony and looked out at the Washington Monument on that chilly December night. I thought of all the movies I'd seen in my lifetime that had this exact scene in them, and here I was, living it with a small group of people I greatly admire. As if the scene couldn't be more perfect, it began to snow.

During the course of the night, conversation eventually turned briefly to Trump. Richard looked at the president and said, "What are we going to do?" We all knew what he meant. He meant, what's going to happen? What can we do to help make this better? How are we going to not lose all of the progress you've made over the last eight years? It felt like (even though Richard is British) we were all turning to our fearless leader one last time (cue *Hamilton*) for hope.

"We'll be okay," the president said simply. And I believed him. He also said a few other things with which I fully agreed, but are better left unsaid here.

Then Richard asked, "After the inauguration, where are you guys going off to go?"

"We'll head to Palm Springs," said the president.

"For some golf?" I asked. Michelle smirked, rolled her eyes, and made a comment about golf.

Then I turned to Richard and Joan and offered, "Why don't you have them down to Necker Island?" I know it sounds a little presumptuous, inviting someone to someone else's private home. But I knew Richard well enough by then to know he'd love the idea. And Richard likewise knew me well enough that unapologetically blurting out my every thought is exactly the kind of thing that I would do.

He looked at me and then at the president. "Well, do you guys want to come to Necker?" The couple exchanged looks between them all and nodded in affirmation. *Amazing! The Obamas were headed to Necker!* I was really excited for them. I knew they'd love it just as much as I do. Then Joan and I popped up to use the restroom, and en route back through the residence she looked to me, slipped her arm in mine, and said, "We better head out. Don't want to wear out our welcome." Those Bransons and their knack for knowing when to leave. I was half-ready to grab a pillow and check into the Lincoln bedroom, but they were right. We said our goodbyes and went back to the hotel. It was a special night that I'll never forget. And if Michelle, Barack, or Valerie is reading this right now: thank you for your service to our country and the warm hospitality you offered me that evening.

That next week I was back in LA and put into motion the plan to get the Obamas out to Necker immediately after the inauguration. My assistant and I were put in touch with their chief of staff and the Secret Service to make all of the arrangements. Helen did all of the planning from the Necker end, coordinating the advance trip for the Secret Service to scout everything, and I did everything else from LA. Trump's inauguration was January 20, 2017. It was a sobering moment watching the Obamas walk across the lawn into the helicopter that would take them away after eight historical years in the White House. As the media inquired where the Obamas would head to later that day aboard Special Mission 28,000 (no longer Air Force One as he was no longer president), I assumed I was one of about 50 people in the world who knew where they were going.

Richard had kindly invited me down to Necker during that same week to be with them, but I respectfully declined. I felt I had played my role already and did not want to encroach. It also happened to be my 40th birthday and I'd planned a huge blowout elsewhere in the Caribbean with 100 of my closest friends, Virgin colleagues, and family. I couldn't cancel, even for the Obamas. But about halfway through my party week, Helen texted to let me know that Richard was disappointed that he couldn't attend my 40th and was sending Helen in his plane to come pick me up and fly me over to Necker when it was over. My parents were also invited, but they politely declined. My mom has mentioned that they count this as one of their biggest regrets. My parents *love* the Obamas. But they're so humble, and I think they didn't want to impose.

On the last day of my celebration trip, I hopped on Richard's plane and headed to Necker. We stopped in Florida on the way to pick up Valerie. When we arrived, it became clear that there wasn't much room on the island. Literally, there were no available rooms. Understandably, the Obamas required so much secret service that this island was at capacity. On arrival, I was informed that Richard had arranged for me to stay on his yacht that was moored right next to the island. This was the icing on my big fat proverbial 40th birthday cake. I was still so high off of spending four days with my loved ones, friends, and colleagues and now I got to spend a few more on this yacht solo. It was exactly the centering moment I needed – a comedown from an all-time high, a time to reflect on the last eight years and the progress our country had made. The progress I had made. What would the future look like? I spent each morning sipping my coffee, staring at Necker from the boat, appreciative of my journey thus far and inspired for the future.

The whole week was spent the exact way it always goes on Necker. Fun, adventure, competition, thoughtful conversation mixed with kitesurfing, Hobie Cats, plentiful food, and bubbles. It felt like our little secret, too. No one in the world knew where the Obamas had gone until Richard posted that infamous photo of him putting the president in a headlock on his blog. "I Beat Obama at Kitesurfing" was the headline, and summed up the friendly competition the two hatched that week.

On the last night, Richard decided that we'd have an intimate dinner party on the yacht. Then we'd hop back over to the island and throw a party for the staff. With all of the extra guests that week, they'd worked especially hard. Everyone joked that we were "going over to Jason's house" for dinner that night. We sat and ate at a small table at the back of the boat together for the last time. The former president asked me so many questions about myself and my ambitions. He wanted to know how I was serving the community beyond onePULSE and what my plans are for the future. He kindly listened, but didn't seem to care much about the success of *Limitless* or other Virgin Produced efforts, like most everyone else I'd met in recent years. He wanted to know what I was doing to make the world a better place. I couldn't believe how much that entire dinner conversation revolved around me, my family, and my interests. The former president and First Lady of the United States, Valerie Jarrett, and the Branson's wanted to know all about *me*. Inside, I still just felt like Peaches from middle-of-nowhere Texas!

After dinner, Richard surprised everyone with a fireworks show before we headed back to land for the surprise staff party. As I stood there, face lit from the light off the water, shoulder to shoulder with some of the most impactful people of our generation, I was deeply moved and challenged. What *was* I going to do with my position and influence? Was I doing enough? Was I focused on the right things? Was I making a difference in the world? Inspired, I wanted that night to last forever.

But alas, the next day, we packed up and jumped on Richard's plane back to the States. I sat across from President Obama, and we got to continue our conversation from the night before. He told me all about his plans for the Obama Foundation, which was still in its infancy, and their forthcoming production deal with Netflix. I was moved by his definitive focus on creating content with purpose. Michelle talked about how excited she was to write her memoir, which became the bestselling book many times over, *Becoming*. I recall her also being excited to have time to attend more spin classes. We jokingly compared passports. Mine was worn and torn as I traveled hundreds of times a year with Virgin. The former president's was crisp and brand new. It hadn't even been stamped once yet. "I haven't held one of these in a long time," he said as he picked it up out of the cupholder. They take all of that from you when you become president and hand back new ones once you're a private citizen again.

I stared out the window as the sun set, knowing we only had about 30 minutes left in the plane ride. Half an hour until this whole experience was nothing but a memory. As Michelle's legs swung up across Barrack's lap, signaling a request for a foot massage, I thought *God, I really love these people*, as she winked at me. It was so refreshing to realize that Barack and Michelle Obama are exactly who you'd hope they are. Not just community organizers and leaders but kind, selfless, and warm people. That's what I always share when people ask me about Richard, too. He's exactly what you think he is: studied, generous, and good-spirited. Hardly anyone in Hollywood ever lives up to their image once you get to know them. But these individuals do. And at that moment, I felt incredibly proud to be in their presence.

As my time with them came to a close, I knew I had to finally share something with President Obama. Though my parents had declined the invitation to join us on Necker, my dad had written him a note about how much he appreciated everything he did for our country. Recalling my Yogi Berra faux pas of years past though, I was always wary of asking for things from famous people.

"I really hate to do this," I ventured, "but my dad wrote you a note and I would love to share it with you if you don't mind." Of course, the former president agreed, and I shared with him the most beautiful letter my dad had emailed me. I waited awkwardly as the president took a few minutes to read it from my phone. When he was finished, he looked up and smiled and nodded at me.

"Could we send your dad a video?" he asked. *Come again?* I thought. *Of course we can send my dad a video! Are you kidding?!* I pulled out my phone and said, "Are you ready?" as I hit record.

Then Mr. Obama went on to say, "Hi John! I just wanted to thank you for your note. And I wanted to thank you for your son. He set up an amazing vacation and has been such a great friend to us this week. We're incredibly grateful to him. Thank you and I hope I get to meet you soon." I beamed with pride. I knew my dad was going to love it. He'd be blown away. Mr. Obama had not only given him the gift of a personalized video and thank you, he'd shown he knows the one true way to a parent's heart: their children. He knew nothing would make my dad happier than letting him know I had some tiny, microscopic bit of impact on the president's life. It was such an act of generosity.

Those last 10 minutes of the flight I looked out the window as the sun set over the Potomac as we approached Washington, DC. There were no words to express everything I'd just experienced. I was so blessed, so grateful, and so incredibly honored by everything that happened in the last week. I couldn't think of anything else to do but try and live a life deserving of it. As we landed, the former president grabbed his brand-new passport emblazoned with the presidential seal, and we all said our goodbyes. The last thing he said as he turned to walk down the plane stairs was, "Well, I guess it's time to get to work."

CUE: "Higher Ground" by Stevie Wonder

PART

IV

That's a Wrap

15

Kaaboom

INSPIRED BY MY time with the Obamas, I did everything I could to ensure the onePULSE Foundation got up and running successfully and began to work more with Virgin Unite, the nonprofit organization of the Virgin brand. I also had to turn my attention back to work, as we currently had plenty of movies in development. There was always a meeting to take, a long list of calls to return, or a dinner to rush to, but I was becoming more interested in focusing on more meaningful content and initiatives, like organizing a prison reform event for Virgin Unite or attending a board of trustees meeting for onePULSE. By this time, I was also much more comfortable in my skin and beginning to understand that I needed balance in my life. But it was hard. That's just not how Hollywood works. It's fast-paced, and to be successful, I had to keep up. Remember, you're only as good as your last hit. It's a tough way to live.

As we gained more attention, Justin took a step back publicly and I took a step forward, which was just how our relationship worked at J2. He hated the spotlight, and although I didn't love it, it didn't bother me. Justin was also married and focused on starting a family by this time, so his priorities had shifted. He'd always been the quieter one, while I would talk to a tree if it could talk back. I started getting invited to be on panels, speak at conferences, and do more profile interviews, and was often interviewed about business moves in industry trades like *Variety*, *Hollywood Reporter*, or *Billboard*. Soon I had speaking engagements almost weekly. It was extra hard to slow down when I was getting so much attention and validation from it. I very much became the face of Virgin in Hollywood, in the entertainment industry. I'd come to terms with the fact that we'd probably never be Virgin Studios, but I was getting that familiar itch again that there was more to do commercially.

It was about this time that my parents invited me to a first-year music festival called KAABOO. As I've mentioned, my parents and I have always shared a love for music. The festival was located in Del Mar, my old stomping grounds with Mary, and where my parents were living at the time. It was advertised as a clean, multi-experiential festival with flushing toilets for a more adult crowd than, say, Coachella or Burning Man. The headliners were a combination of bucket list classic rock artists and modern-day hitmakers. I was psyched. My mom is pretty culturally in tune, and knew full well that people often camp at music festivals. So she invited all of my brothers and me down to their lovely, air-conditioned home and set up tents in the living room for each of us to get the true music festival experience. It was so fun.

During the whole festival weekend, I was intrigued. It was an incredible experience. As advertised, there were no dirty port-a-potties but rather full plumbing with flushing toilets. Everything was clean, not covered in dirt and dust like so many other festivals. The food was actually even tasty. The lobster rolls were a family favorite. There was an artwork exhibit and full-length comedy shows. It really was a multisensory event. I could tell they were doing something really different. It was exactly as my parents had described it, a music festival for adults. As my mind tends to do I found myself wondering, *Who runs this thing?* I found out it was a guy named Chris Brown (no, not *that* Chris Brown) and introduced myself.

"So this is your event?" I asked.

"Yup," he replied.

"It's great," I said, "very multisensory."

"Are you in marketing?" he asked

"Well, I'm in entertainment. I'm at Virgin Produced."

"I love Virgin! You know, we should talk about working together next year. I'll introduce you to my partners Seth and Bryan, the founders."

With that, I got Chris's email address and went about my way with my family. *Maybe a new commercial client*, I thought.

Quickly thereafter, I heard from Chris, who introduced me to Seth and Bryan. They were based in Denver and, as luck would have it, I was heading out there soon for the ribbon-cutting ceremony of the new Virgin America direct flight from LA to Denver. We arranged to meet up at a bar beforehand. When I walked in, I quickly noticed that these guys were not like my normal Hollywood meetings at all. They were dressed in drab blazers and not very animated. Honestly, they were a little banker-y. But they confirmed exactly what Chris had said. They wanted to run a festival that catered to adults and put a great emphasis on corporate partner sponsors. And these corporate sponsors needed content produced. KAABOO itself also needed promo videos created the next year to build more buzz. They seemed very keen on working with us. Especially Bryan, who seemed to have a borderline obsession with Richard Branson. While I found the fanboy aspect a little off-putting, I shook it off. Within days, we received an outline of what a Virgin Produced/KAABOO content alignment could look like and their goals for the new relationship. We signed a contract and were basically in business.

In the next few months, Bryan and Seth flew down to our Santa Monica offices multiple times to meet and greet my team and hammer out more details. My whole team was excited. It made so much sense for Virgin Produced to work with a music festival. Virgin, of course, had its roots in music, and KAABOO was an elevated version of the music festival experience. It felt a natural fit. To kick things off we made a "thank you" video targeted to the attendees. Then we made an artist lineup video for next year's festival that resulted in thousands of ticket sales. Things were going great. The team at KAABOO seemed incredibly grateful and continued to pitch ideas of ways we could work together. Bryan, specifically, seemed especially interested in growing the relationship.

He started calling me regularly and suggesting we meet up at a hotel for a "brainstorm." During one of these meetings he looked me straight in the eyes and asked, "Jason, where do you want to take your business?" I told him that I had dreams of Virgin Produced becoming its own studio, but at the moment we were in the middle of closing a deal with a studio called STX and planned to produce our next few movies. I shared that we had worked with this studio on the hit comedy film *Bad Moms* and the studio's president was interested in a long-term alignment starting with these next two films. "How much are they paying you?" he asked, "a few million dollars? You can do bigger and better than that. What if I took your business and injected steroids?"

"What does that mean?" I asked.

"I want to invest in your business. While you won't be a studio, you can remain independent of any one studio. Work with them all or not at all. Flexibility. My background is in private equity, and I will invest the capital needed to grow Virgin Produced substantially. We could turn Virgin Produced into a major, independent player. You would essentially be your own studio without having to rebrand as Virgin Studios." And there were the magic words. Over the next hour, he went on and on. "I also want Virgin Produced to become the official content producer for KAABOO. You'd remain CEO of Virgin Produced, and also serve a dual role as chief brand marketing officer for KAABOO. Virgin would then have a reach into TV, film, and music festivals. You could dominate all silos of entertainment."

I had to admit, I liked the sound of that. Maybe my dream of being our own studio wasn't completely dead after all. But I told Bryan I needed to see where the deal with STX went first. We were deep into negotiations, and I couldn't just bail. So I waited for a while, and the deal dragged and took much longer than I expected. STX was a newer studio helmed by a Brit named Sophie Watts. Her mother had worked with Richard decades prior and helped shape the brand in early days. I was intrigued to see if I could bring Virgin Produced full circle with STX and Ms. Watts. But I was becoming less and less hopeful that we'd close it due to a corporate restructuring, which would ultimately see Ms. Watts moving on to other opportunities. Because of our past experience, I was also a little wary of excitable suitors like Bryan. We'd been screwed by an investor before (Amanat) and almost lost everything. Although that was years ago now, Justin reminded me of it frequently. In more ways than one, we just barely recovered from it.

With Sophie Watts on her way out of the STX door, I had a decision to make. Stay with STX and maybe get our two films made or accept a proclaimed huge influx of cash, which could be game changing. We did need the money to grow. We'd experienced a lot of success, but in many ways were still seen as a minor player in Hollywood. It felt like we were on the cusp of something big, but to get there, we needed more growth capital. And Bryan had both the desire and the money. That much we could definitely verify. This time around, we did our research and discovered that Bryan was a verifiable real deal. It wasn't smoke and mirrors as it had been with Amanat. Bryan was an experienced venture capitalist and private equity investor, and there was past deal flow to validate that. On a trip to London, he even met with Richard's legal team to pitch the idea of a new license agreement for Virgin Produced. It was a significant investment. With that, a fund controlled by Bryan Gordon officially became the largest shareholder in Virgin Produced.

It didn't take long for it to become clear that his brand, KAABOO, was much more important to Bryan than Virgin Produced. Soon after he invested, he started diverting most of our personnel and resources to the music festival instead of toward our film and TV development. And because he now had control, he could do it. He even fired a few people whom I had hired. This was very concerning to me because I cared so much about my team, most of whom I'd worked with for years, some for decades. I started to worry that I'd made another mistake. I brought all of my concerns to Bryan, and he reassured me, "Jason, you've built Virgin Produced; you're established. Now let's build KAABOO. Together they will thrive." *Maybe he's right*, I thought.

Despite things with Bryan not turning out exactly as I'd hoped, KAABOO was going very well. By 2018, the festival was in its fourth year and had put on another incredible weekend with a lineup that included Foo Fighters, Katy Perry, Halsey, Post Malone, and Imagine Dragons. Bryan and Seth also wanted to expand to the Cayman Islands with KAABOO Cayman and into Dallas with KAABOO Texas by 2019. Since I'd grown up with the Cayman Islands as a second home, I was always open to ideas to help progress the arts and culture there, and benefit the economy of the place I loved so much. I knew this could draw the global attention that I believed it so rightly deserved. Often the Cayman Islands are inaccurately portrayed in movies, TV, and John Grisham novels as a place where drug lords hide their money, or where funds must be wired in order to have a fictional hostage released. It had long been a side project of mine to help reinvigorate and rehabilitate their reputation in Hollywood. Years earlier, Justin, my brother Logan, local friend Brian Braggs, and I had initiated and launched the Cayman Islands Film Commission under the Cayman Islands Investment Bureau, led by Dax Basdeo. The film commission was organized to officially attract, educate, and lobby for movies to be shot within the Cayman Islands, thus creating economic and artistic impact within the community. Producing a KAABOO festival in Cayman was going to be a substantial boom for the economy and local vendors and artists alike. To this day it's still two of the local contributions that I'm most proud of.

By 2019, though, because of personnel diversion and a lack of promised resources and bandwidth, Virgin Produced was struggling. So much so that I was beginning to feel out of options. That year, KAABOO Cayman was the smashing brand and experiential success I'd envisioned it could be. A laundry list of global artists showed up there for the first time, discovering the paradise that I called home for decades. The Chainsmokers, Bryan Adams, Jason Derulo, Zedd, Duran Duran, Maren Morris, and plenty more all performed. Richard attended as well and stayed for the entire event, even enjoying himself on stage with Flo Rida, and The Chainsmokers. It was a proud moment for the brand and for the country. The event resulted in an influx of millions of dollars and significant economic impact to the island. None of it would have been possible without the support of Dart Enterprises, the Cayman Islands Government, and countless local vendors. I will always be grateful for everyone's involvement and belief in the event.

But despite how excited I was about that, the other truth was that Virgin Produced hadn't progressed any of its movies in over a year. We were not making moves or growing into our own studio, as Bryan had pitched. We weren't even striking deals with other studios anymore. Our whole team and resources had been diverted to KAABOO, and I felt like I was out on an island by myself trying to get other projects made. I certainly couldn't produce movies by myself. And even if I could, we definitely couldn't distribute them because we had no studio deal. Without the necessary financing from Gordon's fund or a studio, I was handcuffed to KAABOO, and Bryan knew it. Virgin Produced had fallen into a version of development hell, and we were spinning our wheels. Except this time, the expectations were higher. Virgin Produced had previously been an award-winning force. So many versions of "What's your next movie?" were asked of me everywhere I went. The chatter was getting louder and the fate of the company was beyond my control. I felt Virgin Produced slipping away.

One particularly dark day, I sent Bryan an email reluctantly resigning. "I need to step down. I can't make film and TV deals or progress them. I feel we've been stripped all of our resources. You have me only focused on KAABOO," I told him.

"You can't resign!" Bryan said over an impromptu sushi dinner that evening. "You're the face of Virgin Produced, and you need to stay in place." Following dinner, he went on to convince my COO, producer Tobin Armbrust, and me that we would have the resources needed to progress our film and TV projects. *We just needed to focus on KAABOO partnerships for right now.* I will admit here that he also blew a lot of smoke up my ass about how great I am, and I liked it. That's something he'd done since the beginning of our relationship, very successfully. Bryan painted me to my face as the greatest human in the whole world at everything. Despite Seth being in his life for decades, apparently I was his "favorite partner." And he let me know it constantly. I've always said that flattery is fine as long as you don't inhale. Well, when it came to Bryan Gordon, I inhaled deeply. And I trusted him. I was high as a kite, euphoric on his flattery . . . and it was a big mistake.

In retrospect, what Bryan really liked about me didn't have anything to do with me at all. He liked that I was the key that unlocked his access to Virgin. And he liked that he could tell people who didn't know any better that he was "in business with Richard Branson" to gain credibility and progress all of his related and unrelated deals. Though he never held an official executive title at Virgin Produced, he certainly acted like he did everywhere he could. He had a Virgin email address and the recognizable logo attached right at the bottom of each one he sent. Before I realized how calculating he really was, Bryan was positioning for his final chess move, which was a pitch that would ultimately create a Virgin-branded music festival – Virgin Fest. I have to admit, I was onboard from the start. It made sense. Bryan's expertise in the capital markets combined with the operational expertise of the KAABOO festival team, the Virgin brand, and my reputation in the industry – it sounded great. I convinced myself that this was a smart decision that would bring the Virgin brand full circle and back into music. Bryan hopped a plane to London to cut the deal with Richard's legal team. I trusted him with my most sacred business family and relationship: Virgin. Although I was excited to continue expanding the music festival portfolio, my once very successful brainchild, Virgin Produced, was still just a shell of what it originally had been.

By spring 2019, we had one successful KAABOO Cayman under our belts, one sparsely attended KAABOO Texas complete and were a few months out from September when KAABOO Del Mar was to be held. We also had our inaugural Virgin Fest in Los Angeles scheduled for summer 2020 with Lizzo booked as the headliner. That's when it all started to unravel. Bryan rang me up one day and said, "KAABOO needs funding if we're going to make the festival happen – in a few weeks" *How could that be possible?* I thought. As I understood it, Bryan and a few other investors had pumped many millions of dollars into the business over the last five years, and it had all gone to KAABOO. My team and I were under the impression that KAABOO was profitable. This sudden need for money to save the festival was confusing. Well, surprise, surprise, KAABOO was in dire financial straits, and Bryan and his cofounders hid it from everyone. He needed a seven-figure influx of cash in the next two weeks or it was all going to come crashing down. KAABOO was going to go Kaaboom!

That's when the threats started. "Jason, you'll need to help here," he said. "If KAABOO gets cancelled, then Virgin Fest won't happen."

Stunned, I immediately replied, "That means Virgin Produced is done. My career is over.

"Are you serious?" I continued.

Bryan softly interrupted, "We are out of time. I'll email you next steps." I can still feel the silence as he hung up. My heart started racing and my anxiety ramped up higher than it'd ever been before. Sheer panic. *Son of a bitch.* I had been played. I was the pawn and the

Virgin brand the innocent bystander. The worst part was, I knew he was right. If KAABOO was cancelled, everything we built would go down with it. Before sounding any unnecessary alarm bells with Richard, I needed to go first to the one other shareholder we had in Virgin Fest. I called Marc Hagle. Mr. Hagle, a self-made entrepreneur and former Purdue band drummer had invested in Virgin Fest due to his love of music and his affinity for the Virgin brand. He and his wife Sharon knew the brand well and were even set to be future astronauts in the Virgin Galactic program. They had attended past KAABOO festivals and had been told by Bryan that KAABOO was profitable. So this new venture investment into Virgin Fest initially made sense to the Hagle's as much as it did to me and to Richard's Virgin Group.

"Uh, Marc, I just got off the phone with Bryan Gordon, and he's made it very clear that they have a financial need in order to do the upcoming KAABOO festival," I explained. In the subsequent court trial that would follow, Bryan attempted to rewrite history and claim that he had many other options to save the festival – besides Virgin. But the truth is that only Virgin Fest and its shareholder Mr. Hagle could save it. And Bryan knew this. The only solution on such short notice was clear: we had to buy KAABOO to save it.

Bryan led the negotiations between KAABOO and Virgin Fest for the investment that would ultimately lead to a deal for Virgin Fest to acquire the assets of KAABOO. Virgin Fest agreed with Bryan and KAABOO that they would provide the $10 million needed to fund the 2019 KAABOO festival, alongside a whole mound of legal agreements, which included Bryan's new entity EventPro, obligating them to perform future production services. Although this sequence of events was frustrating, our meeting of the minds enabled us to hold the September 2019 festival, and for Bryan to save face. It also prevented him from tarnishing Virgin's reputation in Hollywood, and from destroying my career in the process. Well, for the moment anyway.

The weekend of our marathon dealmaking, KAABOO went off without a hitch. It was announced everywhere that *Virgin Fest had acquired KAABOO* and made it all sound like it was an exciting, premeditated deal that we'd had in the works for a while. We had another great lineup with Dave Matthews Band, Black-Eyed Peas,

Kings of Leon, Mumford & Sons, and more. Not that we – Virgin Fest nor I – actually did want to own the KAABOO brand. But it appeared that maybe we'd weathered the storm.

And then, on the Monday morning after the festival was over, we got word that Bryan Gordon had fired a roster of experienced professionals he was meant to keep in place at his new shingle EventPro. Those were the very people who were meant to produce future festivals for the brands we now owned – Virgin Fest and KAABOO. After a series of defaults on their agreements with us, EventPro showed little effort to comply with our agreement. Even after we wired the millions of dollars and saved the festival, Bryan decided he wasn't going to hold up his side of the deal. With the inaugural Virgin Fest set for summer, and KAABOO 2020 to plan, we had no other choice but to send two default letters, in hopes that Bryan and his team would comply with the agreement. It was clear; they were to provide *anything and everything needed* to produce the festival and were not doing so.

Instead, Bryan and EventPro sued Virgin Fest for what they called "a Trojan takeover." This is exactly what it sounds like. Someone invests or gets ingratiated into your company somehow and then extorts you if you don't hand over control. If it sounds familiar, it should. Because it's not what we did to Bryan, but exactly what he did to us. We certainly never threatened or extorted him to buy KAABOO. We never wanted to own KAABOO in the first place! So why did he sue Virgin Fest for saving KAABOO? *Billboard Magazine* journalist Dave Brooks asked the same thing in a profile story titled *KAABOO Festival Was Almost Cancelled, So Why Are the Founders Suing the Man Who Saved It?*

With KAABOO tied up in frivolous litigation against Virgin Fest, Virgin Produced was now just a shadow of what it once was. And to make things worse, we still had to somehow put on Virgin Fest in six months. I went down a spiral of shame. How did I let this happen? It had all seemed like such a smart move at the time. How could I still let myself get misled again so severely? Because of my successful run of movies at Virgin Produced, maybe I made the mistake of letting my guard down, trusting but not verifying or thinking that we were impenetrable. Did I feel we were invincible with the Virgin name behind us? (And in front of us?) We had a great record, clout, and respect in the industry. I felt like I'd taken my eye off the ball just for a second and gotten hit in the face with a fast one. Now I was essentially the CEO of two music festival brands mired in frivolous litigation and no control or even visibility into my once thriving film company. Bryan controlled the fate of my brainchild – and my Virgin career. And I sat in Hollywood, angry.

Well as everyone in the entire world knows now, things got exponentially worse just a few months later as we entered a global pandemic. We went into lockdown and spent all day, every day in our homes alone. Of course, we had to cancel Virgin Fest and KAABOO Del Mar for 2020. Though through March and April we were all hoping to "stop the spread" and "reopen by Easter," it became abundantly clear that wasn't going to happen. Then a letter issued from the Los Angeles Mayor's office made it very clear that hosting a festival in 2020 was not possible. We were in this thing for the long haul and had to make some tough calls. Every artist except Lizzo returned their fee. Lizzo refused to give back her $5 million performance fee (even though she was contractually obligated to) and so, to round out my year of litigation, we had no choice but to sue Lizzo and her agency, WME. Lizzo claimed, per her contract, that she was "ready, willing, and able" to perform and therefore was entitled to her fee. We made it clear she could have been "ready," and she may have been "willing" (to break the law), but she certainly was not "able" to break the law and defy a government mandate.

Meanwhile, I found out that throughout the course of all that happened over at Virgin Produced, Bryan Gordon had violated the terms of the Virgin licensing agreement, and therefore it had been revoked. Under Bryan's control, the company was out of compliance because we hadn't made good on developing and producing the movies we were supposed to. On its 10-year anniversary, Virgin Produced officially was no more. Even my email account cancelled, as if I had never existed to Virgin. Everything we'd built was gone.

After I lost Virgin Produced, I didn't know who I was anymore. It was during this period of time, on the heels of the Pulse tragedy, my time with the Obamas, the career disappointments, and coming face-to-face with so many people from high school again, that I began to think more and more about being Peaches. Was I Jason Felts? Or would

I always just be Peaches? In many ways I'd changed, and Peaches was my past. But he wasn't completely gone. He often felt like a little angel on my shoulder whispering in my ear. Like all past versions of ourselves, I guess, he was still there, along for the ride. Sometimes he gave me good advice, sometimes he gave me bad advice. Peaches definitely would have never gotten up on the table at Necker Island in a move that likely changed the course of my life. He's way too timid for that. I'm glad I ignored him then. But he was also the small voice inside of me telling me when something didn't feel right, when someone didn't seem like a good person, that maybe drinking my sorrows away wasn't the right move, and to call my mom. In so many ways I'd moved on from him, and in so many ways I still was him.

With a pandemic raging and everywhere shut down, I spent a lot of time sitting outside on my balcony at night looking out over the now quiet city of Los Angeles, consumed by these kinds of existential thoughts. I thought about where I'd come from and where I was, who I'd been and who I'd become. I had no idea what the future held, but I knew I was angry at Hollywood.

Fuck this town.

CUE: "Hustle" by P!nk

16

What Matters

By April 2020, I had lost the company I built from the ground up and was named in multiple frivolous lawsuits. And, of course, we were in the middle of the COVID-19 pandemic. Like the rest of the world, I was cooped up at home all day and night. The only thing that seemed to be going well was that I was about a year into a great relationship with my partner, Daniel. He's the love of my life and very private, so I'm keeping the details of our love story out of this memoir. But I had fallen in love for real and forever this time. He had moved in with me, and so thankfully neither of us were quarantined alone.

Although I had great company in quarantine, secretly I was completely and utterly depressed. Bryan Gordon had corporately seduced me, flattered me, lied to me, and then taken everything from me. Then he sued me for allegedly doing the exact thing he'd done to me. There was all kinds of media and press coverage about the lawsuit, most of it negative, with reporters favoring clickbait headlines over the facts. Because I decided it was the best legal strategy not to talk to the media, there were a lot of assumptions written by the press that were inaccurate. I learned that a member of Bryan's team had planted a story in the online tabloid *TMZ*, which got his version of events out first. The worst part was that many of them featured Richard's picture, for which I felt a ton of shame. Richard didn't deserve that. I was seething inside.

I was betrayed and disenfranchised. But mostly, I was sad and fatigued. What the hell was I even going to do next?

To say I started drinking heavily again is an understatement. I buried myself in alcohol during the day, and multiples of the highest milligram weed gummies I could find before bed each night. Late one night, I was sitting on the balcony of my high-rise corner apartment, high as a kite and at least one bottle of Pinot in. I was wallowing in depression and thinking about everything that had been taken from me, from my best friend Justin, my friends and fellow investors, and our employees. It didn't matter that I had a dream high-rise condo, a Caribbean beach house, famous artwork, luxury cars, and could fly my family private. I'd wanted those materialistic things for so long, and though I was grateful to have them, they were no consolation. They didn't make me feel anything. I sat there, numb, staring out at the quiet skyline.

The furniture on the patio was quite oversized, way too big for the narrow balcony. I had moved it from the Calabasas house, and it didn't fit right at my new place. It was squeezed in such that there was hardly any room to walk. To get around from one side to another, you almost had to walk on the furniture. So when I stood up to reach the bottle of wine and pour myself another glass, I had to stand on the couch. As I did, I realized how high (in both ways) I really was. The railing only hit me at my thighs. I glanced down to the valet below and thought, *It'd be easy enough for me to step over the railing right now. I should wait until the valet walks inside. I'd probably die instantly. I don't think I'd even feel it. I could just do it now. It'd be easy. I've got millions in life insurance that would go to my family and unfuck this situation for me. Fuck Gordon, fuck this town, and fuck all the naysayers. Would the valet attendant just hurry up and go back inside . . .*

I leaned a little toward the edge to see how it felt. My heart raced. I could end all the pain and shame right now. It was so tempting. The bad feelings were just too much. I wanted to be done with the striving and done with trying to impress anyone. An image of my dad flashed into my mind at that moment. My dad used to put out his arm to stabilize and protect me whenever he'd stop too quickly when driving. Did your parents ever do that? Even though you're buckled into the passenger side, they reach out their arm to stop you from flying through the window in case of an accident. It's a parental instinct, I think. To protect and save their children. I felt my dad in that moment do exactly that. If he had been there on that balcony, he'd have reached out his arm, just like he did when I was a child, and protected me.

Just then, Daniel slid open the door to balcony. I hadn't heard him get home. "Hey," he said brightly, with a huge smile as he shuffled onto the squished patio to come give me a kiss. It was as if his very presence had blown the huge, dark, heavy cloud surrounding me right off into the night. He had no idea what I'd just been thinking. What I'd almost just contemplated.

"Do you want to make dinner?" he asked.

I looked him into his warm eyes and replied, "Sure. Let's make dinner."

As I watched him walk back inside, I heard the voice of my mom in my head, "Jason, get down off that." She never liked me to walk on that patio furniture. It made her nervous. For good reason. I listened. I walked back inside and instead of ending my pain that night, I made yummy zucchini boats with my partner and safe place. Now, everything didn't change in an instant. I was still sad and went to bed with everything still on my mind. But the image of my dad, fortuitous interruption by my partner, and rational voice of my mom reminded me that I did have something to live for. I was deeply loved by those around me, and I still had more I wanted to do in this world. I had to find the will to go on and make as much of this right as I could.

The next morning, I woke up and was reminded of a lyric from one of Ashlee's songs. "Hollywood can chew me up, but it won't spit me out." *That's right.* This town and industry that I'd idolized for my entire life and longed to be a part of had certainly chewed me up. But I wasn't going to let it spit me out. I began to rally and feel a little bit of my spark come back. I wouldn't let this bury me. That early morning, instead of sitting around useless, I showered and put on a favorite bathrobe, and flicked on the light of my home office. I was going to find my purpose again. In my desk drawer I happened on that weathered and beat-up Jason keychain that said *healer* on the back that Gran had bought me all those years ago. She had passed long ago but I still thought of her often. I'd made it to her funeral but always harbored a little guilt that in the hustle and bustle of my career, I hadn't spent much time with her at the end. I wondered what she'd think of me now, of my sexuality and life choices. Despite our conservative upbringing, deep down I believe she'd be proud of me. And that she still wanted me to live with purpose and bring healing where I could. My own life and the world at large both felt like a bit of a mess, but I was going to do something to heal this situation. Whether she knew it or not, my Gran had instilled that in me all those years ago. There was a lot of healing that needed to be done, and I needed to start with myself.

First, I called Marc Hagle to game plan what we were going to do about the Bryan Gordon lawsuit. We agreed that we weren't going to let him rewrite history, and we would litigate the facts and truth without any compromising. We decided we were not going to just sit idly by, but defend ourselves. We would countersue Gordon and EventPro for fraud. I was going to defend my actions and integrity no matter what it took. As it turned out, Bryan Gordon has quite a storied history and this wasn't his first brush with dispute and the courts. I was now well aware that Gordon had sued past employees (even one with terminal cancer) and had almost half a dozen lawsuits that he had settled and had the files sealed. Marc and I were determined to prove he'd finally met his match with us. We weren't afraid of him. My assistant once had described me, fondly (I think), as a brilliant pain in the ass. I am a born perfectionist, and I was determined to become the biggest, most perfect pain in the ass Bryan Gordon had ever experienced. I wasn't going anywhere.

Next I started reaching out to former employees at Virgin Produced, Virgin Fest, and KAABOO to see how they were doing amidst the pandemic. I wanted to help everyone who had been affected. Nothing reaffirms your purpose and gets you out of a funk like helping someone else. I asked everyone if I could be a reference for any job they may be applying to or if I could help make a connection. Did they need rent money? Could they start a business from home? Could I connect them to the right people? Bryan hadn't just screwed me over; he'd screwed us all. And I felt terrible about it. I felt an unwavering duty to make sure those people who I'd worked with were taken care of as best I could.

These tasks became my sort of makeshift work from home "work day." After I'd done whatever I needed to do for the lawsuits and reached out to former employees, I'd spend the rest of the day focused on myself, getting back to a kind of spiritual center. I had come a really long way since my conservative Southern Baptist beginnings, but I had retained that inner knowing that there was something bigger than myself out there. I started spending time meditating in my own way, and doing yoga. Thank you, YouTube. I started reading, and I couldn't tell you the last time I'd read a book before that. I never had time. And I certainly had never focused on my own personal growth. I downloaded Audible and listened to every kind of self-help, personal development–type book I could find.

I also coordinated constant Zoom calls with everyone in my family. We'd eat dinner together over the computer or play family games or even have a virtual cooking class with my chef brother. Those Zooms became the highlight of my week. Then, a few months in, when it became clear that the world would not reopen soon and things were going to stay this way for a long time, I had a realization over one of those calls. We were all isolating separately and would be indefinitely. Why don't we isolate together? None of them were going back to their physical jobs anytime soon. It was certainly a big ask. It meant my brothers all leaving their respective states and homes and my parents giving up their place in San Diego. But they all agreed. Time with our loved ones was the most important thing in the world. If the pandemic taught us anything, it was that.

We decided we would all congregate in a big house we rented in Palm Springs. It was almost summer, and we wanted to be somewhere gorgeous, warm, and with a pool since we were going to be spending all of our time there. Venturing into public still felt scary, and most places in California had strict rules, occasionally even issuing "shelter in place" orders. Everybody packed up, got in a car, and made their way out to the desert. We made our own bubble. My parents, brothers, me, and our partners and dogs.

For the first couple of weeks, it just felt like a big vacation. We relaxed, reconnected, hung out, and threw ourselves themed parties. Then around week three or four, we realized that we needed a little more structure. I think we were all craving some routine. So, we instituted some house rules. Everybody had assigned communal chores, like dishes and taking out the trash, and everyone was responsible for cleaning their own bathrooms and keeping their bedrooms tidy. My chore was cleaning up the backyard and pool area at the end of the day.

We also rotated who made dinner each night for the group. And those also had themes: Mexican, Italian, Hawaiian, French, and so on. We made it as festive as possible. My favorite was "dress like your roommate" night where you had to dress like someone else in the house. And after every dinner, all 10 of us went for a group walk together. Occasionally we did a bike ride instead. For my parents' anniversary, we even set up a whole fake restaurant and a table for two with a candlelit dinner to help them celebrate.

We stayed in that neighborhood together for a few months, and I can confidently say that it was one of the best times of my life. I felt 16 again, living with my family under the same roof, doing chores. It was healing. All of the things that had been so important to me just a year earlier – money, success, acclaim, clout, access, cars, houses, and so on – it faded away. I could hardly remember what was so alluring about it now in light of being with my family. Community was what mattered most. Especially in those days, knowing your family was safe and healthy and close were the most important things. Nothing else even came close. I desperately needed that reminder.

I could also just be myself. Not "Jason the producer" or "Jason the CEO" or "Jason from Virgin" or, for that matter, even "Peaches." I was just Jason. I cannot overstate how little my family cares about any of that, in the best possible way. Once I could settle back into my authentic self with zero pretense or judgment, I realized just how worried I'd been about what everyone in Hollywood would think about me constantly. And before that I was worried what everyone in high school would think of me. It's exhausting. I felt like I could finally breathe.

Toward the end of summer, the government did begin to signal that things were close to getting back to "normal." People were slowly returning to their office buildings, companies were reopening, production was restarting. Our time in Palm Springs had to come to an end, and I felt a sense of dread. I didn't want to go back to my old life. And yet, there were things still left to do. Sadly, come fall, we all packed up and headed back to where we'd come from. But that time we'd spent together changed me. Or rather, reminded me who I really am. I'll always be so grateful for that.

When I returned to LA, I had to figure out what to do with Virgin Fest and KAABOO, which were on life support but still technically in existence. And I was still technically the CEO. As large-scale events were not permitted, we had to officially cancel installations of scheduled festivals and figure out what to do about refunds and tickets. We decided to give consumers the ability to let their tickets roll over to when the company could host the festivals again. We also offered every ticket holder a complimentary plus-one ticket, even though the ability to hold the festivals wasn't our call. California still had a policy against large gatherings, and there was nothing we could do.

I was still tied up, as a key witness, in a lot of litigation, with both the Gordon fraud case and with Lizzo in relation to her unreturned fee for Virgin Fest. Besides dealing with the fallout of those things, I still couldn't figure out exactly what to do next. How was I going to save this business? Can I save this business? Do I even *want* to save this business?

I hated how cynical I'd become about Hollywood. Deep down I still felt like the teenager who was obsessed with pop culture. That part of me would never change, completely. I've always been a cinephile and hardly ever met a movie I didn't like. I love how certain moments mark a period in time and enter the monoculture in such a way that everyone knows what you meant when you said "chicken of the sea" or "sliving." Entertainment has always been much more than a job to me. It was my delight and my escape when I was younger. I was so proud to have achieved my dreams and become a part of Hollywood's infrastructure and contribute to the creation of some amazing projects. But I was so disillusioned by the ego of it all. I didn't want to worry about people not honoring contracts or misleading me or stabbing me in the back. I wanted to stop worrying about everyone else's intentions or when I'd next produce a hit and just *live*.

Most of all though, I felt like I didn't *need* Hollywood anymore. For so long I was just a spectator desperately trying to get inside of it and become part of it. I wanted in the game. I'd been blinded by the glitz and glam of it all. The illusion of grandeur. It's intoxicating when you start winning awards and everyone you meet tells you how much they "love your movies" or they "love your brand." It was just *my* movie, and certainly wasn't just *my brand*. But, I'll tell you what: it's basically a drug. And it was fuel to my striver syndrome. And flattery is okay, as long as you don't inhale. I had inhaled. But when all of that was stripped away, Hollywood wasn't what I'd hoped it would be. Now that I'd been in it for over 20 years, I wanted out. I wanted to go back to being a spectator again and just enjoying the consumption of entertainment – not producing it. I was tired of the machine. I wanted to simply be entertained, not responsible for entertaining. That's when I was always the happiest anyway. Hollywood had given me a lot of experiences, some influence, a chunk of money, and a micro amount of power. I had made some great friends. But it didn't make me happy; it didn't fulfill me. I didn't want to be behind the curtain any longer. I just wanted to be in the audience.

I called Richard to talk to him about it a little. I didn't come right out and tell him I was considering leaving the business yet. We hadn't had a heart-to-heart yet about everything that went down with Virgin Produced and KAABOO so I talked about that. I wanted him to know my heart wasn't in all of it. He was great about it, of course. He's partnered with the wrong people before and been the victim of plenty of dirty business tricks. It's almost a rite of passage. He's been put through the wringer, too. You don't stay in business as long as he has without some of that. He made it clear in his own, non-effusive way that he was appreciative and proud of all I'd accomplished. A while passed where we didn't talk much as I still struggled to figure out my next moves. I still wondered whether I could rehabilitate the business.

Then on July 1, 2021, I got an email from Richard that said, "Hey Jason, I hope you and your partner are well. You may have seen the exciting news that I'm going to be flying with Virgin Galactic on Sunday, July 11. If you happen to be free, I would love to have you at Spaceport America, New Mexico, for the event, although I fully appreciate that it might be short notice. Please see attached all the details. Hope to see you there."

He was going to space. When I read this email, I immediately knew a couple of things. One, I was definitely going to the launch. There was no way I was going to miss this fulfillment of Richard's dream. And two, I was most definitely going to resign from the entertainment industry. Something about reading that Richard was about to achieve his goal made me realize that I had also achieved mine. I had done what I'd set out to do. There was nothing left for me here, and it was time to move on. I was going to head to New Mexico, and I was going find a moment to tell Richard I was officially done. Not just with Virgin, but with the entertainment industry altogether.

Before the launch, there was a breakfast meet-and-greet event in the morning that about 100 of us were invited to. I was a little nervous to attend. I didn't feel like I belonged there because I wasn't really Virgin anymore. I wasn't the one with the big fancy movies coming out, I wasn't the one with big news or making huge deals. I wasn't the favored child; I hardly even felt like part of the family anymore. For the first time ever, I walked into a room full of Virgin folks and felt small.

Within 60 seconds of walking in, Richard caught my eye from across the room and motioned for me to come over there. He put his arms around me and then sat and scooched over in his seat at the table so I could sit beside him and Joan. The first thing out of my mouth was, "You're going to space! This is so exciting!" He smiled and looked at me like, *well . . . yeah.* As we ate breakfast, he asked about my partner and how things were. There was no mention of Hollywood or deals. No talk of lawsuits or what I was working on. It was clear that he and Joan just wanted to know how I was and if I was happy. Though I'd felt out of place just minutes before, it was clear he didn't see it that way. He welcomed me the way he always had, ever since that first day on Necker Island.

God, I thought, *I wish the whole world could see this moment right now.* I think many people who know of Richard Branson perceive him to be a good guy and that he stands for important causes like taking care of the planet and human rights and prison reform. But most people don't truly know him. And I think the stigma that gets attached to most successful businessmen is that they are ruthless capitalists who will do whatever it takes to get ahead. Not Richard. He's incredibly kind and an incredibly good person who puts others first. He takes time to understand people and things, free of judgment or selfish motive. If only more successful and powerful people were like him, the world would be a better, more unified place.

We finished up breakfast and went outside to watch the launch. Now there were closer to 350 people there. Everyone cheered as Richard appeared one more time, now in his space suit, and walked out onto the launchpad to climb inside the Virgin Galactic plane, VMS *Eve* (named after his Richard's mum), and then into spacecraft VSS *Unity*. We were all sitting, waiting to watch it unfold right in front of our eyes and on large TV screens surrounding the area.

Moments later, as the spaceship detached from the carrier plane and blasted perfectly up into space, the spectators were silent. Though it was an exciting moment and everyone was cheering loudly, in my head I was in a little quiet world of my own thinking about how special my time at Virgin had been and how happy I was that it was now over. There were so many days, just a year or two earlier when I couldn't imagine actually being grateful that I'd lost my company. It felt like the worst possible outcome. But now, after the months in quarantine with my family, I was grateful for all of it. Every single ounce of the journey, I was grateful for it. I'm not sure I ever would have found true fulfillment if I'd kept chasing the next thing. All of this was going through my mind as I watched Richard Branson blast into outer space. I was so distracted by the historic moment that the fact that I was standing next to Elon Musk and his newborn son didn't even register. In fact, I couldn't figure out why people kept turning around to look at *me* and my reaction to the launch. Turns out, they were peeping at Mr. Musk's reaction. Which was just like mine – relieved it had all gone smoothly.

When the shuttle landed back down, there was uproarious applause, snapping me out of my little existential daydream. A group of us were permitted to go out on the tarmac and greet Richard and his fellow astronauts on arrival. Of course, Richard was bombarded by people and press. In addition to the Branson family, a few of my favorite longtime Virgin people were out there too: Helen Clarke, Christine Choi, Raul Leal, Gordon McCallum, Peter Norris, Josh Bayliss, George Whitesides, and Gabriel Baldinucci, to name a few. Although I was never the biggest Virgin company, these folks had supported me from day one. Celebrating Richard's moment alongside them meant a lot. They were my Virgin family, and despite how I'd felt earlier in the day, we were still family. The whole time I was thinking, *They have no idea that for me, this is goodbye. There's a chance*

I might never see some of these people again. We all took pictures together and celebrated Richard's safe return.

After all of the excitement was over, I was walking out the door of the Spaceport to catch the shuttle back to the hotel when I passed Richard going the other way. He initiated another hug, the first hello post-space because it was so crowded on the tarmac. I put my hands on his shoulders and said, "You did it! You got to space." Instantly, tears pricked the corners of my eyes. I could barely contain my emotions. It was a hugely powerful moment for Richard, of course. But it had also become a catalyst in my own life to leave something behind and start again. I wanted to tell him everything that was going on in my mind and about the big decision I'd made. But words just wouldn't come.

Instead, he said, "See you at the house tomorrow. We're having a barbeque."

The next day, I showed up at the house the Branson's had rented for the occasion. It was just their closest friends and family and not pretentious or fancy in any way. His grandkids ran around, and it was an overall festival and joyous occasion. Simple, warm, and inviting. We had a delicious lunch, and I got to catch up with some people who were really important in shaping my adult life. Of course, Sam my "Rastafarian Brother" was there, and Helen Clarke, who we joked had become my work wife while at Virgin. Sure, she was Richard's assistant, but to me she was a dear friend and someone I will treasure forever. I love her. Joan Branson, of course, was there as well. To me, she is a woman who has such a magnificent presence. Truly the spiritual center of the Branson family, Joan is a quiet force. She has this ability to zero in on you with her full concentration and make you feel like the most important person in the world. Even if her husband just got back from space. After we ate, I went up to Richard and said, "I have something for you." I'd had a special gift made for the occasion – a Variant3D.io zero-waste blanket printed with the Virgin Galactic logo with astronaut number one sewed onto it. He had achieved his dream.

Then I took a beat and unloaded a mouthful, "I'm really happy for you. Also, I want you to know that I'm going to be making some big changes. I'm stepping down from Virgin Fest. I don't know where I'll end up yet, but I'm retiring from entertainment altogether. I'm doing it all for my personal well-being. It's just something I need to do. I'm not sure exactly what I will do next. But yesterday you bookended my career with Virgin. You followed your dream, and I realized that I have followed mine."

He cheekily wrapped me in that blanket and gave me one last big hug, which Helen had managed to capture on camera. As he leaned into the hug he said, "Thank you, Jason." I thanked him back and said I needed to get off to my flight. Then he ran around to show everyone the gift. Richard and Joan had taught me the art of the perfect exit, and this was it. For me, this party was over. It was time to go home.

CUE: "See You Again" by Wiz Khalifa, featuring Charlie Puth

Epilogue

ON MY FLIGHT home from New Mexico, I took out my phone and furiously typed. I wanted to remember everything about what I'd just experienced. I started with my feelings, which quickly turned into revelations. It was a free flow of lessons I had learned as I prepared to embark on the next leg of my life journey. Things I wish I had known before I arrived in Hollywood. These revelations inspired the book you've been reading and were cut and pasted here, without edit, from my phone:

- Sometimes we all need a declarative moment of no return. A moment where we cannot turn back, and by removing the option to take the easy path and give up, we take the hard path. We do the hard thing because of the immense value it creates.
- Building something worth having means there are always people who may try and take it.
- Starting today, I will only have real friends, not deal "friends."
- Entertainers, politicians, and bankers are similar. It's their location that reinforces their priority. Hollywood for artistic fame. DC for power. And Wall Street for money.

- Being silent and listening is more valuable than talking.
- My fancy corner office was far less productive than my quiet little space at home.
- If someone is on your payroll, for them, their paycheck is likely priority over the relationship.
- Respecting yourself is more important than being liked by others.
- Workaholism is as deadly as any other addiction.
- The mistakes that make me humble are more valuable than the achievements to feed ego.
- The only bad reaction has been inaction.
- I have manifested and earned my success without selling out my values.
- My net worth is only defined only by whom I love and who truly loves me.
- I should not feel guilt for my success, or shame for my failures.
- My experiences bring me more happiness than my possessions.
- Being in healthy relationships brings me my main source of fulfillment.
- Old friends are priceless treasures.
- My new definition of a healer is to not to be a fixer, but to give empathy.
- Bullies become cowards when you stand up to them.
- I have a lot left to do and achieve.
- My striver syndrome isn't gone. I acknowledge it, and I will manage it.
- But in a car, plane, or train, I will now look out the window instead of into my emails.
- I'm very happy and satisfied with my life.
- **I have enough!**

Where Are They Now?

- On May 3, 2022, Jason Felts announced his retirement from Hollywood. Emblazed on the front of *Billboard* was a picture of Jason and Sir Richard Branson (in jeans) and quote from Branson that read, "I look forward to seeing him work less and play more."
- Jason now spends his time as his own boss advising startups and Fortune 500 corporations on their brand strategy, focusing on building a life with his husband, and supporting nonprofit causes that matter to him.
- While Jason is playing more than working, his swan song with Virgin was that he initiated and drafted curriculum for his mentor Richard Branson's online MasterClass. A full-circle, art-imitating-life experience.
- Michael "Doc" Baker still oversees sports medicine at Garland ISD, and no doubt, has had a positive influence on thousands of athletes and student trainers for over 50 years – but only one Peaches.
- Justin is happily married to Liza in his favorite role of life, Dad. He and Jason still adventure and partner in business together.
- Mary is still flying the friendly skies, and along with Melissa, they remain Jason's closest confidants.

- The Hollywood roommates, well, all left Hollywood, with the exception of Riley, who is still a hard-working actor and now a husband and father.

- Ashlee Simpson (Ross) went on to become a successful singer, songwriter, and actress debuting her first album "Autobiography" at number one and selling more than five million copies. In 2024, for old time's sake, she asked Jason if he would also teach her son Bronx how to drive. Jason happily accepted the honor.

- Michael Ovitz went on to become a Silicon Valley venture capitalist, and likely couldn't pick Jason out of a lineup of past assistants, interns, employees, or recipients of his once tough tongue.

- AJ is successfully directing films, and doing it her way.

- Kourtney Kardashian, well, unless one lives under a rock, they know where she is now.

- Omar Amanat was sentenced to five years in prison, in a separate unrelated case: *U.S. v. Amanat, U.S. District Court, Southern District of New York, No. 15-cr-00536.*

- Richard Branson, still based on Necker Island, spends most of his time building businesses that will make a positive difference in the world and working with Virgin Unite and organizations it has incubated, such as The Elders, The B Team, Ocean Unite (which merged into ORRAA), and the Planetary Guardians.

- Former President Barack Obama and Michelle Obama continue to focus on their philanthropic work through the Obama Foundation, which aims to inspire and empower the next generation of leaders.

- On April 12, 2024, a Delaware judge ruled that Bryan Gordon and his colleagues attempted to defraud Virgin Fest, and awarded $2 million in damages for breach of contract. On any future collection of the judgment award, Jason committed his entire portion of any proceeds collected to be divided equally among the former KAABOO staff who lost their jobs due to the actions of Gordon and his colleagues.

- In summer 2024, Jason married his soulmate, Daniel, and enjoys a very private life traveling and adventuring . . . well, apart from the promoting of this book.
- Jason's parents, growing family, and real friends (including those mentioned in this book) continue to remind him that they aren't impressed by or judge his past. They are only focused on making more lasting memories together . . . outside of Hollywood.

Acknowledgments

As I REFLECT on the journey of writing this memoir, I am filled with gratitude for the many individuals who have supported and inspired me along the way.

First and foremost, I would like to express my heartfelt thanks to my family. Dad, you taught me the importance of having inner peace, balance, and ensuring that my own happiness is always a priority. Without judgment, you shaped my beliefs and values and led by example. Mom, I appreciate your unwillingness to allow me to be anything other than who I am, and for your advocacy on equality and justice at home and in life. Thank you for creating a family for all of us with your strength and your tough love. For my brothers Logan and Joe, for being so uniquely you, and always having my back despite where I am at in any given moment of life. I am at my very happiest on the days that I get to spend with both of you, together. For Justin, my best friend and business partner, who believed in me and took that entrepreneurial leap way back when, the roller coaster has been one for the ages and, the sum of all those turns formed my best lessons, memories, moments, and milestones. And to my bonus "sisters" Tina, Jourdan, and Liza, thank you for humoring and loving our crazy modern family. And to the next generation of nieces and nephew, your Uncle Jason can't wait to watch you grow and find your own wonderful place in this world.

For my closest friends and confidants (you know exactly who you are, because we keep in actual touch versus just over social media). Despite the geographic distance with some, you have never been absent. You have inspired me to remain authentic and have provided me with unwavering support, encouragement, and laughter during my highest highs and the lowest lows. Your true friendship has been my personal anchor.

For you Richard, Joan, Sam, and Holly Branson, as well as my extended global Virgin family (especially Abby L., Allie H., Christine C., David C., Debbie D., Dimitrios P., Gabriel B., George W., Gordon M., Greg R., Helen C., Jesse M., Josh B., Latif P., Nathan R., Nirmal S., Peter N., Raul L., Stephen H., Thayer T.), my business associate friends along the way (especially Gary S., Marc H., Sharon H., Michael U., Bill H., Angelo L., Adam L., Katie L., Justin S., Wayne G., Cameron F., Michele L., Mark V., Jackie D., Jan F., and Nathan S.), my attorneys and advisors who've been in some trenches with me (especially Dan M., Steven G., John G., Dallas N., Robert B., John B., Sam B., Jesse B., Ian J., Ian L., Phil B., Philip P., and Mike K.), and close early career colleagues (especially the glue that has held me together Rebecca F.), Huntley R., Rene R., Tobin A., Jenn C., Tatiana V., Ron H., Barrick P., and Harvey M., for your alliance, leadership, creative talent, unwavering trust, and belief in my earliest visions. You have all been my professional anchor. The adventures and achievements with you all are memories I will forever cherish.

To my writing community, thank you for your invaluable feedback and encouragement and taking a chance on a first-time writer. Special thanks to my editors Jennifer K. and Jaime C. for your guidance, and to Liz M., who encouraged me to dig deeper along the way. Thank you to the very talented Michelle B., for capturing my energy and spirit in this book cover, and with appreciation to the Hollywood Sign Trust for preserving the iconic landmark that draws millions to follow their own dreams. A worthy cause, I would be remiss not to spotlight in support www.hollywoodsign.org.

To my publisher, especially Zach S., Amanda P., Michelle H., Susan G., Rene C., and the entire Wiley team. I am incredibly thankful for your belief in this project and for providing me with the platform and support to reach a global audience.

To all the movies, TV shows, actors, artists, musicians, directors, producers, and executives who initially inspired me to go West and follow my dreams. (Especially the late John Ritter, his assistant Susan W., best friend and attorney Bob M., and force of nature wife and heart health advocate Amy Y.).

Last but far from least, to my beautiful husband, Daniel. I was lost without you. I had everything, yet I had nothing. Your encouragement, consistency, and resolute love gives me peace with my past and excitement for our future.

In closing, I want to acknowledge everyone who's stories and experiences have influenced my own story – inside and outside of this book. Each encounter has shaped my understanding of the world, and for that, I hold lasting gratitude. And in acknowledging the journey that has brought me here, I would be remiss not to mention those who doubted my vision, withheld their support, or chose to try and block or attempt to destroy one of my dreams in the name of your own self-interest. I would also be remiss not to mention those who stopped returning my calls or texts the moment you felt I could not serve you or your bank account any longer. You know exactly who you are. May this book serve as a reminder also to you for showing your true colors. I harbor no ill will; instead, I hope that this work inspires you to reflect and strive for a more compassionate and inclusive approach in your own pursuits without judgment.

Thank you all for being part of this journey. I hope that this memoir resonates with you and inspires others as much as your support has inspired me.

Love,
Jason

About the Author

Entrepreneur and brand strategist Jason Felts founded and served as CEO of two Virgin companies with a focus on the development and production of films, television shows, short form content, and live entertainment for Sir Richard Branson's Virgin brand. In 2010, Felts was appointed to Virgin's Global Brand Council and has served as consultant to Virgin-branded companies in the aviation, hotel, space, and telecom sectors. Named by *Variety* in the "Top 10 to Watch" and profiled in *Forbes*, *Bloomberg*, *Billboard*, and *Rolling Stone*, Felts has built, repositioned, and/or launched several consumer brands and media companies. Felts has architected and led full teams responsible for the execution of world-class entertainment and lifestyle experiences, including the coproduction and marketing of blockbuster Hollywood films *Limitless*, *Bad Moms*, *That Awkward Moment*, *Immortals*, *Movie 43*, *The Impossible*, *21 & Over*, and biopic *Jobs*, which cumulatively have grossed over $1 billion worldwide. Felts oversaw the creation of the groundbreaking Virgin America inflight "Safety Dance" video, a viral success earning over a billion media impressions, a $700 million ad equivalency value, and was recognized by a Clio, Webby, and Shorty Award. During Felts's tenure, Virgin launched and operated its own content network with over 100 million in captive audience viewership.

Prior to cofounding Virgin Produced, Felts was a cofounder at J2TV and was responsible for the development, financing, and production of a slate of film and TV shows for broadcast networks including E!, FOX, and Comcast. J2TV is most recognized for introducing the then virtually unknown Kardashians to audiences in 2005 with the creation of *Filthy Rich* on the E! network. Felts currently consults, strategically invests, and serves as a board member to several Fortune 500 brands in the hospitality, media, and tech sectors. Felts also speaks publicly on entrepreneurship, with an equal focus on philanthropic efforts centered on inclusivity and equality and was honored for the same by the State of New York's "Responsible 100," which recognizes prominent leaders in the area of social responsibility. In 2024, Felts received an honorary doctorate from Ripon College in recognition of a life "Breaking Barriers." Trading in hectic Los Angeles highways, Felts now resides part-time on a 22-mile-long Caribbean island, and spends his days consulting, writing, and using his voice for social good.

Index